THE LITERARY PROFESSION IN THE
ELIZABETHAN AGE

PHOEBE SHEAVYN, M.A. (Manchester), D.Litt. (London) was formerly Special Lecturer in English Literature and Tutor for Women Students in the University of Manchester, Tutor in English Literature, Somerville College Oxford, and Fellow and Reader at Bryn Mawr College, Pennsylvania, U.S.A. She conducted the correspondence about this new edition and, at 101 years of age, has seen the proofs.

PHOEBE SHEAVYN

The Literary Profession in the Elizabethan Age

2nd edition, revised throughout, by

J. W. SAUNDERS
author of *The Profession of English Letters*

MANCHESTER UNIVERSITY PRESS
BARNES & NOBLE INC., NEW YORK

© 1967, Manchester University Press
Published by the University of Manchester at
THE UNIVERSITY PRESS
316–324 Oxford Road Manchester 13
First published, 1909
2nd edition revised throughout by J. W. Saunders, 1967

U.S.A.
BARNES & NOBLE, INC.
105, Fifth Avenue, New York, 3

Printed in Great Britain by Butler & Tanner Ltd , Frome and London

CONTENTS

page

Preface to the Second Edition   vii

Introduction   1

I Authors and Patrons   8

II Authors and Official Censors   39

III Authors and Publishers   64

IV Authors and the Theatre   89

V Authors and Supplementary Means of Livelihood   101

VI Personal Relations amongst Authors   127

VII Authors and Readers   148

Appendix I   209
   Complete Works abbreviated in the footnotes

Appendix II   210
   An Analysis of the Social Status of 200 Renaissance
      Poets

Index   239

PREFACE TO THE SECOND EDITION

IN the preface to the first edition Dr Sheavyn defined the limits of her work: 'This little book is, in fact, only a series of studies upon certain aspects of the whole question of authorship and the conditions amid which it was pursued as a profession during the period denoted. No attempt has been made to deal with learned and controversial writings. The inquiry is confined to what may perhaps be styled, for want of a good English word, "belles-lettres"—to the "literature of power", as distinguished from the "literature of knowledge". It includes poetry, story-telling, pamphlets on social topics, and drama. The last has been treated very briefly, because it has already received ample investigation from more competent writers.'

She continued: 'The period chosen for review has also had to be strictly limited. It dates from the accession of Elizabeth to a few years after the accession of Charles I. It has been selected as being a period of comparative internal quiet, preceded and followed by times of serious disturbance—a period therefore fairly favourable for a study of the natural development of the profession of literature.'

In this second edition I have respected Dr Sheavyn's limits, although this occasions several difficulties. It has become clear in the fifty-odd years since she wrote that two of the fields she excluded or treated briefly offered much more *professional* opportunity to writers at the time than *belles-lettres*. As Eleanor Rosenberg states in her book, *Leicester, Patron of Letters* (New York, 1955), the main object of courtly patronage was not *belles-lettres* at all, but translations, handbooks, historical compilations, and works of piety and controversy, designed *inter alia* to provide 'a learned ministry and an enlightened ruling class'. The best-sellers of the age were books like John Norden's *Pensive Man's Practice* (1584), which exceeded forty

editions by 1627, and the Sternhold-Hopkins *Psalter* (1549), 47
editions by 1600. As far as *belles-lettres* are concerned, it is now
clear that, except in the theatre for very special reasons, conditions were not ripe this early for a literary profession in any
proper sense of the term. Idealists like Edmund Spenser were
reaching forward to a profession, and many lesser writers were
seeking what financial independence they could from the
printed-book market, but only the dramatists achieved a living
from writing and its ancillary pursuits. The printing trade was
still in its infancy: between 1500 and 1630 the total national
book production, of new books and new editions, rose from
45 a year to only 460, and was confined by all kinds of limitations, political and social. In these circumstances most of the
writers whom we have regarded as pioneers of professional
belles-lettres made use of their literary gifts as a means to an end
rather than as an end in themselves, and were much more
interested in social promotion at Court, the *carrière ouverte aux
talents*, than in literary independence. We can see now that
many of their complaints were not so much those of frustrated
would-be literary professionals as those of neglected would-be
political placemen.

It is also clear that the really formative periods in the development of the profession of literature came just before and
after Dr Sheavyn's selected age, in the very periods of serious
disturbance she avoids. The social factors which limited the
development of the printed-book profession, and gave the
dramatists their chance, were determined in the turbulent
reign of Henry VIII, when a proud monarch set about the task
of achieving centralized direction of all the nation's affairs,
including its cultural activities, at a Court which he hoped
would be the envy of Europe. Similarly, the forces which
broke the absolute power of the Court and which encouraged
conditions favourable to a literary profession, came to the fore
in the Civil Wars, when there was an enormous expansion of

the printed-book market and the origination of new media later to provide writers with an established professional base.

What I have done, then, in this edition, to bring up to date the central concepts of Dr Sheavyn's thesis, is to modify conclusions about the *belles-lettres* professionals, so that their professional limitations may be more clearly seen, to say a little more about the drama, where the professionals really were professionals, and to emphasize the disadvantages of the Courtly system for those who did not really want to play the Courtly game. Outside the theatre, the profession had to wait the best part of a century before it could establish itself, but in the meantime the struggle of writers to survive, in conditions which enhanced the amateur and crippled the professional, is a theme well worthy of the loving care with which Dr Sheavyn many years ago first approached the subject.

But this remains Dr Sheavyn's book, and I have resisted the temptation to write a new one. To this end, I have retained the original structure of the book, which was conceived as a collection of connected essays on the one theme, although the chapter distribution is rather uneven with a giant at the end. And in the footnotes I have left untouched Dr Sheavyn's references to her historical sources, though these have been largely superseded. Her literary references, however, have been thoroughly overhauled. It is surprising in how many instances the Grosarts and Arbers of Victorian scholarship remain unchallenged on the shelves of University libraries; for some writers, the student still has to go to their much-thumbed editions. But where they have been superseded by a modern standard edition, the references have been revised. The student is now referred to the standard edition most likely to appear on the open shelves of his library. Thus, with Nashe reference is made to the McKerrow edition, as revised by F. P. Wilson in 1958, with the *Parnassus Plays* to the Leishman edition of 1949, and so on. Where there was a choice between a Victorian edition of the complete works, and a modern edition of 'selected', in the main I have continued to refer to the older edition as the more comprehensive and thoroughly useful for the student; but sometimes a good standard selection in general use has been preferred. Where a new edition of the complete works is still far from the end of its publication schedule, as with the Yale *Jonson*, I have preferred the next best thing, in Jonson's case the Herford-Simpson edition. A list of these 'works' is given in Appendix I, in case the student is in doubt about which edition is signified by the footnotes.

Our preference these days for a standard omnibus edition includes also our insistence on getting as near as we can to the original text of the author. One of the inconsistencies of Dr Sheavyn's book was an Edwardian arbitrariness about transcriptions; sometimes she left the text as it stood in her source edition, sometimes she completely modernized it, and sometimes she produced a hybrid, the original text plus certain modernizations of spelling and punctuation. I have taken advantage of this opportunity to reinstate the original text (except for lengthening contractions, and substituting *v* for *u*, and *j* for *i*, in the usual places), except with those authors (Shakespeare and a few of the dramatists, in particular) where we seem to be accustomed to modernized texts. In this way I hope that the book will be a better tool for scholars, while it will retain the unique flavour of Dr Sheavyn's original work.

J. W. SAUNDERS

Introduction

> You have of the Wits that write verses, and yet
> are no poets: they are Poets that live by it, the
> poore fellowes that live by it.
>
> JONSON, *Epicoene*, II. iii
>
> When I doo play my Prizes in Print, Ile be paid
> for my paines, that's once.
>
> NASHE, *Have with you to Saffron-Walden*[1]

IN the following pages an attempt is made to describe, from
evidence afforded by contemporary writers, some of the conditions amid which a profession of letters was pioneered
during the reigns of Elizabeth and James I. The subject is one
of considerable interest, both historical and literary, and the
evidence to be obtained is more abundant than might at first
sight be supposed. The Elizabethan writer is above all things
outspoken and impulsive, even childishly naïve in self-
exposure; and for our purposes, these characteristics are invalu-
able. As he remonstrates with a publisher, grumbles at a patron,
and apologizes to readers, he lets us into the secret of many
things that would otherwise remain unknown or unintelligible.
But his revelations must be interpreted, if their bearing is to be
accurately estimated, in the light of modern researches into the
economic and social history of the age. The Elizabethan writer
was no shrewder than most of us in apprehending the causes of
social weal or woe. It needs the impartial judgment and fuller
knowledge possible only to posterity, to understand and trace
to their origin the special conditions which environed an
author in that epoch.

In the study of Elizabethan and Jacobean society, in whatever sphere, certain ascertained facts of social and economic
history must be steadily kept in view. Since the accession of

---

[1] *Works of Thomas Nashe*, ed. R. B. McKerrow (1958), III, 128.

the Tudor dynasty, the influence and prestige of the older nobility, the aristocracy of feudal creation, had considerably waned. The policy of the Tudors had aimed consistently at depressing the old baronial families, and at substituting an aristocracy which should be subservient to the Crown. In the reign of Elizabeth, accordingly, most of the leading members of the aristocracy belonged to houses ennobled under the Tudors, and deriving their influence less from territorial possessions and jurisdiction than from their wealth and their relations with the Crown.

Moreover, a middle class of *entrepreneurs* and *rentiers* was steadily growing in wealth and power throughout the whole of Elizabeth's reign. In particular, merchant adventurers and lawyers accumulated large fortunes. James Howell was of the opinion that the twenty-four London Aldermen could buy up a hundred of the richest men in Amsterdam.[1] William Harrison knew a shipowner possessing sixteen or seventeen ships worth £1,000 each, exclusive of cargo.[2] By means of their riches such men were enabled to associate with the outer circles of the aristocracy, which was indeed constantly recruited from their ranks. When, moreover, James I began to sell baronetcies and peerages, the distinction between rank and mere wealth became still less evident. The effect of this social revolution, in its influence upon the question of literary patronage, will be considered later on.

A natural consequence of the change was that men began to attach to riches an importance vastly greater than before. The commercial desire for gain spread rapidly; all classes entered

[1] *Epistolae Ho-Elianae* (1629), 1 May 1619.

[2] *Description of England* (New Shaks. Soc., 1877), I, 291.

The average cost of a meal at a respectable tavern was sixpence. Taking into account the low incidence of direct and indirect taxation then prevalent, one needs to multiply these figures by at least forty to get a modern comparison.

into the race for wealth. Further, the existence of a number of
opulent men, the merchant capitalists, tended to raise the
general standard of comfort, and to encourage a spirit of
luxury and display. Harrison bears reluctant witness to the
luxuriousness prevalent in his day; extravagance in food, in
dress, and in furniture, he says, marks all English life. John
Chamberlain tells a characteristic bit of gossip concerning a
bankrupt London tradesman: when the inventory of his
belongings was taken, thirty of his wife's smocks were valued
at three-score pounds![1] Philip Stubbes asserts that whereas, in
his father's day, one or two dishes of good wholesome meat
were thought 'sufficient for a man of great worship to dyne
withall', it was, in his own time, thought necessary to have the
table 'covered from the one end to the other, as thick as one
dish can stand by another'.[2] Many country gentlemen, unable
to bear the increasing expense of housekeeping, gave up their
establishments, and went to follow the Court, with one man
and a lackey for retinue.

Meanwhile, prices were rising rapidly, owing partly to
increased consumption, partly to the influx of silver from the
West. In the latter half of the sixteenth century, corn cost from
three to ten times the average price of the previous three centuries.[3] Sugar rose from fourpence to half a crown.[4] Stowe
tells us that not only corn 'but all things else, whatever was
sustenance for man, was likewise raised without all conscience
or reason'. Rents increased exorbitantly during the same period.
A farm which in the earlier part of the century let for ten
shillings, would fetch in 1583 as much as ten pounds.[5] This
dearth, i.e. dearness, of the necessaries of life is a frequent

---

[1] 15 October 1602. *Letters*, ed. N. E. McClure (1939), I, 166.
[2] *Anatomy of Abuses* (1583). New Shaks. Soc. (1877–82), 102–3.
[3] J. E. Thorold Rogers, *Six Centuries of Work and Wages* (1884), II, 388.
[4] *Description of England*, I, 131.
[5] *Anatomy of Abuses*, 29–30.

topic with Elizabethan writers on social questions. They are puzzled to account for it in face of the evident prosperity of the nation, failing to realize that it was, in some sort, in itself evidence of prosperity.

On the other hand, money incomes had not risen in proportion to the increased scale of expenditure. Under inflationary conditions those with relatively fixed incomes, including wage-earners whose pay increases lag behind rising prices, suffer severely. In 1581 artificers had to pay their journeymen twopence a day more than formerly, and yet the latter found it impossible to live on their wages.[1] It has been reckoned that a man could earn by a whole year's work in 1593 no more food and maintenance than he could have earned a century earlier by the labour of fifteen weeks.[2] The lessened value of a money income is strikingly illustrated by the following contemporary statement:

In times past, & within the memory of man, he hath beene accounted a rich & welthy man, & well able to keep house among his neighbors, which, all things discharged, was clearly worth £30 or £40; but in these our daies the man of that estimation is so farre in the common opinion, from a good house-keeper, or man of wealth, that he is reputed the next neighbor to a begger.[3]

The prosperous were those who sold the products most in demand, material necessaries and luxuries. The seller of labour, the smaller gentry, and the professional man, of more or less fixed income, felt keenly the pinch of high prices. As for the literary man, unless he were maintained by patronage, he was in the economic position of an ordinary wage-earner. He offered for sale a commodity not too greatly in demand, and even—as was also to some extent the case with manual labour

[1] W. S(tafford), *A Compendious or briefe Examination* (1581), New Shaks. Soc. (1786), 16.

[2] J. E. Thorold Rogers, op. cit, II, 391.

[3] *A Compendious Examination*, 82.

—artificially cheapened by legislation. In the modern sense there were no full-time professional authors; but there were many writers seeking to capitalize their talent by selling writings either to the press or to rich men. Nashe was at any rate a professional writer in this sense, for Gabriel Harvey says of him, 'No lesse than *London* could serve him: where somewhat recovered of his wits, by the excrements thereof (for the space of nine or ten yere) hee hath got his belly fed, and his backe clothed . . . hee hath troubled the Presse all this time, and published sundrie works & volumes.'[1] See also the description of the poor University man in *1 Return from Parnassus*: 'I wante shiftes of shirtes, bandes, and all thinges els, yet I remaine thrise humblie & most affectionatlie bounde to the right honorable printing house for my poore shiftes of apparell'.[2]

These men were invariably poor, and this in a society tending more and more to measure men by financial standards. Their earnings by authorship assumed frequently the unsatisfactory form of doles from so-called patrons, in return for the 'gift' of a book; but in one way or another, they relied upon writing, not very successfully, to provide them with a livelihood.

'*Poetry* in this latter Age', says Jonson, 'hath prov'd but a meane *Mistresse*, to such as have wholly addicted themselves to her, or given their names up to her family. They who have but saluted her on the by, and now and then tendred their visits, shee hath done much for, and advanced in the way of their owne professions (both the *Law*, and the *Gospel*) beyond all they could have hoped, or done for themselves, without her favour.'[3] Yet Jonson fared himself remarkably well, combining

[1] *The Trimming of Thomas Nashe. Works of Gabriel Harvey*, ed. A. B. Grosart (1885), III, 68.

[2] I. i. *Three Parnassus Plays*, ed. J. B. Leishman (1949), 143.

[3] *Discoveries. Ben Jonson*, ed. C. H. Herford, and P. and E. Simpson, VIII (1947), 583.

the roles of Courtly satellite and professional writer, and being involved with the theatre. The majority of his fellows could have uttered, as most of them did utter, far more touching complaints of their mistress:

> Let schollers be as thriftie as they maye,
> They will be poore ere theire last dyinge daye.
> Learninge and povertie will ever kiss.[1]

The truth of this may be demonstrated by the experience of almost every professional writer of the time. John Foxe, author of the well-known *Book of Martyrs*, is said to have been found in St Paul's Churchyard half dead from starvation. Michael Drayton is said to have possessed just five pounds at his death. Richard Hooker's children were 'beggars'. Thomas Wilson said 'it were better be a Carter, then a Scholer, for wor(l)dly profite'[2]. Nashe, Dekker, and many others, suffered imprisonment as debtors.

The attitude of ordinary men towards literature was, as will be seen later, largely one of self-deception. They believed themselves to have literary tastes; they certainly read considerably, they talked a great deal about poetry; and they went to the public playhouse. But their taste was far from cultivated, and their methods of criticism were barbarously elementary and their criteria crude. One recalls Prince Hamlet's advice to his players to have care for the opinions of the judicious, 'the censure of the which One, must in your allowance o'reway a whole Theater of others', and Jonson's contempt in *Bartholomew Fair* for the grounded judgments fit only for sweeping the stage and gathering up the broken apples for the bears within. The immense output of literary work during the Elizabethan age was fostered by the enlightened encouragement of only a few; in the main the writers had to withstand the withering

---

[1] *Pilgrimage to Parnassus. Three Parnassus Plays* (1949), 98.
[2] *Arte of Rhetorique* (1560), prologue to the reader.

effects of poverty, official interference, unfair competition and scorn. Only an exceptionally robust vitality could have persevered in the face of such obstacles. Tasteless, formless, crudely barbaric or childishly elaborate though much Elizabethan work may be, it also bears the stamp of this unconquerable vitality.

The succeeding pages of this book are devoted to an attempt to elucidate the conditions, economic, legal and social, which assisted, lured or hampered the would-be professional author. It will be seen that discouragements far outweighed rewards; but they put the writer's mettle to the proof, and fostered in him the strenuousness which gives life.

CHAPTER I

Authors and Patrons

... grand *Maecenas* casts a glavering eye,
On the cold present of a Poesie:
And least he might more frankly take than give,
Gropes for a french crowne in his emptie sleeve.

Hall, *Virgidemiarum*[1]

The priest unpaide can neither sing nor say,
Nor poets sweetlie write excepte they meete
With sounde rewarde, for sermoning so sweete.

Lodge, *A Fig for Momus*, eclogue III

THE prevalence of a system of private literary patronage has usually coincided with the existence of a despotic or at least highly aristocratic and oligarchical form of society. In such a society alone is the bounty of individual benefactors a necessity. In a community where power and wealth are more widely distributed, and literary culture within general reach, there are contrived, almost inevitably, means of rewarding genius, based upon the ability to appeal to large classes of men. Thus Thucydides, to whom the general vote of the citizens of Athens decreed at one time a public gift of £2,400, could afford to be independent of individual benefactors. A more commercial age like our own substitutes for a gratuitous reward a complex pattern of financial returns, of which the main component is often the market value of an edition.

On the other hand, among such conditions as prevailed at Alexandria under the early Ptolemys, in Rome under Augustus, and in the Italy of the despots, the patron of literature is a necessity. There we find a comparatively small wealthy cultured society, under the leadership of men to whom the gratification of literary tastes is a luxury for which they are willing

---

[1] V, 83–6, *Collected Poems*, ed. A. Davenport (1949), 77.

to pay with munificence. And it must be confessed that in such a society literary genius has flourished at least as well as in communities of less concentrated culture. The list of writers who profited by the enlightened liberality of such patrons as Ptolemy, Augustus, Maecenas, Messala, Lorenzo de Medici, Alfonso of Naples and Pope Nicholas, includes some of the most renowned names in literature.

In England the circle of cultivated aristocrats has always been smaller than in Renaissance Italy, nor have we ever been ruled by a monarch who could compare in taste and liberality with the great Italian humanist princes. But the Teutonic custom of befriending and honouring literary abilities in the person of the scôp was handed down to later times by such rulers as Alfred and Henry Beauclerc; and this was, in the fourteenth century, reinforced by the example of Italy, though the practice was confined, during the fourteenth and fifteenth centuries, to the monarch, the royal family, and some of the greater ecclesiastical dignitaries. In the sixteenth century we find a fairly general recognition, on the part of the nobility, of their obligations as patrons of literature. Again, the influential factor was Italian example. According to Castiglione's *Il Cortegiano*, the most persuasive of the many contemporary handbooks of Courtesy, circulating widely throughout Europe after its publication in 1527, the ideal Courtier had to be, in the words of Hoby's Elizabethan translation, 'more than indifferently well seene at the leaste in those studies, which they call Humanitie', and skilled 'in writing both rime and prose, and especially in this our vulgar tunge'.[1] If the prince were to represent in himself the 'floure of Courtlines' (and neither Henry VIII nor Elizabeth were backward in their ambitions this way), he had to write himself, and gather about him a context of men who were experienced in the writing, reading

[1] Ed. J. E. Ashbee (1900), 73, 302, 383.

9

and criticism of English literature. And the nobility followed their leader.

But the conditions of this new Courtly society differed widely from those of England of the fourteenth or Italy of the fifteenth century. In the first place, the emphasis laid upon the ability of Courtiers to write themselves elevated in social prestige the amateur writer above the would-be professional. Secondly, writing was only one of the skills required at Court, though one of the more important: other arts, like music and dancing, were much in demand, and the successful Courtier, and the more successful of his satellites, tended to have an all-round ability, with talents which went beyond the arts to general military and diplomatic service. Thirdly, noblemen were conscious of wider political responsibilities: in a time of religious and social upheaval, there was a necessity to educate, and enlist the support of, the middle classes which with commercial prosperity and wider literacy had become a major power in the land. And fourthly, this was a period of economic transition, with painful consequences for both patrons and protégés. Neither side realized the drift of circumstances: the reigns of Elizabeth and James mark a gradual disintegration of the aristocratic system of private literary patronage, even though it spread its net more widely and more powerfully than in the times of Chaucer and Lydgate. Efforts were often aimed at the conservation of a dying system, which rightly directed might have facilitated the introduction of a new pattern granting much more economic independence to the writer. We shall find that, all through the Elizabethan period, patronage was struggled after all the more feverishly, because of a growing sense of its precariousness.

Moreover, apart from the influence of tradition, it was inevitable that literary production, so far as it existed, should depend upon patronage. Books were only just beginning to be recognized in the world of trade, and in that age all that fell outside the sphere of buying and selling at recognized prices was matter of patronage. Patronage ruled in every walk of life. The halls of great men, the courtyards of country gentlemen, the antechambers of the Court, were thronged with suitors, pleading for every conceivable kind of gift, from the office of Groom of the Chamber to her Majesty to the honourable employment of turnspit in a country kitchen. This was an age when salaries, if they existed as such, were usually very small, and the real rewards of any kind of service came from fees and gratuities, the emoluments attached to all kinds of sinecure offices, the profits from land leases, and the yield from charters, licences and monopolies granted by letters patent. As Sir John Neale suggests, the noblemen were 'poised upon a great credit structure'[1], and in proportion the smaller country gentry shared the same power. At any time the sources of their wealth might be denied, with some change in the balance of power at Court, bringing ruin not only for the principal himself (Essex, for instance, was £10,000 in debt at his fall) but for all those dependent upon his largesse. Nevertheless, while the risks were enormous, the rewards were also very considerable, and this was the magnet that attracted Shakespeare from Stratford and Marlowe from Canterbury.

The elaborate mechanism of Civil Service Examinations, promotion by seniority, and registration, which now shields greatness from the importunate was only to be evolved three centuries later, and the writer who had business, whether he was seeking a sinecure or a dedication fee, had to urge his claims personally amidst a crowd of rival applicants. Yet he had to gain a patron or half starve. Not a single writer of the period was free from obligations to patrons. Again and again they tell us that patronage alone can save, or has saved them

[1] 'The Elizabethan Political Scene', *Proceedings of the British Academy*, XXXIV (1948), 116.

from want. Massinger declares that he could not have subsisted without the support of his patrons.[1] Nashe openly entreats that someone will find him meat and maintenance, that he may 'play the paper stainer'.[2] Lodge depicts a recognized type in his portrait of the unfortunate poet driven by lack of patronage to forsake poetry for the plough.[3]

The old form of patronage, as experienced by Chaucer and Gower, had been a substantial and satisfactory thing. The writer was given an organic place within the feudal community, and enjoyed protection and security. The relationship between writer and patron was one of dignity: the writer served honourably in his special capacity, and there was nothing abject or servile about him. But in Elizabethan days the connexion was usually more casual and less permanent. The names of those writers who were so fortunate to meet with lifelong patronage are few indeed: Roger Ascham, Samuel Daniel, perhaps Ben Jonson as well—it is doubtful if another could be found. Even in the case of these favoured three there are signs enough that their needs were but inadequately met. Ascham, in a suit to the Queen a year before his death, asks no more than to be enabled to leave £20 a year to each of his two sons, 'which', he declares, 'will satisfy my desire, although as small a portion as ever secretary to a prince left behind him'.[4] Jonson was driven more than once to sell part of his library, and grieved that his fortune humbled him to accept even the smallest courtesies with gratitude.[5] By far the most fortunate seems to have been Daniel. He finds no more serious complaint to make than that, being employed

---

[1] *Maid of Honour* (1632), dedication.

[2] *Have with you to Saffron-Walden. Works* (1958), III, 29.

[3] *Fig for Momus* (1595), Eclogue III.

[4] 10 October 1567. *Cal. State Papers, Dom. Add.*, 41.

[5] *An Epistle to Sir Edward Sacvile. The Under-Wood: Ben Jonson* VIII (1947), 153.

as a tutor, he is 'constrayned to live with *children*', when he should be writing 'the actions of *men*'.[1]

The most enlightened and generous patrons of literature known to us were various noble men and women who group themselves round the central figure of Sir Philip Sidney. Though a relatively poor man, Sidney was a devoted lover of the beautiful, and a true friend to the literary artist. Men of letters had special reason to share the almost idolatrous feeling with which he was regarded by his contemporaries. He is honoured with gratitude by nearly every writer of the times, and held up to public view as the ideal patron. Nashe gave utterance to the general sentiment when he penned the following lament:

Gentle *Sir Phillip Sidney*, thou knewst what belongd to a Scholler, thou knewst what paines, what toyle, what travel, conduct to perfection: wel couldst thou give every Vertue his encouragement, every Art his due, every writer his desert: cause none more vertuous, witty, or learned than thy selfe. But thou art dead in thy grave, and hast left too few successors of thy glory, too few to cherish the Sons of the Muses, or water those budding hopes with their plenty, which thy bounty erst planted.[2]

Philip's sister Mary, the wife of William Herbert, Earl of Pembroke, shared his tastes, and continued, as far as possible, the patronage of his many literary protégés after his early death. Spenser dedicated to her one of the sonnets prefixed to his *Faerie Queene*. Breton expresses passionate devotion to her for having succoured him in distress.[3] Daniel acknowledges that she 'first encouraged and framed' him to the service of the Muses,[4] and urged him to the choice of higher themes.

[1] From a letter to Lord Keeper Egerton, prefixed to a presentation folio in 1601: *Complete Works*, ed. A. B. Grosart (1885), I, 10.

[2] *Pierce Penilesse. Works* (1958) I, 159.

[3] *Pilgrimage to Paradise* (1592), dedication.

[4] *Defence of Rime*, dedication to the Earl of Pembroke.

Abraham Fraunce wrote two poems for her.[1] Nashe praises her without stint.[2] She was evidently, like her brother, a genuine friend to literary art.

Mary Sidney's son, William Herbert, third Earl of Pembroke, inherited the tastes of his mother and uncle. He was educated in the love of poetry by his mother's wise choice of Daniel as his tutor. Many literary men later on owed him gratitude for kindnesses. The poet William Browne lived with him at Wilton. He befriended his neighbour and relative George Herbert, and the dramatist Massinger. John Florio was 'under heavy obligations to him'. Francis Davison, George Chapman, John Taylor and Breton dedicated works to him. John Donne was his intimate friend. But the most interesting fact about him is his connexion with Shakespeare. To him and his brother Philip was dedicated the First Folio of 1623, and he is stated by the editors to have 'prosecuted both them (i.e. the works) and their author with much favour'. It seems that, like his uncle, Pembroke was of a most generous and attractive nature, as is shown by the following passage from a contemporary private letter: 'My Lord of Pembroke did a most noble act, like himself; for the king having given him all Sir Gervase Elwaies estate, which came to above £1,000 per annum, he freely bestowed it on the widow and her children.'[3] Every New Year's Day the Earl used to send Ben Jonson £25 to buy books.[4]

Elizabeth, Countess of Rutland, Sidney's daughter, does not seem to have inherited much of his interest in literature. At any rate, though she befriended Jonson, he does not appear enthusiastic about her as a patroness of the arts. He makes appeal to her noble father's memory to stimulate her zeal for

[1] The Countess of Pembroke's *Ivychurch* and *Emanuel*.
[2] Preface to Sidney's *Astrophel and Stella* (1591).
[3] James Howell, *Epistolae Ho-Elianae*, 1 March 1618.
[4] David Masson, *Drummond of Hawthornden* (1873), 100.

letters, reminding her that it would be a sin against her 'great father's spirit', did she not inherit his love unto the Muses.[1]

Sidney's uncle, the Earl of Leicester, was a major patron of the day, but apart from the support he gave the theatre by keeping his own troupe of players, he followed the more general pattern of the day by encouraging rather than *litterateurs* the scholars, particularly Puritan controversialists.[2] He was friendly to Ascham, whose son Dudley was his godson, and works were dedicated to him by Robert Greene, Florio, Edward Hake, and Edmund Spenser.[3] Spenser's relations with Leicester were none too happy, to judge from the dedication to him of the translation *Virgils Gnat*. In this a little gnat, presumably Spenser, eager to save the life of a sleeping husbandman, presumably Leicester, towards whom a 'hideous snake' is making its way, makes use of his only means, his little sting, to awaken the sleeper, by whose first hasty movement he is brushed aside and slain. Spenser alludes to their relations thus:

> Wrong'd, yet not daring to expresse my paine,
> To you (great Lord) the causer of my care,
> In clowdie teares my case I thus complaine
> Unto your selfe, that onely privie are:
> But if that any *Oedipus* unware
> Shall chaunce, through power of some divining spright,
> To reade the secrete of this riddle rare,
> And know the purporte of my evill plight,
> Let him rest pleased with his owne insight. . . .
> But what so by my selfe may not be showen,
> May by this Gnatts complaint be easily knowen.

[1] *The Forest* (to the Countess of Rutland).

[2] Thomas Cartwright, for instance, owed him much for protection, and received from him a pension of £50 yearly for life.

[3] Greene's *Planetomachia* (1585), Florio's *First Fruites* (1598), Hake's *Newes out of Powles Churchyarde* (1579), and Spenser's *Virgils Gnat* (1595, 'long since dedicated').

In the latter part of the poem the ghost of the gnat appears to the husbandman, and reproaches him for the death which has exiled him from all joy into the 'waste wilderness' of Hades. It looks as if Spenser was becoming discontented by his 'promotion' as secretary to Lord Grey in Ireland. The poet had specifically literary ambitions, with a very earnest view about the relation of high literature with society, and he is unlikely to have been contented by political patronage, particularly if this kept him away from London, as was to prove the case under successive patrons.

The favourite of Elizabeth's declining years, Robert Devereux, second Earl of Essex, was also the recipient of many dedications and much eulogy from literary men. He was himself something of a poet, masque writer and artist. Sir Henry Wotton said of him that to 'evaporate his thoughts in a sonnet' was his common way. It was he who took upon himself the cost of Spenser's funeral, a very splendid one, and he was an intimate friend of Henry Wriothesley, the Earl of Southampton, Shakespeare's friend and early patron.

Southampton was probably, after Sidney, the most discerning and generous of all the aristocratic patrons of literature at the opening of the seventeenth century. He gave to Sir Thomas Bodley one hundred pounds, to buy books for his new public library.[1] He was devoted to the drama, at one time, when in disgrace, filling his abundant leisure 'by going to plays nearly every day'. He was a generous friend to Nashe, Barnabe Barnes, Gervase Markham, Florio, John Minshew and Daniel, and he is eulogized by innumerable writers, including Chapman, Joshua Sylvester, George Wither, Richard Braithwaite, Francis Beaumont and Henry Lok. His relations with Shakespeare must have been intimate; there is a perceptible difference of tone between the two dedications (of *Venus and Adonis* and *Lucrece*) addressed to him by the poet, the later of the two

[1] *Reliquiae Bodleianae* (1703), 170.

clearly expressing not so much gratitude as personal affection. He is nowadays generally considered to be the Mr. W. H. of the sonnets.

Other noble benefactors with specific literary interests must be passed over lightly. Most famous is Lucy, Countess of Bedford, the gifted niece of the poet, Sir John Harington. During the reign of James I she was the favourite patroness of the literary world, generously helpful to many, and receiving from writers of acknowledged eminence such as Michael Drayton, Jonson, Chapman and John Davies of Hereford grateful praises. Donne addressed several of his most beautiful and sincere poems to her. Another lady fortunate in her connexion with men of real genius was Alice Egerton, Countess of Derby, who helped Shakespeare, Donne, Spenser, Jonson, John Marston, John Davies of Hereford, and, early in his career, John Milton. Other patronesses were Margaret, Countess of Cumberland, who engaged Daniel as tutor to her daughter, Lady Anne Clifford, and who accepted the dedication of a poem by Spenser; and the Elizabeth Careys, mother and daughter, with whom Spenser claimed relationship in the dedication of *Muiopotmos*, and to whom Nashe twice acknowledged his great indebtedness.[1]

It cannot have escaped notice that all these patrons had many protégés, and it will be surmised that in that case their patronage was probably occasional rather than permanent, and limited in amount.

The rewards of patronage took many forms. Sometimes there was a gift of money, great or small. Charles I, not at all times very generous to literary men, once gave Jonson a present of £100. Nicholas Rowe reports that on one occasion the Earl of Southampton gave Shakespeare the munificent sum of £1,000. Sometimes cash was given in annuity form. Jonson

[1] *Terrors of the Night* (1594), dedication, and *Christs Teares over Jerusalem* (1593), dedication.

had from the Crown an annuity of 100 marks, raised at his own request to £100. Prince Henry gave Drayton a pension of £10, and Joshua Sylvester one of £20. In the last few years of his life, after much trying, Spenser secured from the Queen a pension of £50 a year. Most of these annuities were decidedly meagre.

One form of patronage fairly frequent in the sixteenth century was that of affording hospitality to the author. Nashe was by no means a tactful or delicate-minded man, yet he was housed for some considerable time by the generous Careys.[1] John Donne, with his whole family, was hospitably housed for five years by Sir Robert Drury. Even the dogmatic arrogant Ben Jonson lived as the guest of Esmé Stuart, Lord d'Aubigny, also for five years. Spenser, too, was certainly at one time the guest of the Earl of Leicester—for how long a period is not known. Inevitably, when an ambitious man left his home (and in some cases, as in Shakespeare's, his family) to seek his fortunes at Court, he became in some sense and for some time a lodger.

But the major form of patronage throughout the period, the least burdensome to the patron and the most useful to him, was that of conferring upon the protégé some official appointment. Sometimes these were sinecures, of a minor kind, fulfillable by delegation. William Hunnis, thus, was appointed at one time toll-taker on London Bridge, a sinecure he promptly converted to cash to the value of £40 by selling the post back to the incumbent. Samuel Daniel, already a Groom of the Chamber by virtue of royal patronage, earned from his *Panegyricke Congratulatory* a commission to write a masque and the post of licenser of the Queen's Revels. More dramatically, William Grey, a writer of the mid-sixteenth century with a flair for political ballads, earned the status of Esquire, a seat in Parliament, the post of Chamberlain and Receiver in the Court

[1] Vide *Terrors of the Night*, dedication and opening paragraph.

18

of General Surveyors, and substantial gifts of land and property in the town of Reading (which made him the owner of two of the three inns in the town, 197 houses, four corn mills and two fulling mills). More usually the post bestowed involved the writer in full-time service in a non-literary capacity: Spenser thus became a secretary and civil servant, Marlowe a political agent, Fraunce and Sir John Davies Court lawyers, Herrick a Court chaplain, and so on. Perhaps this is how Shakespeare became a liveried player with the Lord Chamberlain, Lord Hunsdon.

Whether such appointments were likely to aid or thwart a poet in his literary pursuits was a question largely irrelevant at the time. Very few writers, indeed, regarded literature as their chief pursuit. Very few were like Spenser in having a serious ambition to write long works, requiring much leisure, and being impeded by official duties. Most of the better writers were happy with a life which combined a Courtly function with writing. And the throng of lesser writers, struggling with professional print and the minor rewards of patronage, would have been considerably diminished if their talents had been strong enough to win a political appointment. It was a hard fact of the time that the best of the literary talent tended to be creamed off into pursuits only partially literary, while the lesser talent, denied other outlets for ambition, tended to be left with plenty of time for writing in a situation of highly inadequate rewards.

Certainly, the bounty of patrons, though widespread, reached very few in sufficient amount to satisfy either their expectations or their needs. Nor do the writers scruple to express their discontent. The most outspoken are Nashe, who never minced his words, and the author of the *Pilgrimage to Parnassus* (1597). Nashe describes his fruitless efforts to court patronage by his writings:

All in vaine, I sate up late, and rose earely, contended with the colde, and conversed with scarcitie: for all my labours turned to losse, my vulgar Muse was despised & neglected, my paines not regarded, or slightly rewarded, and I my selfe (in prime of my best wit) laid open to povertie. Whereupon . . . I accused my fortune, raild on my patrones . . .[1]

The unfortunate poet in the *Pilgrimage to Parnassus* spent many years in study, looking still to meeting with 'some good Maecenas, that liberallie would rewarde', but alas, so long did he feed on hope that he almost starved.[2]

Why was this bitter experience so common? Daniel attributes it, not to indifference, but to the barriers between the great and their inferiors in station, which keep from them the knowledge of the need for their bounty:

> . . . would they but be ples'd to know, how small
> A portion of that over-flowing waste
> Which run's from them, would turne the wheeles, and all
> The frame of wit, to make their glory last:
> I thinke they would doe something: but the stirre
> Still about greatnesse, gives it not the space
> To looke out from it selfe, or to conferre
> Grace but by chance, and as men are in place.[3]

But the plain fact was that the demands on patronage were too heavy to be met. The system was breaking down under the stress of changed conditions. In medieval times, if patrons were few, so were writers, and there were accepted refuges for the writers in noble and monastic houses. In the days of Elizabeth and James I, however, the monasteries had disappeared, leaving noble patronage to fill the gap, and the additional opportunities provided by the playhouses and the publishers tended to be too limited to absorb the increased number of writers. The whole emphasis given in Tudor times to the Humanities,

[1] *Pierce Penilesse* (1592). *Works* (1958), I, 157.

[2] V. *Three Parnassus Plays* (1949), 126.

[3] Verses to John Florio, 1611, prefixed to *Queen Anna's New World of Words.*

and especially to literature and drama, seemed to open out alluring prospects of fame and profit. Hence, the class of would-be professional writers increased out of all proportion to the class amongst whom patrons were to be found. The noblemen and gentry who took their patronistic obligations seriously were neither very wealthy nor very numerous, and were heavily burdened by increased expenditure due to social conditions. On the other hand, the wealthy *nouveaux-riches* either held such obligations lightly, or held views which rendered them indifferent altogether to the literary art.

Hence, inevitably, changed relations between patron and protégé. Of old, a talented youth might very well be educated by his natural protector, the great man of his birthplace, and later on, fostered and encouraged by him in literary production. The return to be made for this beneficence was simply the creation of learned or artistic work for the gratification of his patron's immediate circle. Now, he had become merely one of a crowd of unattached suitors, with few or no special claims, striving to snatch for himself a share of the bounty which could not suffice for all. He had to live in the midst of perpetual rivalry; he must forever be striving to bid higher than his fellows. Literary productions became, not a graceful and natural outcome of favourable circumstances contrived by the patron, but eager bids, self-advertising bids, for bounty by the needy. If he were so fortunate as to give thanks for favours received, beneath the gratitude could constantly be detected craven fear lest no more should be forthcoming. The reader is saddened by the inevitable prominence given in dedications to the patron's charity, rather than to his taste or judgment. In this, again, Nashe is a most shameless offender: see his reason for eulogizing Mistress Elizabeth Carey: 'Divine lady, I must and will memorize more especially, for you recompense learning extraordinarily'.[1]

[1] *Christs Teares* (1593), dedication.

The bait which such a writer holds out is public eulogy. Under earlier conditions of patronage, such eulogy was out of place: a gracefully turned compliment, a promise of lasting remembrance, the choice of some incident connected with the patron as the subject for part of the work, these sufficed. The fact that manuscript copies were few, and rarely travelled beyond the confines of the community for which the work was intended, made it impossible for the writer to advertise to the outside world his patron's beneficence. Nor would medieval writers have considered their work sufficiently worthy to advertise a patron. But in the Elizabethan age the poet's work most frequently owned no natural patron; the patron had to be attracted by it. He must be bribed by the offer of widespread fame, made possible now by print, and must be extolled for virtues raising him above the common run of benefactors. Hence extravagance in eulogy; hence servile humility in the writer. If anyone should care to know to what lengths of exaggerated praise a man of genius could be carried in his desire to earn the goodwill of a possible patron, let him study the verses addressed by John Donne to the bereaved father of Mistress Elizabeth Drury, a girl of fifteen, and probably unknown to Donne. Transfigured though they are by imaginative power, they yet betray unmistakable signs of the effort to bid high. The verses reached their mark, and Donne became for many years the intimate friend and dependent of the wealthy Sir Robert Drury.

Abundant evidence is forthcoming of the slight nature of the bond between patron and writer. Spenser wrote his *Daphnaida*, a beautiful but conventional lament, at the request of a chance patron on a lady whom he had never seen! How different are those two eulogistic mourning poems from Chaucer's simple touching lament for the death of his patron's wife, Blanche the Duchess. He had known and loved the beautiful, gracious woman whom he honoured in the poem. He had seen her

> ... daunce so comlily
> Carole and synge so swetely,
> Laugh and pleye so womanly,

and his verses convey a sense of reality and sincerity which is lacking in those of Donne and Spenser.

To the student of the lives of writers in this age, nothing is more striking than the signs of the loosening of the personal bond between patron and poet. It is true that instances can be cited from other times and other countries, of men of genius unable to gain permanent patronage. The famous Aretino (1492–1557) passed from one patron to another in rapid succession. But he treated his protectors most shamefully. If the stories concerning him are to be believed, he did not scruple to insult, defame and defraud them. The marvel is that, in spite of this, he should generally have found some rich nobleman willing to subsidize him, though in many cases this was done from fear. In Elizabethan England, it was the exception even for men of real talent, against whom no serious accusations can be alleged, to be able to meet with more than casual benefactions. Many dedications are obviously addressed to complete strangers; more to men whose acceptance of the dedication is clearly the utmost the writer ventures to hope for. Amongst the most pathetic, with its implied reproach to the man on whom the writer conceived he *had* natural claims, is Philip Massinger's to Charles, Lord Herbert, son of the Earl of Pembroke:

However I could never arrive at the happiness to be made known to your lordship, yet a desire, born with me, to make a tender of all duties and service to the noble family of the Herberts, descends to me as an inheritance from my dead father Philip Massinger. . . .[1]

It is a sure sign of the lack of effective patronage, when an author dedicates his works to a great variety of patrons. Thus

[1] *The Bondman* (1623), dedication. The name is printed wrongly: his father's name was Arthur.

poor Robert Greene has not less than sixteen different patrons for seventeen books. Nashe's one brief period of comparative prosperity led to the dedication of two successive books to his generous friends the Careys;[1] his friendlessness is shown by the variety of his other dedications.

Of course, few dedications were in themselves adequate to attract more than a passing charity. A man could not hope for lifelong recognition on the strength of an extravagant compliment at the head of a literary trifle. Therefore dedications were not relied upon to do more than procure a sum of money, varying according to the means and disposition of the dedicatee, and his estimate of the work. Sometimes an unimportant post was offered in lieu of a fee, but as such posts were nearly always bestowed 'in reversion', the applicant often preferred a prompt money reward. The uncertain value of reversions is painfully illustrated by the lifelong waiting of the unfortunate John Lyly for the office of Master of the Revels, the holder of which persisted in outliving him. In vain the unlucky writer pleaded for something more substantial,

... Some landes, good fines or forfeitures. ... That seeinge nothing will come to me by Revells, I may pray upon the Rebells. Thirteene yeeres your Highnes servant: but yet nothinge. ... A thousand hopes, but all nothinge, a hundred promises, but yet nothinge ... my last will, is shorter then my Inventorie: But three Legacyes, Patience to my Creditors, Melancholly without measure to my frendes, & Beggery without shame to my posteryty.[2]

A humbler instance of the futility of many bits of patronage is afforded by the following letter from Christopher Ocland to Sir Julius Caesar (13 September 1589). Incidentally, it throws interesting light upon methods sometimes employed for filling positions under Government:

[1] *Terrors of the Night*, dedication, and *Christs Teares*, dedication.
[2] Second petition to the Queen: A. Feuillerat, *John Lyly* (1910), App. LV, 561–2.

24

I made a booke of late in Englishe and did for some especiall causes dedicate the same to my lorde of Warwike. I was in consideration of the same to see about the Tower and Sainte Katherins for a Gunners roome in the tower (for thei be of my Lorde of Warwikes, being Master of the Ordinance, gyfte) and to finde out a man meete for the same who might give me some competent peece of mony, and my said Lord wolde for my sake bestowe the same roome upon him. Whilest I seeke this, XV or mo daies be spent and the tyme lost. . . . I shall have money for the same Gunners roome at Easter next, and a yeare hence. So frustrate of my purpose I fall into want . . . such is my ill hap and fortune.[1]

A money fee was, then, in most cases preferable, and more usual. It was the sixteenth-century substitute, not so much for genuine patronage, as for the chance charity afforded in medieval times to poor University scholars. The typical scholar was always poor, and lived as a matter of course upon charity —either that of the individual or of the public in general:

> For al that he might of his frendes hente
> On bookes and on lernynge he it spente,
> And bisily gan for the soules preye
> Of hem that gaf him wherewith to scoleye.[2]

The Elizabethan writer, unlike Chaucer's Scholar, did little praying for souls; all the same, he received readily all gifts that fell in his way. The usual fee paid for the dedication of a drama was forty shillings, and occasionally other works earned three pounds,[3] but far smaller sums, as low even as half a crown, were thankfully received.

There is no evidence of much demand for dedications

[1] Ed. Sir H. Ellis, *Original Letters of Eminent Literary Men* (Camden Society, 1843), 71.

[2] Chaucer, *Canterbury Tales*, Prol. 299–302.

[3] Nathaniel Field, *A Woman is a Weathercock* (1612), dedication. The Earl of Northumberland gave George Peele £3, in June 1593, upon the presentation of a congratulatory poem (*Hist. MSS. Comm.*, VI, App., 227).

amongst the wealthy; the supply clearly exceeded it. In this, if in nothing else, the sixteenth-century writer was a little less fortunate than his successor in the later seventeenth century. Then, the universal fashion in the upper classes of parading literary taste and generosity produced a considerable demand for dedications, so much so that writers were known to pen a dedication, and then write the book as a mere appendage to it.

It is to be noted that the approbation of a great man had a value not to be measured by the bounty actually bestowed upon the writer. Its indirect effect upon the general public was at least equally important. Jonson, pleasing himself by anticipating the acceptance of his verses by Lord Digby, already in imagination sees the public clamouring for copies:

> . . . O! what a fame 't will be?
> What reputation to my lines, and me,
> . . . what copies shall be had
> What transcripts begg'd? . . .
> Being sent to one, they will be read of all.[1]

It is certainly true that the *imprimatur* of approval by a noble name, whether in manuscript or in catchpenny print, enhanced the appeal of a work. It is this consciousness of the power of aristocratic example that causes Samuel Daniel to make digni-fied appeal to the

> . . . mightie Lords, that with respected grace
> Doe at the sterne of faire example stand.

He urges them to 'holde up disgraced knowledge from the ground'. Alas, he is constrained sadly to confess

> . . . the small respect,
> That these great-seeming best of men doe give,
> (Whose brow begets th' inferior sorts neglect).[2]

---

[1] '*An Epigram to my Muse, the Lady Digby*', *The Under-Wood: Ben Jonson*, VIII (1947), 263.

[2] *Musophilus*, 313–19, 659–61. *Complete Works*, ed. Grosart, I, 235, 246.

Some of these great-seeming ones were so fully conscious of the value of their smile, that they considered the unfortunate author amply rewarded by the mere acceptance of a dedication. But indeed, such acceptance was by no means, in all cases, the simple thing it would appear. Patrons occasionally realized, to their cost, that certain obligations entailed by patronage were not so easily evaded as the money one. Slight as the bond between patron and author had now usually become, the old tradition as to the responsibility of the great lord for his dependants still held sway. The later sixteenth century was a suspicious age, as will be shown later on, and authors relied upon the protection of a powerful patron as a sufficient answer to accusations political or moral. Spenser, dedicating *Colin Clout* to Raleigh, entreats him to protect it with his good countenance 'against the malice of evil mouths which are always wide open to carp at and misconstrue my simple meaning'. Lodge durst not expose his poems to the ill-will of the world 'except they were graced with some noble and worthy patron'.[1] Edward Hake, when dedicating to Leicester his *Newes out of Powles Churchyarde*, evidently had in view the powerful protection thus procured for his book 'beset with deadly hate'.

This was all very well so long as suspicion did not emanate from, or take root in, high places; but occasionally patrons were called upon to face their responsibilities in somewhat serious fashion. If writers sometimes suffered from an unlucky chance allusion to the suspected favourite Essex, Essex himself had at times reason to wish himself less popular with writers. Here is an interesting letter relating to a bit of Court scandal in 1595, exalted names being represented by cyphers:

My Lord,

Upon Monday last, 1500 (Q. Elizabeth) shewed 1000 (E. of Essex) a printed book of t——t, Title to a——a. In yt there is, as I here, dangerous praises of 1000, of his Valour and Worthyness,

[1] *Fig for Momus* (1595), dedication.

27

which doth hym harm here. At his coming from Court he was observed to look wan and pale, being exceedinglie troubled at this great piece of villanie done unto hym. . . . The book I spake of is dedicated to my Lord Essex, and printed beyond sea, and 'tis thought to be Treason to have it. To wryte of these things are so dangerous in so perillous a tyme, but I hope it will be no offence to impart unto you th'actions of this place.[1]

Another mischief-making dedication to Essex is noted in March, 1559, in the correspondence of John Chamberlain:

The treatise of Henry the fourth[2] is reasonablie well written. . . . Here hath ben . . . many exceptions taken, especially to the epistle which was a short thinge in Latin dedicated to the erle of Essex, and objected to him in goode earnest, whereupon there was commaundment yt shold be cut out of the booke . . . for my part I can finde no such buggeswords, but that every thinge is as yt is taken.[3]

Possibly in both these cases Essex was perfectly innocent and had not even seen the objectionable works.

The Earl of Devonshire found difficulty in disentangling himself from the difficulties in which Daniel, his protégé, had involved him by the acting of his play, *Philotas* (1600). Malicious persons persuaded the authorities that it bore some reference to the unfortunate Earl of Essex, executed in 1601, and Daniel seems to have tried to prove his innocence by asserting his patron's approbation of the piece. The Earl, having been implicated with Essex, was sensitive, and remonstrated, and Daniel wrote to excuse himself:

I said I had read some parte of it to your honour: and this I said having none els of powre to grace mee now in Corte & hoping that you out of your knowledg of bookes, or favour of letters &

---

[1] Letter from Roland Whyte to Sir Robert Sidney, 25 November 1595: J. C. Collins, *Sidney Papers*, I, 357.

[2] Sir John Hayward, *History of Henry IV*.

[3] *Letters*, ed. N. E. McClure (1939), 72.

mee, might answere that there is nothing in it disagreeing nor any
thing, as I proteste there is not, but out of the universall notions of
ambition and envie, the perpetuall arguments of bookes or tragedies.
I did not say you incouraged me unto the presenting of it (i.e. on
the stage); if I should I had beene a villayne, for that when I shewd
it to your honour I was not resolvd to have it acted. . . .[1]

It is pleasant to know that between them the culprits must have
satisfied the authorities, for *Philotas* was published in 1605, the
following year.

The unfortunate effects of the gradual breaking-up of the
old system of patronage are only too patent. The uncertainty
of the relation bred uneasiness and discontent. These feelings
might be absent, it is true, in the case of a man in Daniel's
position, conscious of feeling and of inspiring genuine respect
and confidence. They are absent, too, in Shakespeare's case.
His relations with Southampton, beginning with an ordinary
dedication expressive of admiration and hope, prefixed to a
poem intended to advertise his talents, ripened very rapidly,
as his connexion became established, into the affectionate
intimacy which is the theme of his second dedication, and the
worshipping love expressed in the Sonnets. There is no question here of the relation of patron and dependant. The gratitude
Shakespeare utters is for affection, not for a patron's benefits;
he asks for and offers love, does not barter praise for bounty.
Jonson also betrays very little sense of holding an uncertain,
difficult position. This is due partly to the consciousness of his
greatness, but partly also to a certain lack of sensitiveness. He
never shrank from asking, because he felt he deserved, and
because no delicacy of feeling checked him. Hence he boldly
wrote his *Epistle Mendicant*, calling upon the Lord High
Treasurer to note that it is 'no less renown' to relieve 'a bedrid
wit, than a besieged town'. He felt it no dishonour, but a
natural thing to send to King Charles *The Humble Petition of*

[1] Quoted in *Complete Works*, ed. Grosart, I, xxii–xxiii.

Poore Ben, that his pension of 100 marks might be increased to pounds.

But even Jonson took pride in declaring that, though he accepted, he *chose* from whom he would accept.[1] To natures of finer fibre the necessity of asking was very bitter. Spenser was fortunately spared, for the most part, this unpleasant task; but he incurred the keenest humiliation of his life when, following Raleigh's advice, he went to lay his *Faerie Queene* before Elizabeth. Other men might willingly prowl in antechambers day after day in the hope of snatching a little 'court holy water', but this humiliating experience wrung from him some of the bitterest words ever uttered by a suitor at Elizabeth's Court:

> Most miserable man, whom wicked fate
> Hath brought to Court, to sue for had ywist
> That few have found, and manie one hath mist;
> Full little knowest thou that hast not tride,
> What hell it is, in suing long to bide:
> To loose good dayes, that might be better spent;
> To wast long nights in pensive discontent;
> To speed to day, to be put back to morrow;
> To feed on hope, to pine with feare and sorrow;
> To have thy Princes grace, yet want her Peeres;
> To have thy asking, yet waite manie yeeres;
> To fret thy soule with crosses and with cares;
> To eate thy heart through comfortlesse dispaires;
> To fawne, to crowche, to waite, to ride, to ronne,
> To spend, to give, to wante, to be undonne.
> Unhappie wight, borne to desastrous end,
> That doth his life in so long tendance spend.[2]

Such experiences—and it must be remembered that they were the ordinary lot of all literary men and all Courtly aspirants—were indeed embittering. John Lyly's despairing appeal

---

[1] '*An Epistle to Sir Edward Sacvile*', *The Under-Wood: Ben Jonson*, VIII (1947), 153.　　[2] *Mother Hubberds Tale* (1591), 892–908.

to his Royal Mistress has been noted. Nashe gives us in detail a picture of the galling treatment experienced by those poets who addressed themselves to patrons of lower rank. Nashe was not thin-skinned, and we feel that he would have put up with the insults, were bounty forthcoming, but contemptuous niggardliness aroused his ire:

Alas, it is easie for a goodlie tall fellow that shineth in his silkes, to come and out face a poore simple Pedant in a thred bare cloake, and tell him his booke is prety, but at this time he is not provided for him: marrie, about twoe or three daies hence if he come that waie, his Page shall say that he is not within, or else he is so busie with my L. How-call-ye-him and my L. What-call-ye-him that he may not be spoken withall. These are the common courses of the world . . . give . . . a dog a bone, and hele wag his taile: but give me one of my yoong Maisters a booke, and he will put of his hat & blush, and so go his waie. . . . I know him that had thanks for three yeares worke. . . . We want an *Aretine* here among us, that might strip these golden asses.[1]

Lucky indeed was Camden, more fortunate than Daniel in having been early placed in a permanent position of independence, who could say to Usher: 'I never made suit to any man, no, not to His Majesty, but for a matter of course incident to my place; neither, God be praised, I needed; having gathered a contented sufficiency by my long labours in the school.'[2] But Camden ranks among the learned and historical writers, who apparently received rather more encouragement and were more politically useful than mere literary artists. He received substantial favours from the two Goodmans, and from Fulke Greville and Lord Burghley.[3]

---

[1] *Pierce Penilesse. Works* (1958), I, 241–2.   [2] Quoted in *D.N.B.*
[3] Camden's *Britannia*, ed. E. Gibson (1772), preface. According to John Aubrey, Walter Warner the mathematician and the learned Thomas Hariot had pensions from the Earl of Northumberland of £60 and £200 respectively (*Brief Lives*, ed. A. Powell (1949), 333).

Sordid rivalry among authors was the inevitable consequence of the struggle for favour. Daniel, in his noble poem
Musophilus, devotes a passage to lamenting the undignified
competition for patronage. Because the number of writers has
grown so great that there is not room for all, they 'kick and
thrust and shoulder', and quarrel 'like scolding wives'. Nicholas
Breton expresses the matter in still more homely fashion, in his
wish that

> . . . all Scholers should be friends,
> And Poets not to brawl for puddings ends.[1]

Jonson, with his Court pension, his reputation as masque
writer, and his many noble patrons, was a great mark for envy.
Nor was he at all aggrieved by this, and used it as an argument
when asking for 'more',[2] but he was not himself above envying
others. He told Drummond that Daniel 'was at jealousies with
him', though the feeling seems to have been chiefly on his own
side. He called Daniel 'no poet', he parodied his verses, and he
could not refrain from a somewhat childish expression of his
annoyance that Daniel should be befriended by the Duchess of
Bedford, and be regarded as 'a better verser . . . or poet . . . in
the court account' than himself.[3]

Nor was Shakespeare, in spite of the tie of strong personal
affection which bound him to his patron, free from the literary
rivalry which dogged the footsteps of all Elizabethan writers.
One poet at least seems to have succeeded in stealing from him,
by 'the proud full sail of his great verse', some of his patron's
favour, and Shakespeare was blamed for being less assiduous in
eulogy. The greater poet was not above the retort that at
least his silence did no harm, whereas the words of the other
brought 'a tomb' where they were intended to 'give life'. But

---

[1] *Works in Verse and Prose*, ed. A. B. Grosart (1879), I, xxxiv.

[2] *'The humble petition of poore Ben'*, *The Under-Wood: Ben Jonson*, VIII
(1947), 259.   [3] *The Forest.*

he betrays sensitiveness under this painful rivalry, beseeching his patron friend to judge 'who it is that says most'. Let others, he pleads, be esteemed for their 'gross painting', their 'precious phrase', their 'breath of words'; *he* would be valued for his 'dumb thoughts, speaking in effect'.[1]

Amongst other evils entailed upon self-respecting writers by their dependence upon patronage was the inevitable accusation of 'mercenary flattery', 'fawning eloquence' and servility. Nor are many of them to be wholly acquitted. Even a man as highly placed as Sir Francis Bacon is to be found soliciting from His Majesty a theme for treatment, with the remark, 'I should with more alacrity embrace your Majesty's direction than mine own choice':[2] we cannot then be surprised that meaner writers should at times display servility. Even a writer as high-minded as Philip Massinger apologized for his theme on the ground that his own 'low fortune' prevented his refusing 'what by his patron he was called unto'.[3] From Thomas Churchyard, as later passages will show, we need not look for much self-respect, though he was a writer of some repute in his own day, but the following shows him at his worst. In a dedication to Sir Walter Raleigh, conscious of having shown some servility, he thus seeks to justify himself:

And if the world say . . . I shew a kind of adulation to fawn for favour on those that are happy; I answer, that it is a point of wisdom, which my betters have taught me. . . . I take an example from the fish that follow the stream.[4]

After such an instance of moral debasement may perhaps fitly follow a reference to the dedication in which James I shows, in contrast, a sense of his own exalted position. Since it was

[1] Sonnets LXXXII–LXXXVI.
[2] 20 March 1620. *Works*, ed. J. Spedding (1874), XIV, 358.
[3] *A Very Woman*, prologue.
[4] *A Sparke of Friendship* (1588). *Harleian Miscellany*, III (1809), 261.

impossible for *him* to assume the properly humble attitude of a dedicator to any human being, he actually wrote the following irreverent and bombastic dedication:

To the Honour of our Lord and Saviour Jesus Christ, the Eternal Son of the Eternal Father, the only θεάνθρωπος, Mediator, and Reconciler of mankind. In sign of thankfulness, His most Humble and most obliged servant, James, by the Grace of God, King of Great Britain, France, and Ireland, Defender of the Faith, doth dedicate and consecrate this his Declaration.[1]

On the other hand, if the dedicator escaped the snare of servility, he was liable to fall into another, that of impudence and shameless effrontery. Dekker points out that authors without blushing will claim acquaintance with men as patrons whom they scarcely know.[2] A most flagrant instance is the case of Stephen Gosson's impudent unauthorized dedication of his attack upon poets and others, in the *Schoole of Abuse*, to Sir Philip Sidney, a piece of impertinence for which, as Spenser reports, he 'was for hys labor scorned'.[3] Worse, in the year of Sidney's death, Gosson doubled his effrontery by dedicating to the same lover of art another work in which he rendered thanks for the protection Sidney's name afforded to the earlier one![4]

Happily, there were men who rose superior to these temptations. When we find a writer like Thomas Heywood, again and again, making of his dedications 'a due acknowledgement, without the sordid expectation of reward or servile imputation of flattery',[5] we welcome the proof that he at least preserved the true poet's self-respect. George Wither dedicated his

[1] 'Answer to the work of Conrad Vorstius on the Nature and Attributes of God', *Works* (1616).

[2] *Newes from Hell* (1606), dedication.

[3] *Works*, ed. E. Greenlaw and others, *Minor Poems II* (1947), 612.

[4] *Ephemerides of Phialo* (1579), dedication.

[5] *The Fair Maid of the West* (acted 1617), preface.

Shepherd's Hunting to all the 'known and unknown sym-
pathizers' who had felt for him during his imprisonment; and
we honour the manly lines in which he says:

> I have no Minde to flatter; though I might,
> Be made some Lords companion; or a Knight.
> Nor shall my Verse for me on begging goe,
> Though I might starve, unlesse it did doe so.
>   . . . Oh! how I scorne,
> Those Raptures, which are free, and nobly borne,
> Should Fidler-like, for entertainment scrape
> At strangers windowes: and goe play the Ape,
> In counterfeiting Passion, when there's none.[1]

His words suggest what is only too true, that men of weak
principle were betrayed by their necessities into even worse
than servility—into a deliberate hypocrisy, a degraded pandering to the unworthy. That this was so is clear from the satiric
portrait of the poet given in the *Pilgrimage to Parnassus*. Drain-
ing his inspiration from the pint-pot, he exclaims:

Nowe I am fitt to write a book: woulde anie leaden Mydas, anie
mossie patron have his asses ears deified, let him but come, and give
mee some prettye sprinkling to maintaine the expences of my
throate, and Ile dropp out suche an Encomium on him, that shall
immortalize him as longe as there is ever a bookebinder in Englande.[2]

It is by no means certain that Nashe in his necessities was fet-
tered by very high principles; evidently bounty is a main
passport to his praises. If any Maecenas will bind Nashe to him
by his bounty, then the writer will 'doo him as much honour'
as any poet of his 'beardlesse yeeres' in England.[3] It is only fair
perhaps to interpret these and similar reckless utterances in the
light of a genuine devotion to art detectable elsewhere in his
work.

[1] *Withers Motto* (1621), ff. 13, 132.
[2] II. *Three Parnassus Plays* (1949), 103.
[3] *Pierce Penilesse. Works* (1958), I, 195.

The more scrupulous writers did their utmost to avoid the slightest imputation of fawning servility. They chose for their patrons personages of no particular public reputation; they dedicated to personal friends and benefactors, as thank-offering not as bait; and they protested against the undue servility of their less worthy colleagues by a courteous insistence on the value of their own offerings. Samuel Daniel, for one, writes to his patrons as to equals.[1] George Chapman assures Sir Thomas Howard that the work he presents to him contains matter no less worthy the reading than any others recently favoured by great nobles.[2] And John Webster, in dedicating the *Duchess of Malfi* to Lord Berkeley, takes still higher ground:

I am confident this work is not unworthy your honour's perusal; for by such poems as this poets have kissed the hands of great princes, and drawn their gentle eyes to look down upon their sheets of paper, when the poets themselves were bound up in their winding sheets.

Such words go some way to redeem the honour of the professional writer, soiled by such as Nashe, Gosson and Churchyard.

Nor were servility and effrontery the worst of the evils attendant upon patronage. To them was added fraud. We owe to Dekker an interesting exposure of the tricks played by cheating knaves upon unsuspecting patrons. These rogues first got small pamphlets printed, generally of matter filched from other writers. They then procured the names of some large number of gentry, printed copies of a dedicatory epistle with a different patron's name to each; then went round, and obtained as many fees as possible for this single dedication and pamphlet. If the supposed dedicatee were suspicious, and made

---

[1] Vide his noble and thoughtful epistles to Lord Keeper Egerton and the Bishop of Winchester, and his Funeral Poem on the Duke of Devonshire.

[2] *Revenge of Bussy d'Ambois* (1613), dedication.

inquiries amongst the stationers or printers, the wily knaves were prepared for him. They had already distributed among the trade a number of copies of the work, but without the dedication, for which, of course, they were awaiting permission! 'Thus the liberallitie of a Nobleman, or of a Gentleman is abused: thus learning is brought into scorne and contempt: Thus men are cheated of their bountie, giving much for that . . . which is common abroad, and put away for base prices'.[1]

There is another point of view to be considered—that of the patron himself. To him, it is clear, the endless importunities of struggling writers must have presented a serious dilemma. Amid so many, how decide between their claims? How benefit any considerable number in any practical way? Yet how distinguish between them? Some patrons, like Sidney, had genuine tastes and means of discriminating; others at the opposite extreme were content with a perfunctory response to a succession of direct appeals. To the average young man of rank and wealth, the perpetual appeal of professional writers, most of them with undistinguished talents, must have been simply an unqualified nuisance. He bore with it, as a burden incident to rank and fashion; to a certain extent, he even encouraged it as a recognition of his own superiority. But Nashe was probably perfectly justified in his complaint that

. . . ther is not that strict observation of honour, which hath beene heeretofore. Men of great calling take it of merite, to have their names eternizde by Poets; & whatsoever pamphlet or dedication encounters them, they put it up in their sleeves, and scarce give him thankes that presents it.[2]

Thomas Thorpe's satirical advice to Blount on the correct

[1] *Lanthorne and Candle-light. Non-dramatic works of Thomas Dekker*, ed. A. B. Grosart, III (1885), 249.
[2] *Pierce Penilesse*. Works (1958), I, 159.

behaviour of a patron completely bears out Nashe's words.[1] Patronage, as a refuge for the author, was moribund.

It died hard. Struggling authors could not afford to let it die. They would 'hang upon a young heir like a horse-leech'. They followed up the tracks of gouty patrons as if 'hoping to wring some water from a flint'. They even descended to flattering and pandering to lackeys, in order to gain admission to the presence of an unwilling great man. Generations of needy authors begged, starved, and passed away before the day when Swift pilloried their shameless insincerity in his inimitable bookseller's dedication to the *Tale of a Tub*. Generations were to pass before Samuel Johnson gave the *coup de grâce* to the long tottering system by his scornful retort to Lord Chesterfield.

---

[1] Marlowe's *Lucan* (1600), preface. According to G. H. Putnam, *Books and their Makers in the Middle Ages* (1897), the burdensomeness of dedications seems to have been even greater in Germany. There, local authorities were driven to issue notices that they would in future acknowledge no dedications of literary productions unless written authorization had been previously secured. One family, when a composition appeared dedicated to a deceased musical ancestor of theirs, issued a notice that the dedication must be withdrawn unless authorization from the 'shade' was forthcoming!

CHAPTER II

Authors and Official Censors

> I holde no place better governed, how ever in so
> great a sea of all waters there cannot chuse but be
> some quick-sands and rockes & shelves. . . .
>
> NASHE[1]

IT is difficult for a modern writer to estimate at its full strength
the paralysing influence of 'authority' in Elizabethan days. An
unwary journalist, it is true, is occasionally entangled in the
meshes of the law of libel or the delicacies of parliamentary
privilege; but in the sixteenth century, when the function of
government in relation to literary production was mainly to
pounce upon possible offenders, it was rare good fortune for a
writer to succeed all through his life in eluding its grip.

The representatives of authority, so far as literature was con-
cerned, were four: the Privy Council and Court of Star
Chamber; the Court of High Commission; the Stationers'
Company; and the Corporation of the City of London.

The *Privy Council* and *Star Chamber* seem in their action to
have been practically identical. So far as it is possible to define
their relation to each other, it may perhaps be said that the
latter partook of the nature of a Committee of the Council,
sitting as an open court and exercising judicial functions. It
consisted of some of the most important Privy Councillors,
with or without the addition of a varying number of other persons, chiefly judges. In practice, at any rate when dealing with
matters which affected the press, the Star Chamber seems to
have been almost identical with the inner circle of the Privy
Council.

The *Court of High Commission* was founded primarily as a

---

[1] *Have with you to Saffron-Walden. Works* (1958), III, 130.

means of exercising the royal supremacy in ecclesiastical affairs. It was composed of clergy and lawyers, but it assumed the ancient powers and adopted the procedure of the regular ecclesiastical courts, and tended gradually to supersede these. Its authority over the press arose out of the appointment of the Archbishop of Canterbury and the Bishop of London as supreme licensers for all printed publications.

It does not seem possible to distinguish with any precision between the functions exercised in regard to literature by the Court of High Commission on the one hand, and the Star Chamber on the other. Authors and publishers were cited, now before one authority, now before the other. Possibly, in theory, it was held that political offences fell under the jurisdiction of the latter, and offences against religion and morals under that of the former, but in an age when religion and politics were inseparably connected, such distinctions were not easily carried out in practice. Cases of suspicion were reported indifferently, either to the Archbishop of Canterbury, the Bishop of London, or Cecil, the Lord High Treasurer. For instance, John Harrison, Warden of the Stationers' Company, reported to the Archbishop his discovery of a papistical book which he suspected had been recently printed.[1] Dr Charles Parkins sent to Cecil two 'lewd books', which had reached him from overseas, with the cautious remark, 'I will have no herbs of such smell about me without order.'[2] The Star Chamber and the Court of High Commission often worked in concert. Where the latter found it difficult to secure a conviction, the culprit would be called before the Star Chamber for further examination. Conversely, cases brought before the Star Chamber were not infrequently sent for trial by the ecclesiastical court. There was no constitutional check upon the action of either tribunal. More than once attempts were made to contest the legality of the Court of High

[1] 13 November 1573. T. Wright, *Elizabeth and her Times* (1838), I, 493.
[2] 26 November 1593. *Hist. MSS. Comm., Cal. MSS. Hatfield*, IV, 419, 423.

Commission, but such attacks were arbitrarily suppressed. For speaking against it in Parliament a certain Morrice, the author of a suppressed pamphlet, was imprisoned for some years.[1]

Authority, as exercised by these bodies, was thoroughly repressive. The task of governing a nation distracted by religious discords and political intrigues, and harassed by fears for its future peace and prosperity, was far from easy, and the most level-headed statesman was inevitably guided more by fear than by generosity. And the printing presses were elements in society particularly to be feared. Here was a newly arisen force to be reckoned with, rapidly gaining strength, and as yet practically uncontrolled by any sense of responsibility. No wonder that its power should have been dreaded by a perpetually menaced government.

At first the press was treated with the lenient vigilance which characterized the general policy of the earlier years of Elizabeth's reign. It is true that in 1559 an injunction was issued prohibiting the publication of any book or paper without previous licence from appointed authorities. But it is clear from the records of the trade that the injunction was enforced with little strictness; books continued for some time to be issued with no further formality than the payment of a fee to the Stationers' Company for entry on their register. This entry implied the sanction of the officials of the Company, but no licenser's name was usually given. Gradually, however, supervision became more strict. We find the officials fortifying themselves, in the case of books of divinity, with the advice of some 'discreet minister' before sanctioning. They were probably already beginning to recognize the trend of government policy towards making them responsible for the publication of books thus recognized. They therefore began the custom of adding, in the register, the name of the licenser.

But it was not until 1583 that direct interference began. In

[1] J. S. Burn, *Court of High Commission* (1865), 16–17.

that year John Aylmer, Bishop of London, called upon the Stationers' Company to report to him precisely the names of the owners of all the printing presses, and the number possessed by each. It is significant that during the course of the inquiry it was discovered that one printer, John Wolfe, was keeping two presses illegally secreted in a vault.[1] There were special reasons at the time for more vigilant control. The years 1581 to 1588 were years of secret intrigue marked by the discovery of plot after plot. A Jesuit mission under Edmund Campion and Parsons was despatched to England in 1581, with the definite object of encouraging disaffection among Roman Catholics. Loyalty was deliberately undermined and the assassination of the Queen advocated. In 1583 one plot was discovered just in time, and 1585 and 1586 were the years of Babington's abortive conspiracy and the trial, for complicity in it, of Mary Queen of Scots. Throughout all these intrigues, Jesuit pamphlets, secretly printed, played their part in the endeavour to mould opinion.

The result is seen in the Star Chamber decree of 1586, by which for many years the printing press was bound. It strictly limited the number of printers, and it forbade all printing except within the liberties of the City of London, and in Oxford and Cambridge. No printer might set up a new press without direct permission. All presses were to be accessible to inspection. And finally all books and pamphlets issued had first to receive the *imprimatur* of the Archbishop of Canterbury and the Bishop of London.[2] In 1595, under the influence of the disciplinarian, Archbishop John Whitgift, the Court of High Commission reinforced these licensing regulations. Henceforwards, enactments concerning the press, as in 1615 and 1637, were chiefly concerned with limiting the total number of master printers and of presses.

[1] E. Arber, *A Transcript of the Registers of the Company of Stationers of London, 1554–1640*, I (1875), 248.

[2] The text of the Decree is given in Arber, *Transcript*, II (1875), 807–12.

For the licensing of books the Archbishop of Canterbury and the Bishop of London were mainly responsible, though in some cases inferior Church dignitaries could and did act as licensers under their authority. No doubt the allotment of this function arose naturally out of the traditional position of literature as the product of 'clerks', and therefore *de facto* under ecclesiastical control. But the majority of offences could be read as against religion (or ecclesiasticism) and morality.

For particular categories of books it became customary, for obvious reasons, to delegate the licensing to experts: thus, an eminent surgeon would license medical books, and the Earl Marshal books on heraldry. For plays the *imprimatur* of the Master of the Revels, or his deputy, became essential. A political work would sometimes have to wait for the direct sanction of the Lord Treasurer or the Secretary of State.[1] Michael Drayton's *Polyolbion* must have incurred suspicion for some reason, for it seems to have needed the sanction of four licensers.[2]

The task, however, of controlling the press was not limited to the supervision of the number of presses and the licensing of books. Other important functions were the suppression of unauthorized writings, or such as had been licensed without due caution, and the detection of offending utterances. Nor were the powers of the authorities limited to the suppression of the printed book: in the case of disobedience to regulations fine and imprisonment, sometimes even banishment or death, were inflicted.

Books most open to the charge of heresy, works of theology, sermons and the like, do not fall within the scope of the present inquiry. Nor do the pamphlets of the Martin Marprelate controversy in 1588–90: it is sufficient to note that the secret press from which they were issued was tracked with the utmost

[1] October 1588. Arber, *Transcript*, II (1875), 502, 504.
[2] February 1612, *Transcript*, III (1876), 477.

determination and finally captured, and that, of those implicated in these publications, one died in prison and one was hanged.

The rigour of the ecclesiastical authorities in suppressing supposed heretical writings was quite remarkable. For thirty-five years a *Confutation of the Rhemish Testament*, by the Puritan Thomas Cartwright, was kept from the press despite repeated efforts to obtain permission to print,[1] even though the work was undertaken with the encouragement of Leicester and Walsingham. On one occasion in 1568, Magdalen College, Oxford, was required to search for 'superstitious books', and send those found to the Court of High Commission. Still more noteworthy is the suppression in 1591, *after* licence and publication, of a harmless metrical version of the Psalms, called a *Harmony of the Church*, by Michael Drayton.[2] John Selden was summoned in 1618 before the Court of High Commission because in his learned book on *Tithes*, he was thought to have weakened the ecclesiastical claim of 'Divine Right'. He was severely threatened and obliged to sign a form of apology for the publication, and the book was suppressed.[3] Henry Gellibrand, Professor of Astronomy at Gresham College, was called to the same Court because, in an almanac for the year 1631, he had substituted for the names of saints and apostles, those of martyrs recorded by Foxe. He was however acquitted.[4]

Nor was the activity of the authorities limited to the cognizance of published literature. In the Star Chamber, Sir John Yorke and others were indicted for permitting and seeing the performance of an interlude in which a priest was represented as victorious in argument over an English minister. It was regarded as 'a play in prophanation of religion'. Yorke and his wife were fined £1,000 each, and others of the audience £300![5]

[1] *Transcript*, IV (1877), 27–8. [2] Vide *D.N.B.*
[3] Burn, op. cit., 37. [4] Ibid., 61.
[5] *MSS. of the Duke of Northumberland*, 1 July 1614. *Hist. MSS. Comm.*, III, App., 62–3.

Political topics were even more risky. The most innocent allusion to current politics was liable to be tabooed by a government which knew itself to be menaced by secret enemies on every side. This pardonable uneasiness explains, if it does not excuse, the policy which proscribed certain Irish passages in Holinshed's *History of England* (1577), ordering that the offending pages should be cancelled and replaced by others. Less surprisingly, the Government took strong measures against Parsons' daring treatise on the Succession (1594), advocating the claims of the Infanta: it was high treason even to possess a copy.[1] But the nature of the political opinions expressed was not the sole ground of condemnation: the offence lay in publishing *any* opinions upon matters which the Crown considered out of the legitimate range of criticism of a subject. Any expression of views upon current politics was liable to be construed as a 'lewd libel', with condign punishment meted out to the author. Thus in 1582 a certain Vallinger (?Stephen) was fined £100, imprisoned, and pilloried for the authorship of certain 'libels' against government and religion.[2] And in 1599, when John Stubbes and the publisher Page brought out a pamphlet against the French marriage then apparently projected by the Queen, they were condemned to have the right hand struck off, according to the barbarous Elizabethan custom, by a blow from a butcher's knife.

These, however, were publications written avowedly on political topics, by men conscious that they ran the risk of severe penalties. It was otherwise with many publications, innocent in intention, but suspected by the authorities of hidden political allusions. It is perhaps intelligible that an attempt should have been made to suppress Raleigh's *History of the World*, written during his imprisonment. James I considered that it was 'too saucy in censuring princes'. But perfectly

[1] T. G. Law, *Essays and Reviews* (1904), 140.
[2] Burn, op. cit., 75.

innocent academic works fell under the ban. Drama was especially open to suspicion, as offering exceptional chances of working upon popular feeling. During the last years of the life of the turbulent favourite Essex, and those immediately following his execution, the authorities were unusually sensitive. Jonson's *Sejanus* and Daniel's *Philotas* both brought trouble upon their authors, being construed as expressions of sympathy with Essex. On the other hand, it is difficult to understand why the Lord Chamberlain's Company should have been let off without punishment for an offence much more real. The night before Essex's conspiracy in 1601, they revived, at the request of the conspirators, Shakespeare's *Richard II*, the object being beyond doubt to arouse public sympathy. The players were interrogated, and it was proved that the performance was by request; yet it does not appear that they suffered for their temerity.[1] In contrast, Sir John Hayward, for an incautious dedication to Essex of a history of the last years of Richard II, was imprisoned and threatened with torture.[2] That there was a special risk in the publication of work likely to give offence seems clear from the omission, in the *Richard II* quartos of 1597 and 1598, of the deposition scene.

But, alas, for writers and publishers, the list of dangerous topics did not end with religion and politics. Hidden snares lay around every conceivable subject. No writer must so much as glance at the character of any great man. In Sir John Smith's *Discourse on the Forms and Effects of divers sorts of Weapons* (1590), the author speaks rather plainly about 'a few private men, whom almost the whole realm doth greatly blame for their detestable disorders and cruelties'. The book was in consequence suppressed, and there is extant a remonstrance, written by Smith to Cecil, complaining bitterly of the injustice, in that

[1] S. Lee, *Life of Shakespeare* (1878), 175–6.
[2] H. R. Plomer, 'An examination of some existing copies of Hayward's *Life and Raigne of King Henrie IV*' (Library, N.S., III, 1902), 13–23.

. . . a fewe of our such men of warre, beeinge so notoriously knowen
. . . should carrie so much credit, to procure in their owne beehalfes
. . . the extinguishinge of a little booke, that doth reproache none
but such, as through their guiltie consciences will needes . . . discover themselves.[1]

Nothing might be published which could conceivably injure
the interests of anyone powerful enough to retaliate. Dr Giles
Fletcher's book on *The Russe Commonwealth* (1591) was considered likely to do harm to the trade of the Muscovy Company, as it censured rather severely the Russian Government,
and the company procured its suppression.[2] Even personal dis-
putes between writers as unimportant as poverty-stricken
Thomas Nashe, and the pedant Gabriel Harvey, were not to be
tolerated by the authorities.

During the last decade of Elizabeth's reign (the first decade of
Shakespeare's public career), the press seems to have been particularly feared and hampered by government. This was attri-
butable partly to a series of intrigues, about the succession
question, and partly to the autocratic character of the Archbishop of Canterbury, John Whitgift, and of his coadjutor,
Bancroft, the Bishop of London. Not content with rigorous
suppression of religious and political topics, they exercised at
this time a specially severe censorship over satirical publications
dealing with social abuses. There was perhaps special cause, for
the output of coarse satire, during the years before 1600, was
exceptionally large. Whitgift determined to repress the dangerous tendency to criticize, and on 1 June 1599, issued an order
for the suppression and burning of no less than seven satirical
works, including the satires of Joseph Hall, John Marston, and
Edward Guilpin, and the epigrams of John Davies of Hereford,
three books of alleged immoral tendencies, including Marlowe's *Ovid*, and all the quarrelsome pamphlets of Harvey and

[1] ed. Sir H. Ellis, *Original Letters of Eminent Literary Men* (Camden Society,
1843), 60.   [2] Ibid., 76–9.

Nashe. It was forbidden to print hereafter any 'Satyres or Epigrams', and any book by Harvey or Nashe.[1] It was not until 1613, after the death of Whitgift and Bancroft, that satirical writing was again ventured upon, in print at any rate, by that daring free-lance, George Wither, in his *Abuses stript and whipt*. He had even then good cause to repent of his temerity, for the outcome was a rigorous imprisonment.

Satire was particularly likely to give offence, on account of its coarseness, as well as its freedom in criticism. Though the Elizabethan age was outspoken and unrefined, spasmodic attempts were made, sometimes under Puritan influence, to check literature of openly immoral tendencies. The efforts at supervision of literary morals were, at best, spasmodic and ineffective: each instance seems to stand alone, as an accidental thing. That certain books and pamphlets should have been permitted free circulation, when the comparatively harmless recriminations of Nashe and Harvey were condemned, might occasion us some surprise, did we not know how much more urgent was felt to be the preservation of order than the regulation of morals. While the Stationers' Register records the licensing of hundreds of ballads, many undoubtedly evil in tendency, there is at least one instance of a ballad being stayed until 'the undecentnes be reformed', and finally rejected.[2]

There is on record also an interesting order issued from the Privy Council to the Universities in 1593, forbidding them to allow 'common plaiers' to resort thither, upon the definitely moral ground that many of their interludes and 'plaies' are 'full of lewde example' and most of them full of 'vanitie'.[3] This was an exceptional year of hardship for actors in general, a plague year in London when the public playhouses were closed and

---

[1] *Transcript*, III (1876), 677.

[2] 1591. *Transcript*, II (1875), 576.

[3] 29 July 1593, ed. Sir John Dasent, *Acts of the Privy Council* (1890 ff.), XXIV, 427.

the companies evacuated out of town; an apt opportunity for Puritan interference of this kind.

The delays to which some books were subjected by the custom of licensing were often most vexatious and harmful. Philip Stubbes complains that they were often kept waiting three months, sometimes as much as two or three years, and probably after all might meet with a refusal.[1] Such uncertainty must have seriously affected the author's chance of selling his manuscript, while the alterations and cancellations often required by the authorities after printing must have greatly reduced the publisher's profit, and consequently the payment of authors.

Since offences against State and Church were, as was inevitable, sought out with much greater vigilance than offences against mere morality and decency, we are not surprised at Philip Stubbes' complaint that serious works met with much greater difficulty in procuring a licence than writings less worthy, or even morally vicious. He is thinking, no doubt, of Greene's later pamphlets, when he angrily asserts that books

full of all filthines, scurrilitie, baudry, dissolutenes, cosonage, cony-catching and the lyke ... are either quickely licensed, or at least easily tollerate, without all denyall or contradiction whatsoever.[2]

There was thus, in the later years of Elizabeth, and under James, very strict supervision of printed literature. And yet, such was the irrepressible activity of authors and stationers, this rigorous discipline was not entirely successful. Forbidden books *were* bought and sold. Suppression, as always, made the demand for them more keen, though of necessity it must have limited the sale. We know that Raleigh's *History of the World* continued to be sold, after suppression, without the title-page.

---

[1] *Motive to Good Works* (1593). *Anatomy of Abuses* (New Shaks. Soc., 1877-9), 69*.　　　　　　　　　　[2] Ibid.

Rowlands' suppressed 'Humours Lettinge Blood in the Vayne' (1600) was secretly republished, without date, under the title of *Humour's Ordinary*;[1] and twenty-eight booksellers were fined for dealing in the book after it had been forbidden.[2] Nashe got some productions published after the prohibition in 1599, though it is true that none of the Harvey-Nashe pamphlets were reprinted, and that neither antagonist dared to re-open the quarrel. Moreover, dangerously unlawful seditious books were set forth, scaring law-abiding citizens who chanced to meet with them. Lord Edward Windsor had such a book sent to him by post. 'After he had read it,' it was timorously explained, 'he never spake with any of it, nor showed it unto any, but has kept it to himself.'[3]

The most daring exploit of the age in printing was carried out by certain Jesuit priests, who in 1581 secretly prepared four hundred copies of a work by Edmund Campion, and scattered them in St Mary's Church, before the Encaenia at Oxford.[4]

Wither goes as far as to bring a very serious accusation against some of the leading members of the Stationers' Company in his day. He asserts that they took advantage of their official position:

. . . those bookes which they have taken from others as unlawfull have bene divulged againe by some in office among them for their private commodity . . . they have solde those bookes which did to their knowledge contain matter injurious to the person of the King, and Prince . . . it is already come that whatsoever the State dislykes shalbe imprinted and devulged by them (though both absurd and scandalous) with twice more seriousnes, then any booke lawfully commaunded. . . .[5]

---

[1] *Works*, ed. E. F. Rimbault (Percy Society), IX, introduction.
[2] *Transcript*, II (1875), 832.   [3] *Cal. MSS. Hatfield*, V, 53.
[4] Vide Edmund Campion, *D.N.B.*
[5] *The Schollers Purgatory* (*c.* 1624). *Miscellaneous Works* (Spenser Society), I (1872), 111, 34.

Wither was an angry man, but there was doubtless a grain of truth in this. It shows, were illustration needed, that the press shared in the growing tendency towards repudiation of Stuart authority.

The Stationers' Company was the incorporated body of persons engaged in the mechanical production and selling of books. They were the successors to the scriveners and manu-script sellers of previous centuries, and were so called because they occupied recognized stations, or stalls, in localities devoted to the trade.

At this period stationers were primarily booksellers, though they might also be printers, publishers and scriveners. They had a trade organization, incorporated in 1557,[1] and confirmed in 1559, and they had power to regulate in detail the printing and selling of books, to decide questions as to ownership, and in general to make any regulations considered advisable, so long as not contrary to the law of the land. Except in so far as they acted for the Privy Council and the Court of High Com-mission, they were concerned chiefly with the regulation of the book trade for their own advantage as a close corporation. They were invested by charter with great powers of supervision, and were in the habit of appointing 'searchers' to ascertain any cases of infringement of rules. As the number of printers was not more than twenty-three, and the searchers were as many as twenty-four or twenty-eight, it is clear that the supervision was far from nominal, especially when, at one time, the search was made weekly. The craft of printing could only be exercised by members of the Company, and by a limited number of them. In case of disobedience to regulations, the officers of the Company could inflict fines, and they could seize and destroy not only printed 'copy', but even, a more severe penalty, the type or 'letter' itself. One of their main objects was to protect master printers and publishers in their rights as proprietors of

[1] The Charter was enrolled in the City Records on 3 June 1557.

manuscript or 'copy'. They kept a register of books and pamphlets published, which they entered to the name of the owner, charging a small fee for registration. If a work were secretly published by anyone other than the stationer to whom it was entered, the Company could take disciplinary measures to protect the property. The register contains repeated instances of the seizure of copies, unlawfully, or—as they phrase it—'disorderly' printed. Thus, M. Lawe was fined 20s. for printing *England's Mourning Garment*, 'being Thomas Millington's copie' (7 June 1603).

There can be no doubt that at first the register was simply a means of recording permission to print a given work, and the receipt of the regular fee for this permission. To the Company, the main point recorded was the fee; to the stationer, the point lay in the *imprimatur*. Entry was supposed to be compulsory, and it was the only proof of ownership of a book, but stationers appear to have entered, or neglected to enter, at their will. As however the officials of the Stationers' Company came to be more and more employed as the instruments of a higher authority, they made it a condition of entry that the book should first have been passed by the Government licensers, and entry thus became itself a proof of conformity to the State regulations. Hence it grew more desirable and more customary always to enter books, unless the publisher were careless or wished to evade notice.

From about 1586 onwards the Stationers' Register forms a fairly complete record of books openly published. Out of fifty-three small pamphlets published by Nicholas Breton, forty are entered. Out of twenty-two different editions of plays by Shakespeare issued between 1597 and 1637 (some of them certainly pirated), rather more than half are entered. Five out of eight works by Philip Stubbes are recorded. The absence of registration is not to be taken as proof of neglect to procure a licence, but it suggests it, since it is *prima facie* unlikely that the publisher who had taken pains to comply with the licensing regulations should neglect to register with the Company his right to the book.

Other regulations of the Company were designed in the interests of workmen. Some limited the number of apprentices and the kinds of work to be assigned to them; others fixed the term for the period of apprenticeship, and limited the number of copies permitted to be printed in each separate edition. The general effect of these enactments was to keep up the cost of production, and thus indirectly to keep low the payment for manuscripts. Fortunately for authors, they were not artificially restricted in their choice of publisher. Anyone, whether belonging to the Company or not, could take upon himself the risk of publishing a manuscript,[1] provided he could arrange with a printer and bookseller. There was, therefore, competition for the productions of printers who could hit the popular taste.

In the case of acted drama, still another public body of authorities had to be reckoned with, the *Corporation of the City of London*. It was in their capacity of guardians of the public peace, health and morality, that the City Fathers were concerned with the theatre.

The record again is that of a hostile and repressive authority which attempted continually to prohibit performances, and to restrict the freedom of playing companies by regulations as to days, hours, numbers of actors and so on. The first seriously repressive measure came in 1571 when the Corporation proceeded first against 'all fencers, bearewardes, comen players of enterludes and minstralles wandering abroade', declaring them to be vagabonds and therefore liable to instant arrest and imprisonment. Players who wore the livery of a nobleman were exempt from this regulation, with the result that Leicester's men, for instance, sued their patron to be retitled, formally, as 'household Servants and daylie wayters', without any increase

[1] Unless it fell within the class of 'privileged' books.

in stipends or other benefits. London was cleared of all acting companies except those under the patronage of a particular nobleman. Even this protection proved frail, so that repeatedly the players had to enlist the support of the Privy Council to intercede with the Lord Mayor to put an end to some temporary prohibition, so that performances might be resumed, their want relieved, and rehearsals for Court festivities made possible. Ultimately, after the accession of King James, all the companies placed themselves under the protection of a member of the royal family.

In 1574 the Corporation moved against the innyard theatres, which were regarded as particularly vicious and unhygienic, although they were the only public places in London where the companies were able to erect scaffold stages for public entertainment. Henceforward, the innkeeper had to bind himself to keep order, a percentage of the takings had to be given to the poor, and performances were entirely prohibited on Sundays and Holy-Days, traditionally the most profitable. The response of the liveried companies was to erect, from 1576 onwards, their own theatres in precincts where the Corporation had no direct authority. But the running battle between the Corporation and the players continued, one way or another. All public meetings could be prohibited in the interests of public health, and there were always sufficient plagues or threats of plagues to hit the players hard. This was a direct conflict between the Humanist tradition, to which the Court and the Privy Council were committed, which encouraged drama as a necessary and central part of culture, and the Puritan objection that fiction was worthless, often evil, and at best foolishness in the eyes of God. Puritan writers like John Field, one of Leicester's protégés, could not understand why a nobleman with Puritan sympathies like Leicester, should feel bound to keep and protect his own company of players. But the result of this protection was that, despite all the difficulties, a professional theatre was born and flourished in London, an island of relative peace and prosperity for the professional writer. In the end the Puritan forces won, when the outbreak of the Civil War gave the Corporation the opportunity to close down all public playhouses for the duration, but until 1642, as we shall see, the theatre flourished to the great benefit of the writers who made their home in it.

It was rather different in the provinces. In the earlier years of Elizabeth's reign, civic authorities in provincial towns seem to have viewed the performances of travelling companies with indifference, or even with beneficent interest. Many small touring companies brought professional drama to the towns and villages of the countryside. But as Puritan opinion gathered strength, it permeated the provinces too. The history of Shakespeare's birthplace, Stratford-on-Avon, is typical. In his boyhood travelling companies were welcome and frequent visitors. During the year 1568, when Shakespeare's father was Bailiff, two companies were entertained by the Corporation,[1] and no less than twenty-four troupes performed in the town during the years from 1569 to 1587. But by 1602, opinions, or membership of the Town Council, had undergone such an alteration that this body passed a resolution forbidding, under a penalty of ten shillings, the performance of plays in the Guildhall. In 1612 the fine was raised to the large sum of £10.[2] Thenceforward, touring became restricted to the very

[1] S. Lee, *Life of Shakespeare* (1878), II. During the ten years from 1558 to 1568, the Mayor and Corporation of Gloucester paid for no less than twelve public performances by various companies of players. It seems to have been customary for them also to provide the scaffold, and to entertain the players at a tavern (*Hist. MSS. Comm.*, XII, App. ix, 468–70).

[2] J. O. Halliwell, *Stratford Records*, 17 December 45 Eliz., and 7 February 9 James. The form of the prohibition suggests that it is partly due to a growing regard for good order in public places. The similar prohibition in the records of the Corporation of Southampton assigns as a reason the damage done to 'tables, benches, and fourmes', so that the court cannot sit 'in such decent and convenient order as becometh' (*Hist. MSS. Comm.*, XI, App. iii, 28—6 February 1623).

occasional visits of the noble companies, usually for performances in one or other of the noble houses.

To turn to more general considerations, an unfortunate outcome of the suspicious and censorious attitude of authority towards printed literature was the rise of a class of professional informers, or, to use the Elizabethan terms, 'moralizers' and 'state decipherers'. To judge from the complaints to be met with, these informers only began to cause serious trouble some time after the Government had made clear, by the decree of 1586, its general repressive policy. From 1589 onwards we meet with a steady stream of complaints, and it is abundantly evident that professional writers found themselves seriously hampered in their work, and brought into considerable danger, by the malicious activity of these men. Authors, says Nashe, are like men at Persian banquets:

... if they rowle theyr eye never so little at one side, there stands an Eunuch before them with his hart full of jealousie, and his Bowe readie bent to shoote them through, because they looke farther than the Lawes of the Countrey suffer them.[1]

'Application, is now, growne a trade,' grumbles Jonson.[2]

The simplest expression would be construed by these informers as bearing some sinister meaning. 'Let one but name bread,' cries Nashe, 'they will interpret it to be the town of Bredan in the low countreyes.'[3] If the unlucky writer, driven by necessity to write in haste, neglects to explain and qualify as carefully as he would,

.. out steps me an infant squib of the Innes of Court ... catcheth hold of a rush, and absolutely concludeth, it is meant of the Emperour of Ruscia, and that it will utterly marre the traffike into

---

[1] *A Countercuffe* (1589). *Works* (1958), I, 63.
[2] *Volpone* (1607), dedication.
[3] *Christs Teares* (1594), to the reader. *Works* (1958), II, 182.

that country if all the Pamphlets bee not called in and suppressed, wherein that libelling word is mentioned.[1]

These 'decipherers' made it their trade to interpret names as disguises for great personages thereby libelled, and they were only too successful in arousing these exalted ones to set on foot prosecutions without sufficiently careful inquiry. The most far-fetched interpretation of general meaning could bring a writer into trouble, as in the case of Jonson's *Sejanus* and Daniel's well-meant academic *Philotas*. Nor indeed were all writers as fortunate as these two in being able to clear themselves. To meaner writers, without Court influence, the difficulty and danger were much greater. Nicholas Breton did not exaggerate when he said:

> Who doeth not finde it by experience,
> That points and letters often times misread,
> Endaunger oft the harmelesse writers head?[2]

An author's credit is 'unreprievedly lost' if these 'politicians' once begin to call his innocence in question. They have practised 'deciphering' until it has become a regular system. They buy forbidden books in the hope of detecting clues. They meet and confer together, conning the catalogues of publications, and inquiring after new books at the taverns. They use every art that ingenuity can suggest in order to fasten accusations upon unlucky authors.[3] Theirs is indeed, as writers complain with justice, 'a most lewde and detestable' profession. They keep princes in perpetual misgiving, 'uppon the least wagging of a straw to put them in feare where no feare is'. And all this is done in the merely sordid hope of reward for their pains.[4]

---

[1] *Nashes Lenten Stuffe* (1599). *Works* (1958), III, 213.
[2] *Works*, ed. Grosart (1879), I, xxxii.
[3] Jonson: *Epigrammes*, XCII. *Ben Jonson*, VIII (1947), 58–9.
[4] *Nashes Lenten Stuffe*. *Works* (1958), III, 219.

The severity of the punishments inflicted upon writers unable to prove their innocence was extreme. Any utterance construed as a reflection upon political topics was apt to be regarded as seditious and treasonable, and to be accused of these offences was to be liable, before conviction, to imprisonment and torture. On 11 May 1593, an order was issued by the Privy Council to search for the author and publisher of certain supposed seditious placards. If the suspected persons should refuse to confess the truth, the order ran, 'you shall by authority hereof put them to torture in Bridewell, and by the extremity thereof . . . draw them to discover their knowledge'.[1] The rack and the scavenger's daughter were used for the torturing of Alexander Briant, to induce him to confess about a secret press.[2] Similar orders were not infrequently issued by the Star Chamber; indeed, in 1620, this Court had already attained much notoriety for its vigilance and arbitrary severity. As John Chamberlain reported in a private letter of this date, 'the world is now much terrified with the Star-chamber'.[3]

No wonder that writers constantly betrayed a nervous apprehension of the informer. They did their best to forestall him by assertions of innocence, and they guarded against his malice, wherever possible, by engaging the patronage of some exalted personage. The playwright warns his audience against interpreting as a 'libell' what he had written as a 'play'.[4] He protests against the 'State-decipherer or politique Picklocke', who would search out with ridiculous solemnity 'who was meant by the Ginger-bread-woman . . . or what conceal'd States-man by the Seller of Mouse-trappes'.[5] Nashe warns off those who would

---

[1] 11 May 1593. ed. Sir John Dasent, Acts of the Privy Council (1890 ff.), XXIV, 222.

[2] T. G. Law, Essays and Reviews (1904), 48.

[3] 8 July 1620. Letters, ed. N. E. McClure (1939), II, 310.

[4] Jonson, Epicoene, second prologue.

[5] Jonson, Bartholomew Fair, induction.

pry into a supposed hidden meaning in *Summers Last Will and Testament*:

Deepe reaching wits, heere is no deepe streame for you to angle in. Moralizers, you that wrest a never meant meaning out of every thing, applying all things to the present time, keepe your attention for the common Stage: for here are no quips in Characters for you to reade.[1]

He had reason to take precautionary measures. He had suffered severely, for the most frivolous accusations had been used against him by the fraternity of informers; they had even wrested an innocent phrase out of *Pierce Penilesse*, 'I pray how might I call you?', into an attack upon one of themselves, named Howe, of whom the writer had never heard before![2] For the authorship of a play, *The Isle of Dogs*, in which some real or fancied offence had been detected, he had been imprisoned, and banished from London, where alone a professional writer could hope to exist.

It was all very well for writers to outface the informers. Jonson took this line. He warned them, at the performance of *Every Man out of his Humour*, that he defied 'them and their writing tables'. But he had to answer to the Privy Council for *Sejanus*; he had to omit his prologue to *Poetaster*; he was forced to suppress *The Divell is an Asse*; and he suffered imprisonment, together with George Chapman and John Marston, for *Eastward Hoe*. We have no means of knowing how rigorous was their imprisonment; but we know from George Wither later that his own punishment was no empty form. He was confined in solitude, allowed to see no friends, forbidden to write, and refused the allowance of food allotted to 'close prisoners'. Sometimes for twenty-four hours together he was locked up 'without so much as a dropp of water' to cool his

[1] *Works* (1958), III, 235.
[2] *Works* (1958), I, 154.

tongue. When very ill, he was denied both physician and apothecary.[1]

Writers of learned works fared little better than the playwright. We have seen to what loss and annoyance Raphael Holinshed was subjected. John Stowe's self-sacrificing zeal in collecting documents illustrative of the history of his country met with scant encouragement from the authorities. He was brought before the Privy Council on the charge of having in his possession a copy of Alva's manifesto against Queen Elizabeth (1568); and again, in 1570, was called before the Court of High Commission. He seems to have escaped punishment, but the annoyance and risk must have been calculated to deter a man of weaker spirit. Nor was his a unique experience. W. S(tafford), writing in 1581, complained bitterly of the number of learned men harassed during the previous thirty years, simply for 'declaring their opinions in things that have arisen in controversy'. He asks pertinently who is likely to 'have any courage to study . . . seeinge, insteede of honour and preference, dishonour, and hindrance recompensed for a rewarde of learning'.[2] Still more striking, perhaps, is the testimony of Bishop Goodman, that he would have written some reply to Bacon's *Advancement of Learning* (1603), if he 'durst have printed it'.[3]

It is certain that writers were intimidated, and that some were reduced to silence. Art was, as Shakespeare lamented, 'made tongue-tied by authority'.[4] Nashe published nothing for twelve months for fear of censure;[5] necessity and inclination

---

[1] *Schollers Purgatory. Miscellaneous Works* (Spenser Society, 1872), 3.

[2] *Compendious Examination* (New Shaks. Soc., 1876), 27.

[3] *Court of James I* (1839), I, 283.

[4] Sonnet LXVI. The earlier editions of *Richard II*, for instance, omit the deposition scene.

[5] *Summers Last Will and Testament*, prologue. *Works* (1958), III, 234. This can be read as exclusively referring to *literary* censure.

drove him back to the press, with the unfortunate result we have already seen. The list of writers who suffered from the interference of the authorities includes Thomas Cartwright, George Chapman, Samuel Daniel, Thomas Dekker, Michael Drayton, Dr Giles Fletcher, Sir John Hayward, Raphael Holinshed, Ben Jonson, Thomas Kyd, Thomas Lodge, Christopher Marlowe, John Marston, Thomas Middleton, Anthony Munday, Thomas Nashe, Samuel Rowlands, John Selden, William Shakespeare, Sir John Smith, John Stowe, Philip Stubbes and George Wither. In every sphere of writing the baneful effect of government repression is seen. Writers of history, in verse or prose, were driven to passing lightly over any incidents and speeches which might have been made to bear an evil construction. Thus, Drayton, while reciting the reasons urged for the deposition of Edward II, gives a cautious apology for his temerity:

> Much more he spake; but faine would I be short,
> To this intent a Speech delivering;
> Nor may I be too curious to report
> What toucheth the deposing of a King:
> Wherefore I warn thee Muse, not to exhort
> The after-Times to this forbidden thing,
> By Reasons for it, by the Bishop layd,
> Or from my feeling what he might have sayd.[1]

More noteworthy again than the curbing of Drayton's somewhat exuberant Muse, is the influence exerted by the same fear upon the character of Spenser's greatest poem. Without the dread of authority before him, he might never have written of his imaginary Faery Land. He expressly states that he chose the legendary age of Arthur as 'furthest from the danger of envy, and suspicion of the present time . . . for avoiding of jealous

[1] *The Barons Wars* (1596), V, 9. *Works*, ed. J. W. Hebel (1932), II, 87. In the first edition of *Mortimeriados*, he did nor dare to suggest any reasons at all.

opinions and misconstructions'.[1] Spenser had political interests, and he comments widely on the contemporary scene: even though he took refuge in allegory, every stanza ran appalling risks, and it is unlikely that his genius would have counted for anything, if he had been called to account, a fate he seems miraculously to have avoided.

The worst result of all was the discredit into which malicious 'moralizers' brought the whole profession of literature: 'mens study of Depravation or Calumny' tended to diminish the credit of all writers, 'making the Age afraid of their Liberty' and causing all writing to be regarded as 'Aspersions'.[2] The suspicion of the ignorant towards the scholar is sarcastically represented in the *Parnassus Plays*:

Well, remember . . . what I say: schollers are pryed into of late, and are found to bee busye fellowes, disturbers of the peace. Ile say no more.[3]

A fitting *envoi* to this chapter is provided by the story of Christopher Marlowe. The violence and dark insecurity of the age is epitomized in his career. As a Courtly satellite, he served as a secret agent for the Crown and for Sir Thomas Walsingham. He lived dangerously, carrying arms about with him. He met his death violently quarrelling with his colleague, Ingram Frizer, in a tavern in Deptford to which this particular group had been evacuated during the plague year of 1593. And from his University days he had brushed with the authorities, suspected of atheism as well as other crimes. Just before his death the Privy Council summoned him to appear for the utterance of heretical opinions. When Thomas Kyd was being investigated, that is to say tortured, about another matter, an unorthodox theological document was found among his papers;

---

[1] Letter to Raleigh, prefixed to the *Faerie Queene*.
[2] Jonson, *Discoveries. Ben Jonson*, VIII (1947), 633.
[3] *Three Parnassus Plays* (1949), 299–300.

for this Kyd blamed Marlowe, and the Council followed up the investigation with charges of heresy, blasphemy, and receiving seditious and libellous books.[1] On similar charges, a fellow-undergraduate of Marlowe had been burned to death at Norwich four years before. With Marlowe, as with others of his kind, a violent death, one way or another, seems to have been inevitable: destiny only concealed from him the form it eventually took.

[1] *Harl. MSS.* 6583, f. 520, and 7042.

CHAPTER III

Authors and Publishers

> To disparage the whole profession, were an act
> neither becomming an honest man to doe, nor a
> prudent Auditory to suffer.... While they did like
> fleas, but sucke now and then a dropp of the
> writers blood from him . . . it was somwhat
> tollerable: but since they began to feed on him,
> like the third plague of *Aegipt* without remooving
> . . . I say . . . it is high tyme to seeke a remedie.
>
> GEORGE WITHER[1]

THE man who had a manuscript to dispose of in Elizabethan
days would bend his steps first of all to St Paul's Churchyard.
Here would be found all the best booksellers' shops and stalls,[2]
and if, as was usual, he had no very definite connexion with any
particular bookseller, he would hawk his manuscript from one
to the other until he had made the best bargain within his
power. Some of these stationers were printers also; other
printers had no booksellers' shops, and simply worked for
stationers; or if they brought books out on their own account,
employed stationers to sell for them. If the owner of a manuscript preferred to treat direct with the printer, he would have
to go to some other part of the city, for printing offices were
for the most part situated on less valuable sites than the
Churchyard.

It was practically impossible to dispose of a manuscript
outside London. There were stationers, it is true, in one or two
of the larger towns,[3] but they were for the most part only

[1] *Schollers Purgatory. Miscellaneous Works* (Spenser Society, 1872), I,
9–11.

[2] Dekker, *Lanthorne and Candle-light* (1609), epistle dedicatorie. *Non-
dramatic works*, III (1885), 178.

[3] Vide list in Arber, *Transcript*, V (1894), lii.

booksellers, not publishers. All printing by law was confined
to London since 1556, and a provincial publisher would have
found it impossible to deal satisfactorily with printers in
London.[1] The only exceptions were the printing presses of
Oxford and Cambridge, and one permitted to a Dutch refugee
in Norwich, Antony de Solemne.[2] But the former printed
very few works of general literature, and the latter scarcely
anything but Dutch, for his fellow-refugees. Thus it is clear
that a writer had to live in London, if he had professional
ambitions; there alone could he find an adequate market.

Although in theory the writer had a wide choice of publishers, in practice the system of monopolies favoured by Elizabeth had invaded the publishing trade, and many books, and
classes of books, were 'privileged' or patented to particular
booksellers as their sole right. Thus, books on the Common
Law might be published by Richard Tottel or his successor
only; dictionaries must be brought out by H. Binneman;
Primers and Psalters were the monopoly of W. Seres; Latin
Grammar books must be entrusted to T. Marsh; almanacs and
prognostications to J. Roberts and R. Watkyns, and so on.[3]
Fortunately for the writer on general current topics, these
patents referred for the most part to educational books,
religion, law, and the dead languages; in *belles-lettres* a wide
choice remained. Certain stationers, however, had a reputation
for particular kinds of books, and he would consider this in
offering his manuscript for sale.

For a work of erudition and importance, likely perhaps to
be expensive in production, it would be well to open negotia-
tions with Christopher Barker, or his son and successor,
Richard. Barker was printer in English to the Queen, owned a
number of printing presses, and was willing now and then to

---

[1] *Bibliographica* (N.S.), II, 45.
[2] Ibid., 150-4.
[3] Vide list in *Transcript*, II (1875), 15-16.

risk an adventurous enterprise, if interested in the work. At one time he nearly ruined himself by the heavy costs incurred in printing expensive Bibles. Failing Christopher Barker, George Bishop might be approached. He was particularly interested in learned work, especially in theological controversy. For one work of this nature he is known to have maintained the learned Dr Fulke and two men, with their horses, for nine months, and paid the former £40, besides bearing the expenses of printing.[1]

In addition, there was John Day, a man not very popular with his colleagues, being too highly favoured by the great. He was under the special protection of Archbishop Matthew Parker, for whom he sometimes printed privately at Lambeth.[2] He had it in his power, no doubt, to bring suitable books to the notice of the Archbishop, but such notice was perhaps too risky to be greatly coveted. Day published Foxe's *Book of Martyrs*.

For foreign books, and translations from Continental languages and Latin, the most likely publisher was John Wolfe, but Wolfe would undertake anything indeed if promised gain. He was the son of Reyner Wolfe, a native of Strasbourg settled as publisher in London, and must have inherited a large printing connexion from his wealthy father. He was an active man, kept a number of presses, and published on a large scale, perhaps more than any other. His special line, however, was foreign and dead languages, a line in which he met with some competition from Edward Blount. His commercial keenness is illustrated by some of his entries in the Stationers' Register. For instance, although Marlowe died only in the previous June, by September 1593, Wolfe had registered his *Hero and Leander* and his translation of *Lucan*, securing the rights doubtless. But he did not publish then, and perhaps had not even secured a copy; they were only brought out, one in 1598 and the other in 1600, by other publishers. He even entered a des-

---

[1] *The Times*, 5 January 1877 (article on Arber's *Transcript*).
[2] *Bibliographica* (N.S.), II, 155.

cription of Elizabeth's state entry into London before the procession took place,[1] thus more than anticipating modern journalistic methods.

The owner of a manuscript of genuine literary value in the more ambitious fields of *belles-lettres* would no doubt apply to Edward Blount, William Ponsonby, or failing them, to Nicholas Ling or Cuthbert Burby. The first was a genuine lover of literature, with discriminating and generous taste. The list of his publications does him credit, including as it does works by Sir William Alexander, William Camden, Cervantes, Sir William Cornwallis, Daniel, John Earle, Florio, Jonson, Lyly, Marlowe, Sylvester, and the great Shakespeare Folio of 1623. Moreover, he was a true friend to one poet at least: daring, when all vilified the character of the dead Marlowe, to publish his work with a striking prefatory note, indicative of genuine personal affection, and desire to do justice to his genius.[2]

No less worthy was William Ponsonby; in fact, he was probably a publisher higher in public esteem and more entirely scrupulous than Blount. Ponsonby's connexion was largely with the more aristocratic among writers, and he was sufficiently prosperous, evidently, to disdain the publication of such small ware as ballads and catchpenny pamphlets. Though Sidney's friends were reluctant to put his private poems into print, they chose Ponsonby to forestall unauthorized publication by less reputable men; he also brought out the works of Sidney's sister, the Countess of Pembroke; Spenser turned to him, once he had turned professional, to publish the *Faerie Queene* and other poems; and the list of his productions includes a translation of Guicciardini, and one of Plutarch.

But a man of such reputation was of little use to struggling unknown writers, who had to hit the popular taste, even at the

[1] 1588. *Transcript*, II (1875), 506.
[2] *Hero and Leander* (1598), preface.

sacrifice of dignity. Ponsonby published two of Greene's earliest pamphlets, written in the fashionable Euphuistic style; but he published no more for Greene. Nor did he publish any Nashe, Dekker or Breton. Nor was he the man to buy the manuscripts of dramas from the public playhouse, authorized or not; in drama he preferred more moral works, like Samuel Brandon's *Virtuous Octavia*. Ponsonby however was an exception among publishers. Few could resist the bait of a fair text of a popular play, and most were too poor, or too greedy, to be above accepting the ever saleable ballad, almanac and pamphlet.

Among stationers whose names figure largely in the issue of plays were Thomas Thorpe, Andrew Wise, and James Roberts. Wise showed a discriminating appreciation of the market value, at least, of Shakespeare's plays: out of nine books entered by him during seven years, five are Shakespeare plays. James Roberts brought out *The Merchant of Venice*, and *A Midsummer Night's Dream*, and entered copies of *Hamlet* and *Troilus and Cressida*. As for Thomas Thorpe, best known as the unauthorized publisher of Shakespeare's *Sonnets*, he brought out plays by Jonson, Chapman and Marston.

For the lower forms of literature—ballads, catchpenny pamphlets, and the like—John Danter was the printer most popular. He was evidently rather poor and struggling, glad to print for other stationers, and glad to get hold of popular things, cheap to buy and produce and readily saleable. The list of publications licensed to him includes a large number of ballads. Because he was a publisher of no great reputation, anxious above all things to catch the popular taste, he proved useful to certain needy pamphlet writers. He published for Greene in his later, sensational days, and he was a good friend to Nashe during his acrimonious quarrel with Harvey. And in spite of dealing with somewhat sensational literature, he does not seem to have been more unscrupulous than other publishers in stealing what he could lay hands on. He was quite as ready to publish the sensational religious tract as the secular broadside: both appealed to his class of reader.

Thomas Creede and the Jaggards, father and son, were publishers of medium reputation, able to undertake the publication of serious work, but not anything involving really heavy expense, and, like John Wolfe, willing to print anything likely to sell. Creede's judgment was not so good as that of some of his colleagues, or else he was particularly unfortunate in the manuscripts offered to him: among the seventy-four books licensed to him, there are only about five now known to the general student of literature, and three of these only through their connexion with works by Shakespeare. William Jaggard was the object of an angry attack by Thomas Heywood in his *Apology for Actors* as a most careless and impudent printer. Jaggard had also printed without permission poems by Heywood and Shakespeare, and Heywood declared that the latter was much offended. By a curious irony, it was this very printer who in 1623 printed and published with Blount the first Shakespeare Folio, the authorized monument to his fame.

These publishers and printers include, of course, only a small number of the stationers in London. Many more might be mentioned, from Burby, with a large flourishing respectable business, to Hodgets the bookseller, whose registered publications in nineteen years number only twenty-four. As has been seen, the number of printers was strictly limited; but any one of the Stationers' Company could publish a book, if he could get for it a printer and a bookseller.

The matter of 'book privileges' has already been referred to. Though of the utmost importance in the history of the book trade, and though necessarily affecting writers, as tending to lower the prices paid for work by limiting competition among publishers, their effect upon the literary professional was only indirect. They rendered the struggle for existence more arduous to the unprivileged publisher, by placing beyond his reach most of the books for which there was a steady, large demand, and thus indirectly brought about a spirit of unscrupulous rapacity which regarded any manuscript, however obtained, as fair booty. Further, by keeping the majority of the stationers in chronic poverty, these 'privileges' or 'patents' reduced the possibilities of fair remuneration to the author for such manuscripts as were openly bought. That book traders, as a class, suffered serious injury cannot be disputed. More than twenty-three monopolies were granted under Elizabeth, nearly all of them for whole classes of books. Long and bitter struggles were carried on between the privileged few and the many. Constant complaints were made by the monopolists concerning secret infringements of their rights, and from about 1582 to 1586 there was an organized conspiracy against them. It was headed by the irrepressible John Wolfe, who had begun to publish only a few years before, and an active agent of his was a certain poor printer, Roger Ward. With others, they deliberately printed large editions of privileged books and parts of books, and then appealed to Burghley, employing legal advisers to fight out the matter. The situation was unbearable, they declared: nothing was left for the unprivileged stationer but 'ballets and toys'. In the end they gained something. Certain privileges were relinquished by rich stationers to the Company as a whole, in order to provide work for the most needy (though there was great complaint of the workmanship later on), and the commissioners for the inquiry framed some very sensible regulations designed to mitigate the grievances (1583). In the following year still more book privileges were resigned, and the evil was further dealt with in the great Star Chamber decree of 1586.[1]

Many years later, however, things were not much mended. The books resigned to the Company by monopolists, for the

[1] *Transcript*, II (1875), 753–93, and I (1875), 116, 144.

benefit of poor members, had gradually come to be regarded as the property of the ruling stationers, by whom the younger and poorer were oppressed. 'You would think it were unsufferable,' said Wither, describing their grievances. Printers especially suffered injustice. While the selling-prices of many books, owing to the monopolies, had almost doubled,[1] the printers' charges were by enactment kept low, so that they toiled simply to enrich men favoured by privileges.[2]

From the general point of view of the trade, then, book patents were a source of great injustice; from the point of view of the public, and of writers as a class, there is still less to be said for them. Their effect was to render necessary books dear and scarce, to the great injury of education and learning. The upholders of privileges urged that, by enriching certain stationers, patents rendered possible the production of very expensive works of erudition, upon which otherwise no stationer would venture.[3] And they pointed to Barker's expensive folio Bibles, and to the great editions of the works of Sir Thomas More, and Richard Grafton's *Chronicle*, brought out by Richard Tottel with other printers. But the facts do not quite bear out the contention that patents were necessary for this reason, for most of the more adventurous publications were, after all, brought out by syndicates of unprivileged publishers. Thus the Shakespeare folio of 1623, the Holinshed folio of 1577, the translation of the 'moral works' of Plutarch, and Drayton's *Polyolbion*, were all produced by 'unprivileged' stationers. It was by no means infrequent for wealthy citizens to help to bear the expense of producing works in which they were interested. John Bodenham almost certainly bore the cost of the Anthologies connected with his name—*England's Parnassus*, *England's Helicon*, and others. Thomas Heywood's

[1] *Transcript*, IV (1877), 35–8.
[2] *Schollers Purgatory. Miscellaneous Works* (Spenser Society, 1872), I, 109–10.   [3] *Transcript*, II (1875), 804–5.

Hierarchie of Angels is adorned with a number of elaborate full-page engravings dedicated to various generous friends by whom the cost of them was borne.[1]

In the case of works of erudition and controversy payments to authors seem to have been on a reasonably generous scale, as we have seen in the case of George Bishop's payments for Dr Fulke's *Confutation of the Rhemish Testament*. The six final revisers of the Authorized Translation received each thirty shillings per week.[2] For the catchpenny pamphlet, or the small volume of so-called poetry, the regular payment was forty shillings, with perhaps a pottle of wine.[3] Writers of popular reputation could no doubt reckon upon a good deal more, perhaps double the sum. Nashe swears that he will be paid dear for his pains.[4] Greene's pamphlets were in great demand. And the *Parnassus Plays* represent John Danter, the best-known publisher of such wares, offering to raise his fee of forty shillings to 'anything', upon learning that an offered manuscript is a libel.[5] For mere hackwork, such as translation, the author sometimes had no money payment at all, receiving only a certain number of copies, to dispose of at as good a price as he could get.[6] Such popular wares sold at twopence, three-pence, or fourpence, Greene's *Defence of Conny-catching*, for instance, at threepence.[7]

They were advertised by nailing or pasting the front page, with an attractive catch-title, on the whipping-posts in the streets, on the pillars of St Paul's, and on the walls of the Inns of

[1] This custom lasted at least until the time of Dryden's *Virgil*.

[2] *Transcript*, IV (1877), 12.

[3] *2 Return from Parnassus*, I, iii. *Three Parnassus Plays* (1949), 248. George Wither, *Schollers Purgatory* (Spenser Society, 1872), I, 115, 130.

[4] *Have with you to Saffron-Walden. Works* (1958), III, 128.

[5] *2 Return from Parnassus*, I, iii. *Three Parnassus Plays* (1949), 248.

[6] R. B. McKerrow, *Gentleman's Magazine* (April 1906).

[7] *Life and Complete Works in Prose and Verse*, ed. A. B. Grosart (1881-6), XI, 45.

Court, to attract the lawyers and their country clients.[1] The superior writer objected to advertising. Jonson warned his bookseller that he disliked having his poems made known by the

> . . . title-leafe on posts, or walls
> Or in cleft-sticks, advanced to make calls
> For termers, or some clarke-like serving man.[2]

Of course a popular pamphlet would run into many editions: Nashe's *Pierce Penilesse* 'passed through the pikes of six impressions' in two or three years; and he speaks once of 'many thousands' looking for productions from his pen. Wither swears that of his *Hymns* 'twenty thousand might have been dispersed'.[3] But unless the author supplied new matter, if only a new preface, it is probable that he gained nothing further but fame. Edward Hake expressly states, about the new edition of his *Newes out of Powles Churchyarde*, that he received nothing 'either for writing altering or correcting'.

The time for bringing out new books was the term, when Westminster was thronged with lawyers and clients, and when visitors from the country came up to London to see life. Michaelmas term was the most favourable publishing season, as bringing the most clients.[4] Writers had therefore to get their manuscripts ready for printing well in advance during the summer. Greene handed over his *Orpharion* to the printer during the spring, but to the author's great disgust, the latter delayed the printing so long that it did not come out until the following spring, a time less favourable than the autumn.[5]

---

[1] Joseph Hall, *Virgidemiarum*, V, ii. *Collected Poems* (1949), 80.

[2] *Epigrammes*, III. *Ben Jonson*, VIII (1947), 28.

[3] *Schollers Purgatory. Miscellaneous Works* (Spenser Society, 1872), I, 32.

[4] Vide Dekker, *Lanthorne and Candle-light. Non-dramatic works*, III (1885), 178, and Nashe, *Works* (1958), III, 139; I, 64.

[5] *Orpharion* (1599), to the gentlemen readers. *Works*, ed. Grosart (1881–6), XII, 7.

Most profitable to the publisher were almanacs and prognostications, having a very large sale and requiring 'few persons and small stock' to print them.[1] They were the great resource of the 'poorest sort of the Stationers' Company', and great outcry was caused when, in 1588, they were granted as a monopoly to R. Watkins and J. Roberts. It is not likely that very much was to be gained by the authorship of such 'toys', but, if Nashe is to be believed, there was enough to induce a poverty-stricken parson brother of Gabriel Harvey to try to make money by them.

Plays sold well, if published at the height of their popularity on the stage; otherwise, they were less certain of a market in London, and had to be 'vented by termers and country chapmen'.[2] The selling price was sixpence,[3] the same as for a masque.[4] The players however preferred not to spoil their own market by allowing the text of plays to become common, and did their best to prevent their being printed during a popular 'run'.[5] Texts sometimes were pirated, in more or less garbled versions, from the memorizations of unscrupulous players who were prepared to betray their own company.

The custom of reading in booksellers' shops must have interfered with the sale of books to some extent. We are told that 'many peruse them, ere they be solde'.[6] But as many customers probably bought for country friends rather than for themselves, the practice of allowing them thus to sample the books had doubtless its advantages.

It was no easy matter, frequently, for the author to dispose of his manuscript. Dekker, at a time when he must have

[1] Vide Christopher Barker's report in Arber, *Transcript*, I (1875), 144.
[2] Thomas Middleton, *Family of Love* (1608), preface.
[3] Philip Massinger, *The Bondman* (1624), verses attached.
[4] John Lodge, *Illuminations of British History* (1838), III, 227.
[5] Thomas Heywood, *The English Traveller* (1633), to the reader.
[6] Breton, *Poems*, ed. Jean Robertson (1952), 3.

acquired a fair popularity, complains of the difficulty of suiting the stationers' taste: 'Go to one, and offer a coppy, if it be merrie, the man likes no light Stuffe; if sad, it will not sell. Another meddles with nothing but what fits the time.'[1] The narrowness of the market for books is shown by the fact that the popularity of one or two trifling productions could effectually check any demand for others. Nashe suffered from this, but consoled himself by scoring a jest against his foe, Harvey. He can get no harvest, he says, by writing for the press, because '& for the printers, there is sutch gaping amongst them for the coppy of my L. of essex voyage, & the ballet of the threscore & foure knights', that for the most attractive wares they will not offer even 'the contemptiblest summe that may bee . . . the price of Harveys works bound up togither'.[2] Nor was this all the difficulty. The market was glutted by the practice, indulged in by many stationers, of saving the expense of payment for new work by 'buttering over againe, once, in Seven Yeares' anti-quated pamphlets, and issuing them as new.[3] The needy writer was driven to all sorts of unworthy expedients in the endeavour to produce work attractive enough to compete with these cheap revivals.

It should be emphasized that the writer's reward ended with the sale of his manuscript. This became the property of the buyer, whether he were a bookseller intending to publish, or an acting company buying for production on stage, or a middleman speculating to sell again. There was no system of royalties, nor does it appear that the author was ever regarded as entitled, in law or equity, to share in any extraordinary profits.[4] On the other hand, of course, the publisher was responsible for all losses.

[1] *Jests* (1617), to the reader.
[2] Letter to William Cotton. *Works* (1958), V, 194–5.
[3] Jonson, *The Staple of News*, I, v. *Ben Jonson*, VI (1938), 295.
[4] In a fit of generosity, Philip Henslowe once gave ten shillings to be divided among the authors of a successful play.

Strangely enough, authors never complain of the injustice of a system which compelled them to sell outright a manuscript which might afterwards prove of unexpected value. Even Wither, in his diatribes against the iniquitous stationer who sucks the blood of the unfortunate writer, and steals the product of his studious labours, fails to put any blame on the selling custom. No doubt stationers would have resented bitterly any innovation calculated to reserve to the author a pecuniary interest in the manuscript after it had once left his possession. Their doctrine, upheld by legal opinion, was that only members of the Stationers' Company could lay claim to the benefit arising from the sale of books to readers.[1] Thus, they placed the claim of the stationer before that of the producers, writer and printer, regarding these latter as bound to produce for their benefit.[2] This was a natural bias at a time when the socially superior writers, the Courtiers and their friends, did not normally seek print, and the writers who did seek print were *ipso facto* inferior socially to the stationers. The fact that this position was seriously maintained is made clear by Wither's famous quarrel with the Company. In order that he might benefit by the sale of his own work, he had asked for and obtained a privilege, giving him sole right in publishing his *Hymns and Songs*. There were special circumstances, it is true, about this privilege which were calculated to rouse opposition; but it was contested on the principle that Wither, being no stationer, could derive no profit from the sale of books. Wither was not the only instance of a 'privileged' author: Daniel got a patent for his *History of England* in 1618; John Norden had a ten years' patent for his *Speculum Brittanniae*; Arthur Golding got the sole right for

---

[1] George Wither, *Schollers Purgatory. Miscellaneous Works* (Spenser Society, 1872), I, 27.
[2] Ibid., I, 10.

publishing his own works;[1] and Alexander Nevill even obtained the prohibition of every translation of Livy except his own.[2] But there does not appear to be a single instance of the granting of a patent to authors except those of learned or religious works. The ordinary writer had no resource but to dispose of his manuscript for the largest sum he could secure.

If, however, writers had no subject for complaint but an inconveniently hard and fast system of selling, they would have called for no special sympathy. This was a grievance sure to be redressed sooner or later by the effects of competition in the publishing trade, once print became the normal and entirely respectable channel of communication between authors and their public. They suffered a more extraordinary injustice in the fact that the law regarded, or was popularly believed to regard, the mere possession of a manuscript, apart from any previous entry in the books of the Stationers' Company, as implying ownership, and consequently the right to dispose of it. There was thus a regular trade carried on, to the injury of writers, in the illicit procuring and selling of manuscripts: a trade rendered more feasible by the existing custom of preserving work for some time in manuscript and circulating it privately, in the Courtly fashion, in copies made by the scriveners. In his dedication to *Terrors of the Night*, Nashe illustrates the facilities thus afforded for stealing from authors:

A long time since hath it been suppressed by mee; untill the urgent importunitie of a kinde frend of mine (to whom I was sundry waies be-holding) wrested a Coppie from me. That Coppie progressed

[1] Vide lists of privileges given in Arber, *Transcript*, I (1875), 111–16, and V (1894), lvii–lviii.

[2] *Transcript*, II (1875), 312. This was standard practice throughout Europe at this time. According to G. H. Putnam, the possessor of a 'privilege' for a book in a particular subject was regarded as holding a monopoly of the *subject*. In the case of an edition of a classical author, the privilege thus barred the production of any other edition.

from one scriveners shop to another, & at length grew so common, that it was readie to bee hung out for one of their signes. . . . Whereuppon I thought it as good for mee to reape the frute of my owne labours, as to let some unskilfull pen-man . . . startch his ruff & new spade his beard with the benefite he made of them.

Nashe was lucky in that no possessor of one of these numerous copies had yet carried it to the stationers for sale. Manuscripts far less commonly known frequently met that fate, to the permanent injury of the author's prospects of reward. No complaint is so often met with as that of the theft and illicit sale of manuscripts. Lodge protests against the wrong done to him by the piratical publication of certain of his poems, 'owing to the base necessity of an extravagant melancholy mate'.[1] Daniel grumbles at an instance of the 'unmannerly presumption of an indiscreet printer', who had ventured to print a garbled text of a masque by him, acted by the Queen and her ladies,[2] and again rebukes 'the indiscretion of a greedy printer' who had published some of his manuscript sonnets.[3]

Playwrights, more perhaps than other writers, suffered from the wrongful publication of their works; only in their case the loss was rather in reputation than in money. The financial loss fell upon the players who had bought the manuscript, which it was in their interest to keep from publication. Copies were procured by the agents of grasping publishers in various ways. Though Thomas Heywood protests vigorously that he at least is above the dishonest practice of selling his labours twice, 'first to the stage, and after to the press',[4] it is clear from the protest that some authors did make money by this means: in time the practice became quite common. Sometimes it was found possible to procure the full text, the prompt copy, and

[1] *Glaucus and Scylla* (1589), dedication.
[2] *Vision of Twelve Goddesses* (1604), epistle dedicatory.
[3] *Delia* (1592), dedication.
[4] *Rape of Lucrece* (1608), to the reader.

print from this (perhaps amusingly, and usefully for modern historians), prompt notes and all. Sometimes an actor's copy, a single part with cues helped out by a more or less inaccurate memory, proved useful. And some publisher's agents found the new device of shorthand writing extremely useful, as is instanced by the fortunes of the *Play of Queen Elizabeth* (*If you know not me, You know no bodie*). As Thomas Heywood relates in the prologue to the 1637 edition:

> it . . .
> Did throng the Seates, the Boxes, and the Stage
> So much: that some by Stenography drew
> The plot: put it to print: (scarce one word trew:)
> And in that lamenesse it hath limp't so long,
> The Author now to vindicate that wrong
> Hath tooke the paines, upright upon its feete
> To teach it walke, so please you sit, and see't.

The worst of it was that a book once printed and entered in the Stationers' Register became the property of him who entered it, and no other person could safely publish it, however necessary might be an amended edition. Wither states the case clearly:

The Stationers . . . by the lawes and Orders of their Corporation . . . can and do setle upon the particuler members thereof, a perpetuall interest in such Bookes as are Registred by them at their Hall . . . and are secured in taking the ful benefit of those books, better then any Author can by vertue of the Kings Grant, notwithstanding their first Coppies were purloyned from the true owner, or imprinted without his leave.[1]

[1] *Schollers Purgatory. Miscellaneous Works* (Spenser Society, 1872), I, 28–9. They managed these things better in Italy. Ariosto held the copyright of his *Orlando Furioso*, and Tasso, Aretino, Geraldi and others held the copyright of their own works. In 1544–5 a Venetian decree forbade anyone to print or sell a work without first producing written proof of authorization by the author or his representatives. Vide G. H. Putnam, *Books and their Makers in the Middle Ages* (1897), II, 363.

It must indeed have been galling for the author whose work had been stolen and mangled, to have to make terms with the thief in order to secure the issue of a truer text!

We are undoubtedly indebted to this practice of surreptitious publication for many authorized and correct printed copies of works that otherwise would never have passed through the press. It seems to have become more and more customary for authors to see their works through the press. Thus, Jonson carefully issued all his; Massinger and Middleton about half theirs. Repeatedly the author in his preface explains and excuses publication on the ground of the necessity to forestall or to supplant inferior pirated editions. Thus, Chapman prints *All Fools*:

> Lest by others' stealth it be imprest
> Without my passport, patched with others' wit.

Sometimes, against his will, the author found himself forced to authorize a projected piracy in order to get the opportunity of ensuring that it should at least be correct. In such cases he probably gained little besides the satisfaction of protecting his reputation: the manuscript was no longer his property.

The playwright suffered from piracy chiefly in reputation; the ordinary writer both in reputation and in purse. He was defrauded of the price of his manuscript, and it was mangled, pieced out by other work, and attributed to other men's labour, so that he found himself cheated of his due reward on all sides. Thus a printer who named himself as Richard Joanes published a little book called *Brittons Bowre of Delights*, at which Nashe unkindly sneered in his preface to *Astrophel and Stella*. But in fact, out of all the poems in it, Breton had written only three or four of the best, and he was justly irritated, both by the theft of these and by the injustice done to his poetic skill (the printer had used an anthology in a commonplace-book of the time). Again, to take another sphere of authorship,

the learned Dr Turner complains, in a dedication of his
Herbal (1568) to no less a personage than Elizabeth herself,
of the manner in which

> a crafty, covetous, and Popish printer handled me of
> late, who, suppressing my name, and leaving out my
> Preface, set out a book (that I had set out . . .) with his
> preface, as though the book had been his own.

Shakespeare was saddled with the authorship of inferior plays
such as *Sir John Oldcastle* and *The London Prodigal*. The ingenious preface to *England's Helicon*, by Nicholas Ling, suggests
that much pains would have been required to trace the authorship of some poems in this anthology; it almost hints that Ling
would regard the task as unreasonable and superfluous.

In other ways again the unscrupulous publisher was capable
of doing injury to an author. If Wither is to be believed, and
though hot-tempered he was an honest man, they would even
go so far as to arouse suspicion in the minds of the authorities,
caring little for the good name and personal safety of the
author, so their own interests are served thereby: the bad
stationer

> will not stick to belye his Authors intentions, or to publish secretly
> that there is somewhat in his new ymprinted books, against the
> State, or some Honorable personages; that so, they being questioned
> his ware may have the quicker sale. He makes no scruple to put out
> the right Authors Name, & insert another in the second edition of
> a Booke; And when the impression of some pamphlet lyes upon
> his hands, to imprint new Titles for yt, (and so take mens moneyes
> twice or thrice, for the same matter under diverse names) is no
> injury in his opinion.[1]

Mere carelessness caused a good deal of harm, cheating the
public with imperfect copies, and thus hindering the sale. The
unfortunate Drayton, who had great difficulty in inducing

[1] *Schollers Purgatory* (Spenser Society, 1872), I, 121.

stationers to accept the risk of publishing his *Polyolbion* at all, suffered from their carelessness even then. He complains that

some of the Stationers, that had the Selling of the first part of this Poeme, because it went not so fast away in the Sale, as some of their beastly and abominable Trash (a shame both to our Language and Nation) have either despightfully left out, or at least carelessely neglected the Epistles to the Readers, and so have cousoned the Buyers with unperfected Bookes.[1]

It is not impossible that this was mere accident, due to distribution of the book among several master printers, a practice not infrequent when the number of presses allowed was strictly limited. But such dealing was not calculated to encourage the sale of the Second Part of the poem.

When a manuscript had been openly agreed for, the author usually superintended its passage through the press. In fact, unless absent from London, or unless a personage of too great importance, he was expected to attend personally to supervise during the actual printing. Nashe speaks of being 'cald away to correct the faults of the presse' that escaped during his absence from the printing house.[2] Bartholomew Young and Nicholas Breton both crave the reader's indulgence towards printer's errors because they were prevented by more important affairs from 'attendance at the press'.[3]

But the publisher would not scruple to ignore the author's natural desire to superintend, if he could thereby secure an earlier sale. Nashe's *Pierce Penilesse* was 'abroad a fortnight ere' he knew of it, offering itself 'uncorrected and unfinished . . . to the open scorne of the world'. The second impression

---

[1] *Polyolbion*, second part, introduction. *Complete Works*, ed. J. W. Hebel, IV (1933), 391.

[2] *Nashes Lenten Stuffe*, to the reader. *Works* (1958), III, 152.

[3] Bartholomew Young, preface to translation of Montemayor's *Diana* (1598); Nicholas Breton, *The Wil of Wit. Works*, ed. Grosart (1879) II, 63.

was also well in hand before Nashe was informed.[1] It certainly rested with the publisher to determine whether or not a work should be re-issued; if courteous, however, he would probably give the writer a chance of seeing it through the press.

It is not surprising, considering all the disabilities under which printers laboured, and the frequently surreptitious manner of production, that the standard of workmanship should have been very low. It is a fact that some of the (probably illicit) books of the period are in passages quite unintelligible, so that the marvel is that readers were obtained for them. Authors had good reason for complaint, as Thomas Heywood shows:

The infinite faults escaped in my booke of Britaines Troy by the negligence of the printer, as the misquotations, mistaking of sillables, misplacing halfe lines, coining of strange and never heard of words, these being without number, when I would have taken a particular account of the *errata*, the printer answered me, hee would not publish his own disworkemanship, but rather let his owne fault lye upon the necke of the author.[2]

How lightly even a University printer estimated his responsibilities may be judged from the following jaunty preface by the Oxford printer, Joseph Barnes, prefixed to a pageant composed by John Lyly:

I gathered these copies in loose papers I know not how imperfect, therefore I must crave a double pardon; of him that penned them, and those that reade them. The matter of small moment, and therefore the offence is of no great danger.[3]

In the published text of *The Famous Victories of Henry the Fifth*,

---

[1] Epistle to the printer. *Works* (1958), I, 153. The difficulty of literal interpretation is that the whole letter may be a publisher's device to cover imperfections.

[2] *Apology for Actors* (Shakes. Soc., 1841), 62.

[3] *Speeches . . . at the Progres . . . at Bissam* (1592).

verse is written as prose and prose as verse, and passages are quite unintelligible. The 1598 edition of Greene's *James IV* contains a publisher's note stating that in the earlier edition the text had been so mangled that in some parts it was impossible to follow the thread of the discourse. The lapses of some of the Shakespeare quartos provide a familiar subject for modern scholarship, and we must not embark here on a topic so highly technical. Texts were botched not only by bad printers. But we might remind ourselves of the first quarto version of Hamlet's celebrated soliloquy on death; whatever the fault, this is an extraordinarily impoverished text:

> To be, or not to be, I there's the point,
> To Die, to sleepe, is that all? I all:
> No, to sleepe, to dreame, I mary there it goes,
> For in that dreame of death, when wee awake,
> And borne before an everlasting Judge,
> From whence no passenger ever retur'nd,
> The undiscovered country, at whose sight
> The happy smile, and the accursed damn'd.
> But for this, the joyful hope of this,
> Whol'd beare the scornes and flattery of the world,
> Scorned by the right rich, the rich curssed of the poore?

On the other hand, low as was the general standard of the printing-press, instances can be met with, during this period, of excellent workmanship. Bacon's *Essays*, issued in 1612 from the printing-press of James Beale, is a most excellent production. The type is clear, well-formed, and pleasant to the eye, the margins generous, the text enclosed within a plain framework or border. Another edition of the same year, printed for J. Jaggard, though less pretentious, is beautifully clear and accurate. Clearly it was not that skilled labour was lacking, but that the conditions of ordinary production fostered careless work—a carelessness, by the way, not infrequently shared in or condoned by authors.

The basic difficulty was that the Courtly writers thought publication of their works in the printed-book market an undignified irrelevance. Their *belles-lettres* were intended to grace Courtly life. As his good friend, Fulke Greville, said of Sidney's *Arcadia*: it was intended 'for entertainment of time and friends, then any accompt of himself to the world.'[1] Greville's own consent for even a posthumous edition of his poems was decidedly lukewarm: 'These pamphlets, which having slept out my own time, if they happen to be scene herafter, shall at their own perill rise upon the stage when I am not.'[2] Indeed, he is said to have burned all the manuscripts of his plays rather than run the risk. Courtly works did reach print for a variety of reasons, but often the Courtly author of an unexceptionable work, of divinity or utility, appears to be most embarrassed by hobnobbing in print with the humbler professionals.[3] While this attitude prevailed, as the Oxford printer put it, 'the matter' of professional writers was apt to continue to be 'of small moment'.

There are one or two instances on record of writers being made to pay for the privilege of getting into print: minor country gentlemen of no particular significance. A less expensive method of circumventing the power of the stationer was through subscription patronage, a device innovated at this time but to become very familiar in the eighteenth century. John Foxe's *Tables of Grammar* (1552) were thus published, eight Lords of the Privy Council subscribing. A method somewhat analogous must have been pursued by Daniel, when he printed sumptuous editions of his works, and of his *History of England*, to be privately presented to certain persons.[4] He

---

[1] *Works of Fulke Greville*, ed. A. B. Grosart (1870), III, 20-1.

[2] *Poems and Dramas of Fulke Greville*, ed. G. Bullough (1939), I, 24.

[3] Vide J. W. Saunders, 'The Stigma of Print' (*Essays in Criticism*, I, April 1951), 146-7 *et passim*.

[4] *History of England*, note to reader at end of Part I.

must have had some guarantee beforehand that he would be recouped. A writer of a very different order of merit, John Taylor the Water Poet, made a practice of collecting subscriptions beforehand for nearly every pamphlet he published. For one little production, *The Pennyless Pilgrimage*, he obtained 1,600 names. But apparently most of his patrons inconsiderately expected, and tried to exact, their full moneysworth. On one occasion, to his great indignation, half the 'mongrel' subscribers refused to pay up.[1] The method was finally perfected by Jacob Tonson, publishing the fourth edition of *Paradise Lost* in 1688; thereafter it was taken up by many authors, not only in England but elsewhere in Europe. It is an interesting half-way house between the patronage system and outright professionalism.

It is not clear upon what terms Gabriel Harvey published his pamphlets against Nashe. He undertook, certainly, the expense of publication, but Nashe expressly states that the manuscript was the 'copy' of the printer, to be disposed of at will.[2] Perhaps the arrangement was that, if the sale did not pay expenses, Harvey was to make good the deficit.

Under the existing conditions, it was inevitable that the bond of relation between author and publisher should be usually of the slightest. True, there are honourable exceptions. William Ponsonby published everything that is known of Spenser's, except his first work, the *Shepheardes Calender*. So also Simon Waterson published nearly all Daniel's writings, and was appointed executor at the poet's death. But most writers seem to have formed no such lasting connexions. We even find instances of two successive parts of the same work being issued by different publishers. Thus, Stubbes's *Anatomy of Abuses*, Part I, was brought out in 1583 by R. Joanes, but Part II, in the same year, was published by W. Wright.

[1] *A Kicksey-Winsey* (1619), preface.
[2] *Have with you to Saffron-Walden. Works* (1958), III, 96, 27.

Greene's *Mamilia* was licensed to T. Woodcock in 1581, and the second part to W. Ponsonby in 1583. Bacon employed several different publishers, Greene had dealings with seven or eight, Samuel Rowlands published with a great number.

But perhaps the most remarkable instance of the entire absence of any sentimental connexion between the stationer and those whom he published is seen in the relations of John Wolfe and Cuthbert Burby with Nashe and Harvey. Everyone knew that Nashe and Harvey were at daggers drawn, and that Wolfe was the publisher of Harvey's attacks. Yet this very publisher is found (17 September 1593) proposing to publish a book by Nashe. There had probably been a quarrel with Harvey, for Cuthbert Burby brought out Harvey's next diatribe: yet Burby followed it up within a few months by a pamphlet from Nashe himself. Harvey was evidently unable to enlist a publisher in his interest.

This detachment of interest is the more remarkable in cases where the writer was definitely employed by the publisher. It seems to have been quite customary, as it was much later in the case of Oliver Goldsmith, for the stationer to lodge and board the writer while he was engaged upon the stipulated work. Nashe lived for some considerable time in the house of the printer, John Danter, provided for by the good man's wife. In the same way, John Wolfe provided board and lodging for Harvey, though he seemed to have little faith in him.[1]

It is possible that some of the evidence here quoted should be taken with a little allowance. Both the complaints of authors and the statements of satirists are apt to be highly coloured. But then, as now, publishers had to live, and merely from the pages of the Stationers' Register it is easy to see that the publishers of the late sixteenth and early seventeenth centuries, with some honourable exceptions, cared chiefly for their own livelihood, No doubt the struggle for existence among the

[1] *Have with you to Saffron-Walden. Works* (1958), III, 115, 90.

unprivileged was very severe, and they preferred matter which gave them the best return, however cheap and sensational. Public taste left much to be desired, but the stationer cannot be entirely absolved from the charge brought against him by Wither, that he refused the work of the self-respecting artist and expert, in order to escape paying a fair reward,

seeing he cann hyre for a matter of 40 shillings, some needy *Ignoramus* to scrible upon the same subject, and by a large promising title, make it as vendible for an impression or two, as though it had the quintessence of all Art.[1]

Not for the last time in literary history was it discovered that, for immediate reward, clever emptiness pays.

[1] *Schollers Purgatory*. *Miscellaneous Works* (Spenser Society, 1872), I, 130

CHAPTER IV

Authors and the Theatre

And must the basest trade yeeld us reliefe?
Parnassus Plays[1]

NEARLY all the talented writers of the period tried their hands at dramatic writing. Some, like Nashe, failed entirely. Others, like Drayton, secured a fair amount of employment as theatrical hacks for a few years, then threw it up for more congenial work. But others, like Shakespeare, Jonson, Marlowe, Middleton, Greene, and many more, found the theatre a congenial home for professional writing, and have left behind them great literature. There is an extraordinary contradiction at the roots of the Elizabethan theatre, but one from which great professional drama developed. On the one hand, acting was the 'basest trade', the lowest of the low; the public playhouses were raucous places, rowdy and vulgar, little better than the bearbaiting rings, unsavoury not only to Puritans, places where hundreds and indeed thousands of people of all classes crowded together cheek by jowl, refreshed by bottled ale, places where the prostitutes made their assignations; and many writers working there have been censured for leading lives unworthy of their talents, lives of low associations, squalor, coarseness and violence. On the other hand, drama was the Courtliest of the arts, actively encouraged by the Queen and her leading noblemen, protected through long years of Puritan opposition by the patronage of the highest in the land, and some of these base players did well for themselves: Edward Alleyn became a prominent London gentleman and patron of the arts, wealthy enough to spend £10,000 on Dulwich College, and William

[1] 2 *Return from Parnassus*, IV, iv. *Three Parnassus Plays* (1949), 343.

Shakespeare retired to Stratford as an esquire with his own coat of arms. It was undoubtedly this felicitous combination of Courtly and popular support which made the Elizabethan theatre the first real home of the professional man of letters.

In the early years of Elizabeth's reign there were simply a multitude of cheap touring companies: groups consisting sometimes of only four men and a boy, carting their scaffold stages and boxes of traverses and properties round the inn-yards of London and the market places of the country towns. This *théâtre de foire* was highly professional compared with the amateur gild companies of the Middle Ages, and the interludes they played were often written by Courtly and University gentlemen: John Heywood, Thomas Norton, Thomas Sackville, Thomas Watson, Nicholas Grimald, William Gager, Nicholas Udall and the like. And the players themselves were often well-bred, the product of the royal choir schools or servants of a noble house. But life was hard and casual for these companies, and they became indeed the 'vagabonds' the Puritans called them. In the end, they had no future, being eliminated throughout the country by various kinds of Puritan legislation. We are concerned with the noble companies, particularly with those formed after 1559 with Leicester as one of the first patrons. Since it was highly necessary for the Queen and all her leading noblemen to have players at hand for the dramatic performances which were an integral part of Courtly culture, arrangements were made with groups of players for this purpose. The connexion was at first quite casual. The players were simply servants on the fringe of the noble house called in for special occasions, for which they received *ad hoc* fees but no annual salary, and free to fend for themselves at other times. Since masques and Courtly plays usually had fairly large casts, these companies tended to be larger than the ordinary run, with an interest in adding to their number actors of talent and a need to find a continuing supply of boys from the choir schools to play the women's parts, social convention forbidding the use of actresses. By their very nature these companies were relatively respectable units of society, whatever the context in which they worked for most of the year. There were several such companies, but the two most important were the one to which Shakespeare became attached, under the protection successively of Lord Strange, Lord Hunsdon (the Lord Chamberlain), and King James, the company which built the Globe and the Blackfriars and whose chief impresario, if that is the appropriate term, was James Burbage; and the rival firm, which operated under the protection successively of Lord Howard of Effingham (the Lord Admiral), Prince Henry and Lord Palgrave, which built the Fortune and the White-friars, and whose chief impresario was Philip Henslowe.

These noble companies responded to Puritan legislation by making stronger links with their patrons, being formally enrolled as 'household Servants and daylie wayters' and exploiting their protective livery. But the essentials of their life changed little. About 1600 the company could reckon on earning £35 from one performance before the Queen or a noble gathering. Its dramatists earned anything between £5 and £30 for a play or masque specially written for a Court occasion. And often there were other fees and gratuities: in 1604 Shakespeare's company were commanded to close down their public performances to present themselves at Court as supernumerary grooms, specially to impress a visiting Spanish envoy, earning £20 a man. But such casual earnings were not enough: it was understood that the companies supported themselves at other times by touring in the provinces and by public performances, after 1576, in playhouses of their own building in London. Hence, a felicitous combination of patronage by both a Courtly élite and by the general public, hence an innate contradiction deriving from mixing one day with the lords and ladies and the next with the bakers, butchers and candlestick-makers, and hence a great deal of opportunity and indeed security for the writers.

Let us study the facts of professional earnings by these writers. For an accepted drama the usual rate of payment to the author, if we are to judge from the payments made by Philip Henslowe, was £6, rising occasionally to £10. He paid Thomas Heywood, in two instalments, £6 for the play of *A Womon Kylled with Kyndnes*.[1] But Henslowe was a hard bargainer, apt to take advantage of a needy author, and it appears that he acted as a middleman for his company who in their turn had to purchase the play from him. Letters written to him show that authors seeking good terms for themselves were in the habit of 'playing off' the company against him, alleging a high price the players were willing to pay direct for the manuscript in question. Francis Daborne, a practised haggler, swears on one occasion that he could get £25;[2] and if we are to believe him, the company would often gladly pay £20. Alternatively, and even more effectively, Daborne threatened to sell to the rival company.[3] On one occasion, as a matter of fact, he succeeded in screwing Henslowe up to an offer of £20[4] for a play with the intriguing title *Matchavell and the Devill*. But by August of the same year this successful bargainer was down again to £12, with the addition of 'the overplus of the second day', and by December he was offering at the £10 rate. It looks as if the company, as customers, were unable to compete permanently with Henslowe, and we may conclude, from all the evidence, that £10 was a good market price for a play. From his own statements, Ben Jonson seems to have

[1] *Henslowe's Diary*, ed. R. A. Foakes and R. T. Rickert (1961), 224. In comparison, he paid £6 13s. for a 'womones gowne of black vellvett' to be worn by a performer in this play.

[2] *Alleyn Papers*, ed. J. P. Collier (Shakes. Soc., 1843), 65.

[3] Ibid., 67.

[4] 17 April 1613. Ibid., 56–7.

made an average of £12 or £14 a play.[1] Henslowe must have had things all his own way when in 1601 he was entreated, as a favour, to make up a sum already paid to £5, and to accept the 'papers'.[2] For plays written in collaboration, the fee of £6 or so was divided among the collaborators.[3]

Henslowe was frankly commercial in his approach. His was the capital which built theatres, and he charged companies rent for the use of the premises. Indeed, he treated companies as hardly as the authors: he lent money on security of the costumes on ruinous terms; he interfered with the hiring of actors; he seems to have succeeded in ruining five of the minor companies in three years. All kinds of complaints are raised against him: for instance, on one occasion it was said, 'We have paid him for play-books £200 or thereabouts, and yet he denies to give us the copies of any one of them.'[4]

As indicated above, there is evidence that at times, in addition to the money fee paid down, authors received the 'overplus' of a day's takings, the company no doubt reserving a fixed sum for themselves.[5] This 'benefit' day seems to have been the second or third day on which a play was performed. Thus, Dekker, in the prologue to *If this be not a Good Play . . .* (1612), attacking authors for their greed, represents them as willing to write any 'filth', so long as they get a 'cram'd third day'. Later, Jasper Mayne alludes to

---

[1] Vide calculations about Jonson later in this chapter.

[2] *Alleyn Papers*, 23.

[3] An unscrupulous playwright might occasionally make a little more by sharp practice. Greene is said to have sold *Orlando Furioso* twice over, to the Queen's and Lord Admiral's companies. Vide *The Defence of Conny-catching. Works*, ed. Grosart (1881–6), XI, 75–6.

[4] *Alleyn Papers*, 80. It is possible that Henslowe was himself responsible for defrauding players by the surreptitious release of play-texts for publication.

[5] Ibid., 66. Vide calculations about Daborne later in this chapter.

> One whose unbought muse did never fear
> An empty second day, or a thin share.[1]

It is difficult to estimate the probable value of this benefit day. In 1625 the average takings from a performance at the Globe were only £6 13s. 8d., and from a performance at the more lucrative 'private' house, the Blackfriars, £15 15s. And we do not know what proportion of the takings was reserved by the company. The author could scarcely have earned more than a few pounds, even on the best of occasions.

It has been assumed that Burbage's company, operating at the Globe, was on a somewhat superior footing compared with its main rival,[2] and that it paid its authors more highly. Certainly, the Lord Chamberlain's company was a more cooperative enterprise, finding its own capital and not dependent on an *entrepreneur*, but there is little evidence the authors were better paid. Perhaps the best writers did better there. Jonson, who wrote for some considerable time for this company, told William Drummond of Hawthornden in 1618 or 1619 that he 'never gained £200 for all the plays he had ever produced'. As he had written by this date about twelve plays single-handed, and three or four probably in collaboration, it is clear that £12 or £14 was the average price received. We may also infer that this yield, spread over twenty-three years of relative success, less then than £10 a year, was not enough as a sole source of livelihood. Shakespeare's earnings, from this one source, may be calculated as about double Jonson's, and Chapman's rather lower than Jonson's. Massinger probably did as well as Shakespeare, but a dabbler like Drayton probably did not do half as well as Jonson. Play-writing alone, then, had

---

[1] *A City Match* (1639), prologue.

[2] F. E. Schelling, following Fleay's *Table of Court Performances*, reckoned that during the period 1594 to 1603 Burbage's company performed twice as many plays at Court as its four competitors combined (*Elizabethan Drama* (1908), I, 318).

its limitations, even though these rewards were considerably higher than those available in the printed-book market.

As already suggested, this income was supplemented, in Jonson's case, and in that of a number of other writers, by masque writing for noble patrons. The ordinary payment for a private unambitious masque was £5, but Court masques earned more.[1] Thomas Middleton, when City Chronologer, received for various literary services, chiefly as masque-writer, gifts from the City varying from £13 6s. 8d. to £20: the Court could not give less. We may assume that Jonson earned from his career as a masque-writer—he wrote 36 masques and 'entertainments'—about £720.[2] Allowing something for collaboration and non-extant plays, we may calculate that Jonson earned from all his plays and masques an average income of £25 a year.[3]

It was a relatively handsome sum, but not enough. In his later years, despite an additional pension, he undoubtedly fell into indigence. Yet few Elizabethan authors produced so large a body of work as Jonson, and few were so fortunate to spend so long in the lucrative branch of masque-writing. If this is marked success, what must failure have been? Maybe some writers had extravagant habits, but we need no theories about vicious habits of self-indulgence to account for the incessant

[1] *The Puritan* (anon. n.d.), II, iv.

[2] Jonson wrote 36 masques and 'entertainments'. Daniel, with Henry Evans, received £20 for two interludes or plays performed 1 January and 3 January 1605 (P. Cunningham, *Extracts from the Accounts of the Revels at Court*, Shakes. Soc., 1842). Jonson and Inigo Jones each received, for the Queen's Mask, Christmas 1610, the large sum of £40. For a Mask at Court on New Year's Day 1611, Jones received only £16 (J. P. Collier, *Life of Inigo Jones*, Shakes. Soc., 1848, 11–13). For each of Jonson's masques, then, £20 is probably a very liberal computation.

[3] Jonson altogether wrote twenty-four plays, including two in collaboration, four not extant, and two unfinished. He may have possibly collaborated in others.

cry of poverty. The theatre was indeed a refuge and relative haven, but its prosperity had its severe limits.

Dramatic writers occasionally added to the profession of playwright that of actor. Certainly nine known playwrights also acted: Nathaniel Field, Robert Greene, Thomas Heywood, Jonson, George Peele, Anthony Munday, William Rowley, Shakespeare and Robert Wilson. Though Marlowe and Kyd never acted, as far as we know, most of their contemporaries seemed to combine the two professions. Later on, the practice becomes rarer; we may surmise all kinds of reasons, but the most likely was that acting became more highly skilled, as the years went on, and the career more competitive and professional.

In the early years, at any rate, innumerable references prove that actors as a class were regarded as poverty-stricken. Gibes at their gorgeous raiment and empty pockets are common. A phrase in one of Stephen Gosson's pamphlets suggests that the ordinary pay of a hired actor was six shillings weekly in 1579.[1] This is no great sum, the equivalent of the earnings of an unskilled labourer today, or those perhaps of an ordinary modern repertory actor, but they were enough to be regarded as a resource, if the basest, for the poor scholar. There is an excellent scene in *2 Return from Parnassus*, in which Burbage tests the acting powers of the poor University man by making him recite from the old play *Hieronymo* and Shakespeare's *Richard III*.[2] The scholar shows his reluctance to enter upon this calling by exclaiming, 'And must the basest trade yeeld us reliefe?' The hired actors provided the casual labour of the

---

[1] 'The verye hyerlings of some of our plaiers, which stand at reversion of vi⁸ by the weeke': *School of Abuse* (Shakes. Soc., 1841), 29. A poor actor, about to go abroad, told Alleyn that in England he earned hardly anything, sometimes a shilling a day, sometimes nothing (*Alleyn Papers*, Shakes. Soc., 1843, 19).

[2] IV, iv. *Three Parnassus Plays* (1949), 341–3.

company. Above their rank the companies employed a number of regular actors on fixed salaries. How much they were paid we do not know, but in 1635, after a considerable rise in nearly all money incomes, the job was worth as much as £180 a year.

Better prospects opened out to the man who could attain in a company the positions of 'sharer' and 'householder'. The householders owned the theatre and took half the takings as rent. The sharers were those who ran the company, being responsible for the management of the theatre and the production of plays; they paid the hired players, bought properties, and met other expenses out of the half of the takings which fell to them, and divided the profit left.

It is extremely difficult to estimate the probable profits of a sharer, owing to the frequent interruptions when theatres were closed during plagues, during vacations, and for other causes. Overhead expenses too were variable, including the cost of 'hirelings', new properties and costumes, plays and much else. But we can reckon that something like a third of the takings for each performance fell as profit for perhaps a dozen or so sharers. This was not a great fortune, but it was steady and cumulative, and sufficient to make the sharers envied men, 'glorious vagabonds' they are called in *2 Return from Parnassus*. It was the great ambition of every player to rise to be a sharer, by buying a share or half-share. In fact, only three dramatists appear to have had sufficient business acumen to join the sharers: Shakespeare, who owned four shares in Burbage's Globe and two in the Blackfriars; Samuel Rowley, a sharer with Alleyn in the Admiral's Company; and William Rowley, sharer in the Lady Elizabeth's Company from 1612 to 1625. It is possible, though not certain, that Thomas Heywood was a sharer. Three non-dramatic writers are also known to have been sharers: William Barksted, William Basse, and William Bird. And perhaps the actor, Robert Armin, could be included as a writer. How Shakespeare managed his startling success, rising from poverty to the possession of six shares worth over £1,000, is a matter for conjecture. We can detect in him a shrewd sense of business management, and his flight from Stratford was doubtless far more calculating than melodramatic interpretations would suggest, but he may have been given initial impetus from a patron.

The most prosperous men in the theatre were 'housekeepers', the owners or part-owners of the different theatres. The richest of them all—Alleyn, Henslowe, Burbage—fell into this category. Joseph Hall is referring to Burbage when he exclaims:

> Who can despaire that sees another thrive....
> When a craz'd scaffold, and a rotten stage,
> Was all rich Naevius his heritage?[1]

The actor's life was not enviable. It must have been very wearing, both physically and mentally. This was repertory acting, ringing the changes on twenty or more plays, all to be kept in memory at any one time. Audiences were rowdy and addicted to interruptions: indeed, companies employed stout stage-keepers whose job it was during performances to prevent the open stage from being besieged and to keep general order. Actors were used to playing in village halls, in barns, and in the houses of the country gentry, when they appear to have made a green-room of the kitchen. During the tedious journeys from one town to another, along miry, rough, country tracks, it was by no means infrequent for players, in an age when travellers normally rode on horseback, to trudge on foot after the vehicle which carried their properties. Dekker repeatedly taunts players with being compelled to 'travel upon the hard hoofe from village to village for chees & buttermilke',

---

[1] Joseph Hall, *Virgidemiarum. Collected Poems* (1949), 54. Richard Burbage inherited the Blackfriars from his father in 1597.

[2] *The Bel-man of London. Non-dramatic works*, III (1885), 81.

and 'strowting up and down after the waggon'. He describes them as driving 'the poore country people . . . like flocks of Geese to sit cackling in an old barne' while they played to them.[1] No doubt these remarks apply primarily to the poor unlicensed troupes and not the liveried companies. Jonson certainly rode a horse on tour: his enemies jeeringly describe him as ambling by a play waggon in the highway.[2] But even Shakespeare himself, in his early years, felt something of loathing for a profession which, in that age, rendered him vile:

> Oh, for my sake do you with Fortune chide
> The guilty goddess of my harmful deeds,
> That did not better for my life provide
> Than public means which public manners breeds.
> Thence comes it that my name receives a brand;
> And almost thence my nature is subdued
> To what it works in, like the dyer's hand.[3]

On the credit side, the theatre offered a great deal. Rewards, though far from generous, were reasonably secure and continuous; and there were opportunities for supplementary work. In the best companies, a good writer was a valuable property: in Yeats's phrase, this was a theatre in which the spoken word was sovereign. For all the pressures from the 'groundlings' for blood and thunder, jigs and antics and knockabout farce, the support of noble patronage, and often the physical presence in the Lords' rooms of the public playhouses of judicious patrons, left the writers free to write as well as they could. Other times might well envy these Elizabethans their happy fusion of a mass public with the support of the intelligentsia. Above all, there was a rough and ready *camaraderie* in the great companies, a throwing together of talents in competition of art. The Courtiers had their circles of intimate friends who read and

[1] *Jests. Non-dramatic works*, II (1885), 352.
[2] *Satiromastix* (1602), IV, i.
[3] Sonnet CXI.

sharpened each other's work: Sidney, Dyer and Greville joined together in an 'Areopagus' with Spenser and the best of their professional friends. But there were no such friendships to quicken and bring out the best in the printed-book market. Only in the theatre did the professional writer find a natural context of colleagues: a classless society, in a sense, where noble patrons rubbed shoulders with apprentices, and dedicated professionals like Shakespeare, Middleton and Massinger, rubbed shoulders with the gifted amateurs like Marlowe, Jonson and Marston. There was a home here for those who spent a lifetime in the theatre, and for those who only made periodic forays from their main interests elsewhere; for those who made a living from plays, and for those who only dabbled in plays when they were looking for a quick income; for those who could do nothing else but write, and for those to whom writing was part of a varied Courtly career. There must have been many compensations for being involved in the hardships of the 'basest trade'.

CHAPTER V

Authors and Supplementary Means of Livelihood

> Let schollers be as thriftie as they maye,
> They will be poore ere theire last dyinge daye.
> Learninge and povertie will ever kiss.
>
> *Parnassus Plays*[1]

SUCH, then, were the economic conditions amidst which the Elizabethan professional writer sought to pursue a career. The hope of patronage lured him on, and led him to accept for his work payment insufficient to keep body and soul together; patronage itself was fitful and scanty, and often entailed bitter and degrading experiences. The press, accepted by the writer largely as a stepping-stone to the desired haven of patronage, treated him accordingly: the average stationer drove hard bargains, preferred inferior work, snubbed and insulted the writer, and when possible, stole his manuscript from him. Drama and the masque, the most paying forms of literary work, could not suffice to provide *in themselves*, even for the most popular writer, a living wage: whatever the consolations of working in this relative haven, the plain fact is that writers had to take on non-literary responsibilities to make writing pay. Authority, as presented by the Government and the Stationers' Company, ignored any special claim on the part of the author to the produce of his own labours; indirectly encouraged theft from him; limited the number of copies produced for sale; kept up artificially the cost of publication, and finally, harassed the writer by suspicious vigilance, and by accusations likely at least to spoil his market, and at the worst, capable of costing him his life.

In short, this was no age to support a literary profession. We

[1] *Pilgrimage to Parnassus*, I. *Three Parnassus Plays* (1949), 98.

have seen how the writer needed many strings to his bow: no single occupation was sufficient to support him. The most successful writers made use of their writing either to open out a career at Court or to develop the varied opportunities of the dramatic companies. Some had a stake in all the camps: patronage, the printed-book market, and the stage. It is time to examine in more detail some of the fringe activities, literary and non-literary, available to the writer, the varied means by which writers sought to supplement their livelihood. Jonson was comparatively fortunate, though we know that he was miserably poor in later life. Besides the sale of his manuscripts, he had some friendly patronage; he had the position of King's Poet, later known as the poet laureateship, worth about 100 marks a year (£66 12s. 4d.), though paid with little regularity; and he held for a short time, as an antiquarian, the appointment of City Chronologer, worth about £10 yearly. Middleton also held the latter post for some years. But these appear to have been the only public appointments open to literary men as such. The writer of good education had to seek afield in diverse and devious ways.

If possessed of sufficient learning and acuteness, the writer would probably find it most lucrative to turn his pen to controversial work, especially in theology. This was the field, in any case, in which patrons were most interested. Officials and clerics were fully alive to the necessity of answering some of the many polemical treatises issued by Jesuit writers, from Louvain and elsewhere, and a fair remuneration seems to have awaited the man who could give adequate proof of his orthodox zeal, his learning, and controversial ability. The most famous instance of a great writer founding his career in this field was John Milton, but he had a number of Elizabethan predecessors. Thomas Ball, a converted Jesuit, who wrote thirteen works against the Papists, and also made himself useful by assisting to discover disguised Jesuits, received a pension of

£50 a year, no mean income in those days (as good as the hard-won pension of Edmund Spenser, who incidentally gives many indications of hankering after the life of a polemical writer, had he had the right kind of opportunities). Nor was it only the orthodox who were prepared to pay well for a learned and forcible exposition of their views. George Wither, who like many others had published a little sacred poetry, told his readers, 'I have been offred a larger yearely stipend, and more respective entertaynments, to employ my selfe insetting forth hereticall fancies, then I have yet probabilitey to hope for, by professing the Trueth.'[1] Learned work of a scientific nature appears also to have been well rewarded by those interested.[2]

Translation, also, afforded employment to a number of writers. Some patrons, Leicester for instance, put protégés to work on translation from a sense of public duty. And some publishers had a special interest in this field: John Wolfe, for instance, entered in the Stationers' Register no fewer than seventy-seven translations, from Latin, Italian, French, Dutch and Spanish. This was work which engaged the attention of all classes of writer, from the Courtly amateurs like Sir Thomas North, Sir John Harington and Lord Morley, to the serious scholars like John Florio, Philemon Holland, and Sir Henry Savile, to the publishers' hacks, like George Turberville, Thomas Drant and George Pettie. Rewards doubtless varied with the status of the translator. One hack, Richard Robinson, who produced many indifferent versions of dull Latin works for various publishers, appears to have received no money payment at all. The proceeds of a certain number of copies, to be disposed of by himself to friends and patrons, eked out, if luck willed, by a dedication fee, formed his only remuneration.[3]

Correcting for the press also provided some employment,

---

[1] *Schollers Purgatory. Miscellaneous Works* (Spenser Society, 1872), I, 68.
[2] Vide supra 31 and 72.
[3] Vide R. B. McKerrow, *Gentleman's Magazine* (April 1906).

especially for men sufficiently educated to read proofs in foreign and dead languages. John Foxe was a press corrector for some time while abroad, and possibly acted in the same capacity for the printer John Day. It was reckoned among the serious expenses incurred by the printer, as compared with the publisher, that the former had his 'learned correctors' to maintain constantly. They seem to have been engaged permanently, or at least for long periods. They were needed to correct reprints from classical and foreign languages, and such works as were not superintended in the customary manner by the authors themselves, if considered worth much correction.

The scholar in *2 Return from Parnassus* probably represents aptly enough the contempt of the University-bred man for such technical routine correction. 'Whatever befalls thee', he cries, 'keepe thee from the trade of the corrector of the presse. ... Would it not grieve any good spirritt to sit a whole moneth nitting over a lousy beggarly Pamphlet?'[1]

Lower still, in the infernal circles in which literary sinners were condemned to toil and suffer, was the degrading employment of the news factor, the prophetic almanac writer, the ballad and jig writer, and the versifier of bawdry. Sometimes for political reasons a writer of some social status was employed with these ephemera. Among the balladists of the period are to be found Bishops, ministers, University fellows and Inns-of-Court men. But the street ballads were normally written by mere uneducated scribblers. The perpetual gibes of men like Nashe, Dekker, Joseph Hall, Edward Hake, and even Jonson and Drayton, show that they felt keenly the competition caused by these scribblers, and felt too that by the public the more worthy writer was by no means always clearly distinguished from the base.

The spread of elementary education and the introduction of printing went together in extending this class of literature,

[1] I, ii. *Three Parnassus Plays* (1949), 228.

although it was a popular section of the earlier manuscript industry. It was profitable merchandise: when the cupboard of the Stationers' Company was checked in 1560, it was found to contain only forty-four books, but 796 ballads. Certain writers, such as William Elderton, Thomas Deloney and Robert Armin, 'the riffe-raffe of the scribbling rascality', acquired a widespread popularity by their ephemeral productions. Such works could earn £2 or £3 a time: hence, writers of greater capabilities, such as Breton, Dekker, Greene, Middleton and Rowlands were attracted into this field. Very few, even of the best, could boast that they had never been induced by need to cater for unworthy tastes. Lodge could not, for in his *Glaucus and Scylla*, he registered a vow:

> To write no more of that whence shame doth grow,
> Or tie my pen to pennies-knaves' delight,
> But live with fame, and so for fame to wright.

Nashe confessed with his usual frankness:

Twise or thrise in a month, when *res est angusta domi*. . . . I am faine to let my Plow stand still in the midst of a furrow, and follow some of those new-fangled *Galiardos* and *Senior Fantasticos*, to whose amorous *Villannellas* and *Quipassas* I prostitute my pen in hope of gaine. . . .[1]

So much for the literary fringes. There remained to the writer non-literary employment, at the Court or outside the Court. A young University man of talent, in need of a settled income, might perhaps naturally hope for preferment to a fellowship. But to qualify was expensive, and many promising young men found it impossible to reside for a sufficient length of time. University education in Elizabethan days was becoming a costly matter. It had undoubtedly become more expensive since it had grown to be a custom for the sons of rich men

[1] *Have with you to Saffron-Walden. Works* (1958), III, 30–1. Harvey, with how much truth we cannot say, accused Nashe of having written 'filthy Rymes, in the nastiest kind' (*Pierces Supererogation. Works* (1885), II, 91).

to spend some time at the University, *en route* to a Courtly or
mercantile career.[1] Gabriel Harvey boasted that his father had
spent £1,000 on the education of four sons,[2] a very large sum
then even for the moderately wealthy man. An allowance of
£50 to £60 seems to have been customary for young men of
good family. But there was one advantage in the presence in
the University of these undergraduates in easy circumstances:
they provided paid employment for poorer fellow-students as
personal attendants. Sometimes University students eked out
their scanty means, as many of their predecessors had done, by
begging. In January, 1580, a 'scoller of Oxforde' was accused
of wandering through the country with a fellow-student, with
a forged licence to beg, in order 'to get moneye . . . for their
better exhibition'.[3] There were, of course, many scholarships
to the University from grammar schools: Marlowe and Spenser were indebted to such provision. The records of Beverley
Corporation mention a number of exhibitions granted to
grammar-school boys on their admission to the University, the
sums varying from thirty shillings to two pounds yearly.[4] But
despite all the machinery built up to fashion a *carrière ouverte
aux talents*, the lot of the scholar was hardly enviable. 'Schollers', said Breton, are 'hardly brought up, therefore they should
away with hardnesse the better: their allowance in colledges is
but small, therefore little meate should content them'.[5] Moreover, as we shall see later on, scholarships and sizarships, like
most other privileges of the day, were usually obtained with
influence.

[1] J. Bass Mullinger, *The University of Cambridge from 1535 to the Accession
of Charles I* (1884), I, 274.

[2] *Greenes Memoriall*, sonnet xx. *Works*, ed. J. W. Hebel, I (1931), 250-1

[3] *Hist. MSS. Comm.*, V. App. Part I, 579.

[4] A. F. Leach, *Early Yorkshire Schools* (Yorks. Archaeological and Topographical Association, 1899-1900), I, liii.

[5] '*The Wil of Wit*', *The Scholler and the Souldiour*. *Works* (1879), II, c
26.

Private benefactors would not infrequently support promising youths at the University, as Lady Burghley supported
Thomas Speght, and Alexander Nowell supported others. But
the course was long, seven years before proceeding to the M.A.
degree, and it sometimes happened that length of time, and the
accidents of life, brought to an end the benefactor's generosity. No University preferment could be looked for, naturally,
by one whose career had stopped short of the degree, unless
indeed, once more, by the way of 'influence'. In any case, the
holding of a fellowship, or even mere residence after taking
the M.A. degree, entailed certain obligations not very congenial to the candidate for fame and money in the field of
belles-lettres. Every resident M.A. was required to give lectures,
that is, to interpret and comment upon the somewhat arid
'texts' which formed the staple of University study in Dialec-
tic, Law and Theology. His remuneration for this work was
confined to the fees paid by undergraduates.

Further, there were practical reasons which made residence
in Oxford or Cambridge inconvenient for any man who
wished to take up writing professionally. The distance of both
Universities from London, the only centre of the publishing
and theatrical trades, was a serious bar.[1] Nor had he much hope
of getting work published by the University printing-presses.
Their output was limited in kind and in quantity. Indeed,
between 1522 and 1584 there was no printing at all in Cambridge, and when in 1584 a press was started under the auspices
of the University, it met with most determined opposition
from the Stationers' Company, as an alleged infringement of
their rights, and the University had to call upon Burghley to
intervene. The Oxford University Press published about 160
works during the years 1585 to 1603, all but eight of which

---

[1] It was otherwise with the University of Paris which, situated in the
metropolis itself, could and did exercise controlling powers over all publications.

were in Latin or Greek, or were theological works. The eight exceptions are nearly all occasional verses on recent public events. Three only attain to any literary merit: Breton's *Pilgrimage to Paradise* (1592), Davies's *Microcosmos* (1603) and an anonymous translation of Six Idyls from Theocritus.[1] Later on, Cambridge published Giles Fletcher the younger's *Christs Victorie and Triumph* (1610) and Phineas Fletcher's *Purple Island* (1633), but the writers' father had held an important position in the University.

John Lyly, in 1574, applied to Burghley to use his influence to obtain for him a fellowship;[2] but this was before the days of his authorship, which was perhaps indirectly brought about by his failure to obtain the desired preferment. Nashe, on the other hand, declares that he 'might have been Fellow', if he had chosen. No doubt, we are to infer that he scorned it.[3] In fact, he left the University before the end of his seventh year of residence,[4] and moreover does not appear to have been able to reckon upon the influence necessary in these circumstances. 'It is in my time an hard matter', says William Harrison, 'for a poore mans child to come by a felowship. . . . Not he which best deserveth, but he that hath most friends . . . is alwaies surest to speed.'[5] Gross corruption and interference from highly placed personages for the most part decided the choice of fellows. 'Learning nowadays gets nothing if it come empty-handed; promotion . . . is becoming a purchase.'

There was one other determining factor in the question of residence at a University—one, if possible, still less favourable to the profession of literature as an art. During the greater part of the reigns of Elizabeth and James, the policy of the Univer-

[1] F. Madan, *The Early Oxford Press* (1895), 14–57.
[2] *Complete Works*, ed. R. W. Bond (1902), I, 13–14.
[3] *Have with you to Saffron-Walden. Works* (1958), III, 127.
[4] *Nashes Lenten Stuffe. Works* (1958), III, 181.
[5] *Description of England* (New Shaks. Soc., 1877), I, 77.

sities was governed by considerations theological rather than educational or scholarly. During the greater part of Elizabeth's reign, there was great dearth of men fit for the ministry, and in consequence, the authorities imposed upon the Universities as their primary duty the training of men to enter Holy Orders. The Universities had always been the homes of theological study, and the training ground of priests, but this was now made almost their exclusive concern. The other medieval studies, civil and canon law, medicine, and the liberal arts, were dying out at the Universities, falling into disuse, or becoming attracted to London. Every effort was made to encourage the study of divinity, and turn the Universities into mere feeding supplies for the Church. Pains were taken to secure that the profession 'of the study of divinity' required from many fellows, should not be nominal.[1] The five years' liberal education which formerly preceded the study of divinity was curtailed, and sometimes even dispensed with, to the disgust of the broader-minded.[2] No doubt the average Englishman thoroughly approved of this view of the functions of the University.[3] It was practical; and, moreover, theology at this time was a subject of great interest to most men. The policy, however, had an unfortunate effect. It fostered hypocrisy, and it lowered the educational standard, causing candidates for preferment to be selected on theological grounds rather than for their intellectual qualifications. A show of religious zeal not only added to the chances of an aspirant for honours; it even assisted him materially by accelerating his attainment of degrees.

[1] J. Bass Mullinger, *The University of Cambridge from 1535 to the Accession of Charles I* (1884), I, 307-9.

[2] W. S(tafford), *A Compendious or briefe Examination* (1581), (New Shaks. Soc., 1876), 25.

[3] Breton represents, in *Wits Trenchmour* (1597), a rustic father complaining of the neglect of his son's education in divinity: 'New Schoolemen, have a new fashion in their teaching' (*Works* (1879), II, b, 17).

Nashe grumbles about this:

If at the first peeping out of the shell a young Student sets not a grave face on it, or seemes not mortifiedly religious (have he never so good a witte, be hee never so fine a Scholler), he is cast of and discouraged.... Your preferment ... occasioneth a number of young hypocrites.[1]

Nashe's view is probably biassed; but he represents the natural resentment felt by the unclerical writer towards an evil which really existed. It is difficult, under the circumstances, to believe that he himself was ever 'religious' enough to have stood any chance of a fellowship!

The vocational pressures of the Church certainly damaged the scholastic ability of the Universities. In 1580 Greek was almost extinct, in this age of humanism, at St John's College, Cambridge, formerly the home of Roger Ascham, and Ascham himself protested at the changing times:

I know Universities be instituted onelie that the realme may be served with preachers, lawyers, and physicions, and so I know like-wise all woodes be planted onelie eyther for building or burnyng; and yet good husbandes, in serving, use not to cut down all for tymbre and fuell, but leave alwaise standing som good big ons, to be the defense for the newe springe.[2]

It has been shown from a survey of the classical authors mentioned by Francis Meres, that English printers, compared with the whole of European production, were only responsible for 'eighty-eight of eight hundred and fifty-two editions of the Latin authors. Even here the English editions are often no more than reprints of continental texts or fragmentary trans-lations.'[3] Apparently, much English University teaching de-pended upon commonplace-books, direct imitation and literal

---

[1] *Christs Teares. Works* (1958), II, 122–3.

[2] Letter to Sir William Cecil, 1553. ed. Sir H. Ellis, *Original Letters of Eminent Literary Men* (Camden Society, 1843), 16–17.

[3] D. C. Allen, *Francis Meres's Treatise 'Poetrie'* (1933), 27.

borrowing, and in 1616 James was forced to issue a decree forbidding the use of compendia and abbreviators and ordering Cambridge students to turn to the study of the original texts. The good scholars were few, and unable or unwilling to devote themselves to lifelong scholarship like their continental counterparts, and the bad scholars, including some Regius Professors of Greek, seem to have published nothing, nor left any other mark of their tenure of office.

If this theological vocationalism did not deter a man from University residence, then a further discouragement would probably confront him. Both Oxford and Cambridge, during the latter part of the sixteenth century as earlier on, seem to have been hotbeds of contentiousness. Their quarrels were notorious. The State Papers are full of appeals to the Crown, now from one side, now from the other, in bitter college feuds. Theological bias was one cause, the tyranny of heads of colleges was another, and frequently the two combined. Certain changes made in internal administration had given greatly increased powers to the heads of colleges, who seem frequently to have been at open war with their respective bodies of fellows. Thus in 1565 the head of Caius College is said to have expelled twenty fellows, and to have punished some even with beating and the stocks.[1] In 1576 the visitor of New College, Oxford, found the college distracted by such grievous factions that four ringleaders had to be ejected and others chastised.[2] The fellows of Magdalene, Cambridge, petitioned the Chancellor against their President on the ground that he had 'rooted out' a Welsh lecturer simply for his nationality, and that he pastured his cows in the college grounds, as if they were his private property.[3] Yet again, we learn that the Warden of

[1] J. Bass Mullinger, *The University of Cambridge from 1535 to the Accession of Charles I* (1884), I, 201.

[2] *Hist. MSS. Comm., Cal. MSS. Hatfield*, II, 137.

[3] Mullinger, op. cit., I, 287n.

Merton College, Oxford, after a severe tussle got the better of his fellows, fined and punished them, and expelled one, who is said to have died 'of greife or curst hart' within five days.[1]

In such turbulent and unscholastic times, it is not surprising that the college libraries seem to have been regarded as suitable places for detention! In 1611, John Baber, a fellow of Lincoln College, Oxford, being found guilty of misdemeanour and bad example, was ordered as a penalty 'to studie in the Library every day in the week', from 8 to 9 a.m. and from 1 to 2 p.m. for a month. In 1624 we find a similar use of the library recorded.[2]

Such surroundings were not likely to prove congenial to men seeking leisure and peace for the work of artistic creation. The inevitable effect was to drive from the University many men of dignity, worth and genius. As far as the writers are concerned, John Foxe was forced to resign his fellowship at Magdalen, Oxford, on account of his objection to the theological requirements exacted, and, with the exception of Thomas Heywood, who is stated to have been a fellow of Peterhouse, no writer of any repute kept up his connexion with either University. A spell at college was useful for the acquisition of literary skills, or for meeting people from whom advancement at Court might ultimately be obtained, but there was no permanent haven available at Oxford or Cambridge for those who wanted merely to write.

Moreover, from the practical point of view, a fellowship was hardly worth the sacrifice of leisure, peace and principle involved. Although under Elizabeth the Universities increased in prosperity, if not in scholarship and dignity, the value of preferments remained very small, amounting to the very barest living. Fellowships at King's College, Cambridge, were worth little more than £5 13s. 4d. yearly; at St John's most of the

[1] John Chamberlain, *Letters*, ed. N. E. McClure (1939), I, 52.
[2] *Hist. MSS. Comm., MSS. Lincoln College*, II, App., 132.

fellows received £3 5s. 4d.; at Peterhouse 2s. a week. If Nashe is to be believed, Gabriel Harvey, a fellow of Pembroke, was unable to pay his own commons, and had to be helped by the charity of the rest of the fellows.[1] And John Lyly was in debt at one time for his battel, 23s. 10d.[2]

The heads of colleges were little better off. When in 1561, John Pilkington announced to the Vice-Chancellor his resignation of the Mastership of St John's College, Cambridge, he stated that its annual value was only £12.[3] In 1591 the Master of the same college, a man esteemed for his classical training, was so poor that the Dean of St Paul's had taken charge of one of his sons, by way of charity to him.[4] There is some justification for Nashe's assertion that half-educated University men 'betake themselves to some trade of Husbandry, for any maintenance they gette in the way of almes at the Universitie'.[5] Even these poor endowments were threatened by the rapacity of Courtiers.[6]

The general poverty of members of the University is strikingly illustrated by a chance remark uttered by a boasting snob in 1 Return from Parnassus:

I cannot come to my Inn in Oxforde without a dozen congratulatorie orations, made by Genus and Species and his ragged companions. I reward the poore ergoes moste bountifullie, and send them away.[7]

Private tutorships, it is true, provided one source of emolument for senior members of the University. On account of the

---

[1] *Have with you to Saffron-Walden. Works* (1958), III, 88–9.
[2] *Complete Works*, ed. R. W. Bond (1902), I, 15.
[3] Mullinger, op. cit., I, 185n.
[4] Alexander Nowell, 29 April 1591, in *Letters of Eminent Literary Men*, ed. Sir H. Ellis (Camden Society, 1843), 87.
[5] *Anatomie of Absurditie. Works* (1958), I, 37.
[6] Ibid., I, 36.
[7] III, i. *Three Parnassus Plays* (1949), 181–2.

youthful age at which undergraduates came up, these involved duties very much more exacting than those of the tutor of the present day or than those of the present master in a public school. They amounted to the fulfilment of the functions of teacher, matron and guardian. The tutor superintended the expenses of the undergraduate, bought necessary apparel and bed-linen for him, bought his books (and sometimes was left to pay the bill!), taught him privately, and superintended his religious and moral welfare.[1] The tutor of the Earl of Essex writes regarding the young earl's extreme necessity of apparel: 'he will, if not soon supplied, be not only threadbare but ragged'.[2] As late as 1646 we find a father requiring his son's tutor to see that he has employment on Sundays and fast-days, and to take care that he reads the Scriptures morning and evening. He usually had to share his room with his pupil. One of the characters in 2 Return from Parnassus recalls the time when he was in Cambridge, and lay 'in a Trundlebed' under his tutor.[3] For all this wearisome attendance upon the youthful undergraduate, during an academic year arranged to give little more than six weeks' vacation, the remuneration was one pound a quarter.[4]

[1] J. Bass Mullinger, Cambridge Characteristics in the Seventeenth Century, 489. If the tutor had a wife, she superintended the health of the youthful undergraduate: thus, Mrs Wilkinson provided an eye-lotion for her husband's pupil, Ned Harley. Wise mothers sometimes sent presents to the tutor's wife. Vide Letters of Brilliana Harvey (1638–9) (Camden Society, 1854).

[2] C. H. Cooper, Annals of Cambridge, II (1843), 353.

[3] II, vi. Three Parnassus Plays (1949), 285.

[4] John Coke's father, during Michaelmas quarter 1626, paid tuition fees of only ten shillings, though he seems usually to have paid one pound (Cowper MSS., Hist. MSS. Comm., App. I, 191, 284). Henry Brougham' tuition at Queen's College Oxford, thirty years later, was still one pound a quarter, at a time when a suit of clothes cost £9 10s. 5d. (Le Fleming MSS. Hist. MSS. Comm., XII, App. VII, 23). But a great lord paid more: for the young Earl of Rutland, in 1588, twenty pounds was paid for tuition, pe

Clearly, no one who aspired to a career in literature could afford to take upon himself duties so exacting for a reward so inadequate. John Florio, it is true, was at one time a tutor in Oxford; but he seems to have renounced the position for the more promising occupation of private teacher of languages, with a good connexion, in London. The income gained from this seems to have sufficed for him, and in the intervals of teaching he was able to write. Preferable too was the position of tutor in a noble household, where other servants attended to the more mundane needs of the pupils, and where cultured company afforded many compensations besides many opportunities for social promotion.

Thus, with preferments given almost entirely through 'influence', or according to theological requirements or pretensions; limited to those in Holy Orders, or proceeding to take them; and finally, far from sufficient to maintain the holder in bare necessaries; with obligations to lecture and conduct University exercises in subjects unlikely to be congenial to a mind of literary and artistic bent; the only other means of subsistence, acting as tutor, being an engrossing duty which would leave no time or energies for creative work; it is not surprising that the University should have proved the very last home for a would-be writer.

As to the openings offered by the lower teaching profession, not much can be said here.[1] A few remarks about the economic position of the teacher must suffice. There is reason to believe

---

quarter or per year it is not clear (*Rutland MSS.*, *Hist. MSS. Comm.*, App. IV, i, 248). By 1684 tutors' fees seem to have risen greatly: the MSS. of the Rev. W. Pyne record a payment in that year of £22 0s. 4d. for tuition, it is not clear whether for a half-year or a year (*Hist. MSS. Comm.*, IX, ii, App., 495).

[1] Much of the information here on this topic is drawn from A. F. Leach, *Early Yorkshire Schools* (1899–1900) and *English Schools at the Reformation* (1896).

that teaching at the great grammar schools connected with the collegiate churches of Eton, Westminster, or Winchester was sufficiently lucrative.[1] They were large schools, richly endowed, and frequented by the sons of the wealthy aristocracy. Camden's prosperous career seems to point to this conclusion, though he also held the office of Clarenceux King-of-Arms. But it is certain that the ordinary stipend of a grammar school afforded but a very scanty provision for his needs, especially if he were married. Salaries ranged from about £5 or £6 to £20, with occasionally a much smaller allowance for an usher to teach the 'petties', boys of seven to ten years of age.[2] They had formerly been of greater value, but the ill-judged measures taken under the Chantries Act in the reign of Edward VI, by substituting a fixed payment for endowments derived from property, had greatly impoverished the schools throughout the country. So serious was the depreciation that, under Elizabeth, it was found necessary in some districts to combine the funds of no less than five schools, in order to secure enough to pay a schoolmaster. Five Yorkshire grammar schools in 1583 could raise only £25 7s. 2d. between them for the support of the master and other expenses.

It was not that there was lack of good schools, or schools which had done good work—even the pessimist Philip Stubbes admitted that there were 'excellent good schooles, both in cities, townes and countries'[3]—but they were seriously crippled in their resources, and afforded little inducement to men of learning and genius. This was fully recognized by authorities

[1] Colet had offered to the High-master of his new school, St Paul's, the exceptional stipend of £35, an indication that he meant to secure the services of more than a mere common grammarian: F. Seebohm, *Oxford Reformers*, 219.

[2] John Trap, schoolmaster of the Free School at Stratford-upon-Avon, received, in 1629, a salary of five pounds, in addition probably to a house and garden: J. O. Halliwell, *Stratford Records*, 98.

[3] *Anatomy of Abuses* (New Shaks. Soc., 1877–82), II, 19.

whose duty it was to care for education in the various districts. In an appeal (1548) to the protector Somerset against the proposed sale of the endowment of Sedbergh Grammar School, the town authorities plead for more generous treatment of schoolmasters:

Quinetiam doctus nullus provinciam hanc surbibit si quando vacuus fuerit locus, ubi ad tantas angustias stipendium adigitur, parum nimium parum sunt decem pondo ad doctum quemvis alendum hoc sibi soli satis non est, uxori et familiae multo minus erit. Quis ullius spei aut eruditionis juvenis academiam deseret locum amaenitatis plenissimum . . . et cum non minore fortassis stipendio ex collegio, ut ad populum rudem, regionem vastam, horridam gentem, omnis elegantioris culturae expertem, ad immensos labores et non ferendos abeat, praesertim cum tam vile praemium laborum ferat [sic].[1]

It should be noted that nearly all the grammar schools were free,[2] the master being paid a fixed salary, derived from landed property. It is true that there is evidence of extra payments given for extra tuition, or by way of free presents; but there is not sufficient to warrant a belief that this was a frequent custom.[3]

[1] A. F. Leach, *Early Yorkshire Schools* (1899–1900), II, 252–3. They say no learned man will come to the place, if vacant, for besides other hardships the salary (£10) is 'much too small to maintain a learned man, to say nothing of wife and family'. 'What young man of hope or learning,' they ask, 'will leave the University, a place full of delight . . . and possibly affording him no smaller income, in order to come to a rude people, a desolate region, a barbarous folk, devoid of all refined culture, to unlimited and intolerable toil, and that, too, when he is to reap so wretched a reward?'

[2] A. F. Leach demonstrated that the term 'Free School' bears the obvious meaning, i.e. 'a school giving gratuitous education': *English Schools at the Reformation* (1896) 110–13.

[3] A. W. Pollard adds that at an earlier period, and the custom may have continued, the schoolmaster expected frequent invitations to dine or sup with the parents of scholars. The early manuals of Latin contain ready-made forms of invitation from the boy to his master, and doubtless the latter saw to it that the boy used them.

We know that one schoolmaster, Christopher Ocland, was constantly in financial distress, and we know the stipend upon which he had to depend. When the school of St Olave's, Southwark, was founded[1] or remodelled on an improved footing, in 1571, Ocland was engaged as head master, with the former head, if willing, as his assistant. Ocland's salary was fixed at 20 marks yearly (£13 6s. 8d.), for which he was to teach the 'gramaryens', and help the usher with the 'petytes'. He was to be allowed, apparently, to receive also six or eight boarders to eke out his income 'for that twentie marks was not sufficiente lyving'.[2] He found it quite impossible to live upon these meagre resources, and was constantly petitioning great officials for some substantial patronage. In 1580 he gave up teaching, and tried to gain a living by writing, with little success. In 1590 we find him living at Greenwich, because his debts make it impossible for him to be in London; he is teaching again, but his labours 'wyll not fynde' him 'bread and drynck'. He petitions Burghley in most abject terms: 'Helpe, my very good Lord, my singular good Lord, helpe I praie and most humbly desyre your honor for Gods sake, yower poor and infortunate *Christopher*.'[3] Still later, we find it proposed to relieve the poverty of his widow, by giving her the next vacant post as 'coal-treasurer at the waterside'.[4]

Teachers in the elementary schools, and those with private schools of their own, fared even worse. The ordinary rate of payment was from twopence to sixpence a week for each child, in the private school; in the public school, probably, a fixed

[1] There was evidently a school of some sort existing before, since there was a schoolmaster, with some claim to a continuance of employment.

[2] ed. Sir H. Ellis, *Original Letters of Eminent Literary Men* (Camden Society, 1843), 65–6.

[3] Ibid., 73–4.

[4] 7 June 1593. *Acts of the Privy Council*, ed. Sir John Dasent (1890 ff.) XXIV, 297–8.

salary. That the pay was low is only too clear. Stubbes states that in the 'inferior schools . . . such small pittance is allowed the schoolmasters, as they can . . . hardly maintaine themselves . . . they teach and take paines for little or nothing'.[1] Gibes at 'hungry scholars' who spend their time teaching children their horn-books, or drudging over *Pueriles Confabulationes* with 'a companie of seaven yeare olde apes'[2] are frequently met with. 'As lousy as a schoolmaster'[3] was a comparison that could be used apparently without inappropriateness.

The labours of the schoolmaster were by no means light. Then, as now, they were too exacting to allow time for much other work. The ordinary grammar school hours averaged from seven to eight hours a day; and, if we may judge from the account given by a seventeenth century schoolmaster of Rotherham the curriculum was sufficiently varied. The 'petties' learned accidence, syntax, and easy Latin translations; the boys in the higher forms studied Terence, Ovid, Cicero, Virgil, Horace, Seneca, Juvenal, Persius, Isocrates, Hesiod, Homer, and sometimes even Hebrew. They wrote themes and Latin verses, and they held disputations. The task of superintending such a mass of work, even with the assistance of an usher and a few of the older boys, can have left little leisure or energy for writing poetry or emulating the literary productivity of Nashe.

Other duties less congenial than that of reading classic authors fell to the lot of the schoolmaster. Even the collegiate schoolmasters were required to attend to details which must have been very irksome, and they were at times treated with scant courtesy. Here is a letter from the irate parent of a boy whose epistolary skill appears to be defective:

[1] *Anatomy of Abuses* (New Shaks. Soc., 1877–82), II, 20–1.
[2] *Pilgrimage to Parnassus, Three Parnassus Plays* (1949), 128.
[3] *The Puritan* (anon., n.d.), I, ii.

Roger Coppey to J. Harman at Winchester, 1593, Dec. 18. Look to Anthony Coppey, your scholar, and command him not to write unto 'my' but to make you privy to it, for his hand is very bad, and the manner of writing worse, as you see by this letter that he send unto 'my', and from henceforward let him not write but in Latin when he can do it of himself, and not else; and, I pray, good Mr. Harman, speak to one that may teach him to write very fear [*sic*]. The bearer hereof is my brother, and he shall tell you my mind at large.[1]

As has already been suggested the lot of the tutor in a private family was more comfortable. But even here there were considerable variations. Samuel Daniel was treated as an honoured friend; so also was William Browne.[2] But in an ordinary middle-class family, especially of *nouveaux-riches*, his position was certainly far from pleasant. The satiric picture of the tutor in *1 Return from Parnassus* is doubtless highly coloured; but it must have borne some relation to fact. He is to be content to fare like the servants, living on bread and beer and bacon; he is to wait at meals; to work all harvest time; and never to begin his teaching without an obeisance to his pupil. For all this he is to receive five marks a year, and a gift from his master's cast-off wardrobe.[3] The employer was held responsible for the orthodoxy of the private teacher, a penalty of £10 being imposed in 1580 upon all who had in their houses schoolmasters who did not attend church.[4]

Besides Daniel and William Browne, three other writers held the position of family tutor (John Foxe, Stephen Gosson

[1] *Hist. MSS. Comm., Cal. MSS. Hatfield,* IV, 438.
[2] On the other hand, Sir Daniel le Fleming gave William Baxter, a tutor or schoolmaster, forty shillings a year 'and his diet', with permission to take other pupils. The wages he gave a maidservant were three pounds a year. But this was in 1656–63 (*Le Fleming MSS., Hist. MSS. Comm.,* XII App. vii, 365, 373).
[3] II, i. *Three Parnassus Plays* (1949), 166.
[4] J. S. Burn, *Court of High Commission* (1865), 9n.

and William Webbe). Only three, Camden, Ocland and James Shirley, are known to have been school teachers, and the two latter gave up the profession when they turned to writing.[1] John Davies was a 'writing-master' and John Florio a 'master of languages', but their position with a private aristocratic *clientèle* was rather special. Shakespeare may have taught for a while in the country. Two other occasional writers who were also schoolmasters are Richard Knolles and Francis Meres.

Nor could the Church offer a very enviable refuge to the needy literary man, except in the higher ranks. Throughout the greater part of this period, in spite of strenuous efforts at improvement, the financial position, social status, and intellectual qualifications of the average country clergy were such as to bring great discredit upon the profession of Holy Orders. This was largely the result of the uncertainty of the last three reigns, which had driven out of the ranks of the clergy many of the most earnest and best qualified men, and had discouraged those who would have naturally entered Holy Orders.

Moreover, the necessity in the earliest years of Elizabeth's reign of supplying pastors to the many communities left without any ecclesiastical leader,[2] was so urgent that it forced bishops into filling up the vacancies with most injudicious haste. Parker, in 1559, ordained one hundred and fifty clergy in one day. Grindal ordained one hundred in his first year of office. The results were most disastrous. Large numbers of those ordained were quite unqualified, and served only to degrade their order in public estimation. They were held in

[1] Arthur Acheson (*Shakespeare and the Rival Poet*, 110 ff.) would add Chapman, suggesting that he may have kept school 'on the hill next Hitchen's left hand' so qualifying for identification with Holofernes, who educated youth at the change-house 'on the top of the mountain'.

[2] In the period 1560 to 1563 enquiries ascertained that ten parishes were vacant, and 'all together would not make three men's livings'. In Winchester eleven out of fourteen parish churches were vacant: W. H. Frere, *The English Church in the reigns of Elizabeth and James I* (1904), 103–5.

general contempt: 'Some doo bestow advousons of benefices upon their bakers, butlers, cookes . . . and horssekeepers'.[1] They were ignorant: some of them 'such as can scarcely read true english'. And many of them were of unclean life, utterly unfitted, even morally, for their office: 'They will read you their service . . . and when they have done, they will to all kinde of wanton pastimes and delights . . . and all the weeke after, yea all the yeere . . . they will not sticke to keep companie at the alehouse from morning till night, tipling and swilling'. They are 'fitter to feed hogs, then christian soules'.[2]

Undoubtedly the zealous efforts of the higher clergy and the government did much gradually to improve this situation. Already, by 1577, Harrison notes a considerable advance in intellectual qualifications: men are no longer ordained upon such slender acquirements as availed twelve or fifteen years before, 'when there was small choice'. He is even enthusiastic as to the learning and zeal of the higher clergy at the time when he writes; but this is largely due to his patriotic pride in the fact that they are now chosen from among Englishmen, and are no longer 'strangers, especiallie out of Italie'.[3] It was more than ten years afterwards that Ponsonby published Spenser's bitterly satiric sketch of the country parson in *Mother Hubberds Tale* (published 1591):

> . . . read he could not evidence, nor will,
> Ne tell a written word, ne write a letter,
> Ne make one title worse, ne make one better:
> Of such deep learning little had he neede,
> Ne yet of Latine, ne of Greeke, that breede
> Doubt mongst Divines, and difference of texts,
> From whence arise diversitie of sects,
> And hatefull heresies, of God abhor'd:
> But this good Sir did follow the plaine word,

[1] Harrison, *Description of England* (New Shaks. Soc., 1877), I, 26.
[2] *Anatomy of Abuses* (New Shaks. Soc., 1877–82), II, 76–7.
[3] Ibid., 14–15.

Ne medled with their controversies vaine.
All his care was, his service well to saine,
And to read Homelies upon holidayes:
When that was done, he might attend his playes;
An easie life, and fit high God to please.

There was thus very little inducement for the man of
attainments to select the career of parish priest, though it is
possible that, in the earlier years of the period, he would have
been readily beneficed. But when we come to investigate the
value of the average benefice, we are no longer surprised that
few writers should appear to have even dreamed of qualifying
for one. The poverty of the clergy is a standing topic. It supplies on one occasion a telling simile for Dekker, who describes a footpath as being 'beaten more bare, than the livings
of Church-men'.[1] The same writer published a small collection
of private prayers, including one for the clergy, which reveals
incidentally the light in which they were commonly regarded
—as objects for charity. 'As they breake unto us', runs the
prayer, 'the bread of life (which thou sendest . . .) so graunt
(O Lord) that we may not suffer them to starve for earthly
bread, but that like brothers wee may relieve them'.[2]

Harrison testifies that 'the greatest part of the more excellent
wits choose rather to imploy their studies unto physike and the
lawes, utterlie giving over the studie of the scriptures, for
feare least they should in time not get their bread by the
same'.[3] Ten, twelve thirty pounds at most, is the common net
annual value of a living.[4] Stubbes says they range as low as

[1] *Newes from Hell. Non-dramatic works*, II (1885), 98.
[2] *Foure Birdes of Noahs Arke. Non-dramatic works*, V (1886), 49.
[3] *Description of England* (New Shaks. Soc., 1877), I, 37.
[4] John Thornton asks for the vicarage of Helmsley, worth £26 12s. 4d.
yearly: he would keep a school for further maintenance (April, 1578). The
vicarage of Newark is worth 'above twenty pounds' (1587) (*Rutland MSS.,
Hist. MSS. Comm.*, XII, App. iv, i, 116, 224). Thirty pounds was considered
by the Commissioners a satisfactory stipend for a 'godly learned preacher'

£5, £4, and even £2 a year, 'Yea, and table themselves also of the same'.[1] The whole first year's income has to go to the Crown, besides a yearly tenth; so that out of a benefice of £20, 'the incumbent thinketh himself well acquitted if all ordinarie payments being discharged, he may reserve £13 6s. 8d. towards his own sustentation, and maintenance of his family'.[2]

Nor are these legal payments all that are incurred by the unhappy parson. Patrons, infected with the prevalent greed or need of money, demand heavy fees from the unlucky incumbent, amounting at times to as much as three-quarters annually of the total income. They will reduce £40 to £10 by their exactions.[3] The patron will covenant that

> If the living yerely doo arise
> To fortie pound, that then his yongest sonne
> Shall twentie have, and twentie thou has wonne;
> Thou hast it wonne, for it is of franke gift. . . .[4]

In 1609, Ralph Cleaton, curate-in-charge at Buxton, possessed the large income of £5, all the tithes going to the patron.[5] Or patrons demand the payment of a lump sum down: 'Stake three yeares stipend: no man asketh more', says the ironic Joseph Hall.[6] There is an amusing scene in *2 Return from Parnassus*' (1601):

---

at Ripon, and fifteen pounds for an assistant minister. These salaries were in addition to assigned lodgings (*Duch. of Lancs. Survey* 32 Eliz., vide Hubert Hall, *Society in the Elizabethan Age*, 172). But in considering the value of these livings, the remarks following must be taken into account.

[1] *Anatomy of Abuses* (New Shaks. Soc., 1877–82), II, 75.
[2] *Description of England* (New Shaks. Soc., 1877), I, 24.
[3] *Anatomy of Abuses* (New Shaks. Soc., 1877–82), II, 80.
[4] Spenser, *Mother Hubberds Tale*.
[5] John Lodge, *Illustrations of British History* (1838), III, 390.
[6] *Virgidemiarum*, II, v. *Collected Poems* (1949), 28. The newly-appointed Bishop of Sarum is said to have paid to the Duke of Buckingham £3500 Vide A. Welldon, *The Court and Times of James I* (1650), 129.

Acad. Fain would I have a living, if I could tel how to come by it.
    Eccho. Buy it. . . .
Acad. What, is the world a game, are livings gotten by playing?
    Eccho. Paying.
Acad. Paying? but say what's the nearest way to come by a living?
    Eccho. Giving.[1]

Unfortunate vicars, unable to keep house upon their scanty stipends, were driven to lodge at the ale-house; one, in despair of making ends meet, even begs to be allowed to sell ale himself.[2] Nashe had probably sufficient grounds for his irritating sneer at Gabriel Harvey's parson brother Richard, whom he called 'a dolefull foure nobles Curate, nothing so good as the Confessour of Tyburne', declaring that he 'hath scarce so much Ecclesiasticall living in all, as will serve to buy him cruell strings to his bookes, and haire buttons'.[3] We know that the poor fellow had to eke out his living by recourse to the lowest form of writing, astrological almanacs.

It is true that during the later years of Elizabeth, and under James, matters somewhat improved. In point of learning, morality and social status great reforms were effected, and it is probable that under Charles I and Archbishop Laud still more was done. In 1633, for instance, we find a certain Hugh Thomson receiving a stipend of £60 upon his entry into the ministry, a sum later raised to £100.[4]

In short, a clerical career appears to have been quite unattractive for literary aspirants. A few writers in fact took orders:

[1] II, ii. *Three Parnassus Plays* (1949), 263–4.
[2] John Lodge, *Illustrations of British History* (1838), III, 391.
[3] *Have with you to Saffron-Walden. Works* (1958), III, 10.
[4] *Egerton MSS.*, 784. It should be remarked that it is not clear whether Thomson was an Anglican pastor, or belonged to one of the dissenting sects. In 1640 the 'minester of Brocalbe received thirty pounds a year', though it had been reported that the income was fifty pounds (*Letters of Brilliana Harvey*, Camden Society, 1854). An able divine is promised an income of £100 in 1658 (ibid., 237).

Lancelot Andrewes, John Donne, Abraham Fleming, Richard Hakluyt, Robert Herrick, Joseph Hall, William Harrison, John Marston, Francis Meres and James Shirley; and some clerics turned their hand to writing pious literature. But the links between the two professions were frail: Shirley gave up the ministry when he 'set up as a play maker'; Marston abandoned drama for the Church; Herrick made a formal 'farewell unto poetrie' when he was presented with his living, and did not print his poems until about the time of his ejection in 1648. For the Courtly amateur like Donne writing and the ministry combined happily enough, but it is plain that the Church offered no refuge for those whose primary concern was to write professionally.

CHAPTER VI

Personal Relations amongst Authors

> I have ever truly cherished my good opinion of
> other men's worthy labours. . . .
>
> WEBSTER[1]
>
> How I doe love thee *Beaumont*, and thy Muse!
>
> JONSON[2]
>
> Forbeare to tempt me, *Proule*, I will not show
> A line unto thee, till the world it know
>
> JONSON[3]

THE period under consideration was marked by the gradual
rise of a <u>fellowship of authors</u> which affords a strong contrast
to the comparative isolation of English writers of earlier days.
A number of factors combined to concentrate literary production in London: Courtly society was organized in a group
system, whereby a nobleman gathered round himself his own
retinue and circle; all forms of power were centralized in the
capital, while the great baronial families in their provincial
centres were in decline; in addition, it was in London and the
South East that middle-class literacy became established first,
and in practice printing and publishing was also centralized
there. And London in the sixteenth century was very far from
being the vast agglomeration of heterogeneous districts known
to us now. In 1592 its population was estimated at no more
than some 300,000, and all its life concentrated in a few points,
like Whitehall, the Exchange and St Paul's. It was inevitable
that most men of any kind of distinction were well known both
to each other and to the public. The writers were no exception.
This pre-eminently Courtly and class-conscious society was

[1] *The White Devil* (1612), to the reader.
[2] *Epigrammes*, LV. *Ben Jonson*, VIII (1947), 44.
[3] *Epigrammes*, LXXXI. Ibid., 54.

organized like a miniature solar system revolving round the person of the monarch. Some writers were close satellites in their own right, noblemen like Sir Francis Bacon, Lord Chancellor; Sir John Davies, Lord Chief Justice; the Earl of Essex, Earl Marshal; Sir Edward Dyer, Chancellor of the Garter; Fulke Greville, Chancellor of the Exchequer; Sir Walter Raleigh, Privy Councillor; Sir Philip Sidney, Joint Master of the Ordnance, and the Earl of Oxford, Lord Great Chamberlain. Other lesser Courtiers included George Chapman, Sewer to Prince Henry; Samuel Daniel, Gentleman of the Chamber; John Donne, Dean of St Paul's; Abraham Fraunce, Queen's Solicitor; Ben Jonson, the King's Poet; Anthony Munday, Queens Messenger of the Bedchamber, and Edmund Spenser, Sheriff of Cork. Beyond these were outer satellites, like Shakespeare, Drayton, Marlowe, Webster, Lodge and others. And so on, outwards, through the Greenes, Peeles, Nashes and Dekkers, to the hack writers with little or no social status, like William Elderton, Samuel Rowlands, Tom Coryat and John Taylor. But the interesting thing is that the world they all lived in was so small that they all knew each other and were, in some sense, rivals.

Writers display a close knowledge of each other's habits, dress and conversation, and they allude to each other by initials, and nicknames, or by the mention of small personal peculiarities, certain of being understood, not only by the person alluded to but by their audience as well. 'Who in London hath not heard,' asks Gabriel Harvey, 'of his (Greene's) dissolute and licentious living; his fonde disguisinge of a Master of Arte with ruffianly haire, unseemely apparrell, and more unseemelye Company?'[1] Everyone in the reading and theatregoing fraternity knew Jonson's pox-pitted face and burly figure. There was thus point, as well as coarseness, in the scenes in *Satiromastix* in which Dekker twitted Jonson with the

[1] *Foure Letters. Works* (1885), I, 168.

defects of his personal appearance—his face 'puncht full of Oylet-holes, like the cover of a warming-pan', or 'like a rotten russet Apple, when 'tis bruiz'd'.[1] The public doubtless shared in the curiosity felt by his literary colleagues concerning the retired scholarly poet, Samuel Daniel, who was wont to 'lie hid at his garden-house in Old Street' for months together, 'as the tortoise burieth himself all the winter in the ground'.[2] Marlowe's imputed atheism aroused widespread hostility. Drayton's rebuff from King James was so well-known that it caused his friendship to be none too welcome to his colleagues, as he bitterly complains:

> I scarce dare praise a vertuous friend that's dead,
> Lest for my lines he should be censured;
> It was my hap before all other men,
> To suffer shipwrack by my forward pen. . . .
> He next my God on whom I put my trust,
> Had left me troden lower then the dust.[3]

The whole town maliciously relished the humour, conscious or unconscious, of the parodying of majestic Ben Jonson by John Taylor, the lowly Thames water-man. When the great Ben took his famous journey into Scotland, he was followed afar off by this humble imitator, to the joy of all London. Taylor was at pains later on to explain that his journey was not undertaken 'either in malice or in mockage',[4] but the town clung to its jest.

Evidence of the intimate nature of the intercourse of writers is afforded by Thomas Heywood, writing on the use of familiar names:

> Greene, who had in both Academies ta'ne
> Degree of Master, yet could never gain

---

[1] V. ii; IV, iii. *Dramatic Works*, ed. Fredson Bowers (1953), I, 381, 362.
[2] Bishop Fuller, *Worthies of England* (1662), vide under *Somerset*.
[3] *To Master George Sandys. Works*, ed. J. W. Hebel, III (1932), 206.
[4] *The Pennilesse Pilgrimage* (1618), preface.

> To be call'd more than Robin; who, had he
> Profest ought save the Muse, serv'd and been free
> After a seven years prenticeship might have
> (With credit too) gone Robert to his grave.
> Marlo, renown'd for his rare art and wit,
> Could ne'er attain beyond the name of Kit.
> Although his *Hero and Leander* did
> Merit addition rather. Famous Kid
> Was call'd but Tom; Tom Watson, though he wrote
> Able to make Apollo's self to dote
> Upon his Muse, for all that he could strive.
> Yet never could to his full name arrive,
> Tom Nash (in his time of no small esteem)
> Could not a second syllable redeem.
> Excellent Beaumont, in the foremost rank
> Of the rar'st wits, was never more than Frank.
> Mellifluous Shakespeare, whose enchanting quill
> Commanded mirth or passion, was but Will,
> And famous Johnson, though his learned pen
> Be dipt in Castaly, is still but Ben.
> Fletcher and Webster, of that learned pack
> None of the mean'st, yet neither was but Jack.
> Dekker but Tom, nor May, nor Middleton,
> And he's now but Jack Ford that once were John.[1]

Bishop Fuller's story of the 'wit-combats' at the Mermaid between Shakespeare and Jonson bears the impress of truthful gossip:

Many were the wit-combats betwixt him and Ben Jonson, which two I behold like a Spanish Great Galleon, and an English Man-of-War; Maister Johnson (like the former) was built far higher in learning; solid, but slow in his performances. Shakespeare, with the English Man-of-War, lesser in bulk, but lighter in sailing, could

---

[1] *Hierarchie of Angels* (1635), IV, 206; text here as quoted by F. S. Boas, *Thomas Heywood* (1950), 129.

turn with all tides, tack about and take advantage of all winds, by the quickness of his Wit and Invention.[1]

There is plenty of evidence for the fraternal gatherings of the 'Disciples of Ben'. And we know of other close friendships, writers sometimes living together like Beaumont and Fletcher, and Marlowe and Kyd, or working in groups round a central figure, Sidney or Donne or Spenser.[2]

Such close familiarity amongst writers naturally favoured the practice of collaboration, a custom which was especially common in the theatre. All dramatists collaborated; some, such as Beaumont and Samuel Rowley, have left nothing written alone. Even the independent, censorious Jonson wrote with others at times, although in one instance at least he replaced his colleague's work when preparing a play for print.[3]

It should be said that in every writer's close circle of friends and acquaintances, his first audience in fact, there were people who are not known as writers themselves. Donne's circle, for instance, included Sir Henry Goodyere as well as Sir Henry Wotton, Sir John Davies and John Hoskyns. Indeed, the function of the group was only partially literary: Donne's friends were associates from politics and the Inns of Court. The whole Courtly structure of society demanded that individuals grouped together for mutual support and survival: an inevitable law of patronistic organizations. Groups of friends tended to include individuals of divergent social rank, and the writers among them adopted different attitudes towards literature as a profession. Some writers, like Daniel, tried to live a retired life in the household of a patron, secluded from the clannishness of the day. But most were entirely happy to live within

[1] *Worthies of England* (1662), vide under *Warwickshire*.

[2] vide Robert Herrick, *Ode to Jonson*. For further information vide A. Alvarez, *The School of Donne* (1961) and J. W. Saunders, *The Profession of English Letters* (1964).

[3] *Sejanus* (1603), preface.

the group system. When Spenser found himself cut off in Ireland, he established his own group, including Lodowick Bryskett and local representatives of the Church and the Army.[1] Other gentry, removed from the centre of life in London, imitated the Courtly system by setting up similar local groups: Richard Carew in Cornwall, Humphrey Gifford in Devon, William Vallans in Hereford, and Richard Robinson (of Alton) in Cheshire.

Such group intimacy is the source of some of the difficulties that beset the study of Elizabethan literature. Its extreme allusiveness has left for the modern student many a problem where the contemporary reader found only an open riddle. We know why Harvey was furious when Nashe reminded him of his father's lucrative occupation: ropemakers thrived when hangings were so common! But we have lost the key to many of the taunts by which Harvey and Nashe exasperated each other. We have long recognized with interest Greene's jibes at the 'upstart Crow, beautified with our feathers', who 'is in his owne conceit the onely Shake-scene in a countrie'.[2] But it has been harder to identify the objects in Nashe's contemptuous allusions to those who 'leave the trade of *Noverint* whereto they were borne', and like 'the Kidde in *Aesop* . . . forsooke all hopes of life to leape into a new occupation'.[3] We are doubtful whom Greene intended by 'Young Juvenall, that byting Satyrist, that lastlie with mee together writ a Comedie'.[4] We cannot know for certain the identity of the rival poet of Shakespeare's sonnet. We are wholly ignorant of

[1] H. R. Plomer and T. P. Cross, *The Life and Correspondence of Lodowick Bryskett* (1927), 82–3.

[2] *Greens Groatsworth of Wit* (1596). *Works*, ed. Grosart (1881–86), XII, 144.

[3] Nashe's 'To the Gentlemen Students' in Greene, *Menaphon. Works*, ibid., VI, 15–16.

[4] Greene, *Greens Groatsworth of Wit. Works*, Ibid., XII, 143.

the objects of Chettle's denunciation in *Kind-hart's Dream*: the two ballad-mongers, son of 'old Barnes the plumber', sent out into London streets to sell lascivious ballads, and thus spoil the market for honest writers' wares, doubtless familiar figures to most of Chettle's readers.[1]

In the drama, personal allusions are common. Jonson's audience knew that in the person of Antonio Balladino, 'pageant-poet to the city of Milan . . . when a worser cannot be had',[2] he was ridiculing his rival in masque-writing, Anthony Munday, and doubtless the sketch contained for them more humorous points than are obvious to us. And if Shakespeare were indeed making fun of John Florio in the character of Holofernes, contemporary theatre-goers were doubtless able to relish the jest.

It is not surprising that extraordinary interest should have been shown in the personal quarrels of authors. Even in serious controversies, like 'Martin Marprelate' (1588–90), coarse personal banter and abuse contributed much to popular interest. Such titbits of scandal and gossip as the following, concerning well-known personages, were sure to be relished:

I have heard some cleargie men say that M. Bridges was a verie patch and a duns when he was in Cambridg. . . .

Who abuseth the high commission? . . . John London . . . Who hath cut down the elmes at Fulham? John London. . . . Who goeth to bowles upon the Sabboth? Dumbe dunsticall John of Good London hath done all this.[3]

The most resounding of the literary squabbles which agitated Elizabethan and Jacobean life arose from some more reasonable basis than mere personal antagonism. Below the surface of the conflicting personalities of Nashe and Harvey lurked a genuine divergence of literary aim and outlook. In the dispute

[1] *Kind-harts Dream* (1609). (New Shaks. Soc., 1874), 48–9.
[2] *The Case is Altered*, I, i.
[3] P. Dearmer, *Religious Pamphlets* (1898), 116, 126–7.

Harvey shows up as a narrow University pedant, arrogant, dry-as-dust, censorious, trusting to the weight of his learning to help him bear down the upstart impudence of a renegade; he has Courtly pretensions and he seeks to give the impression of a writer in the Court's amateur tradition. And Nashe is the self-confident, emancipated young man of the world, despising the other for his narrow outlook, and flouting his pretensions to superiority; a popular writer with all the instincts of a professional. Nashe makes fun of his opponent's 'Lawiers english' and 'inckehornisme', his 'Hermaphrodite phrases, being halfe Latin and halfe English'.[1] He denies that to be a University man and a scholar confers any distinction in itself. Harvey's college, St John's, Cambridge, has many hundred perfecter scholars than Harvey, who have not 'shakte off obscuritie'.[2] And he utterly repudiates Harvey's standards of literary judgment in style, preferring the effective and incisive, and the lively in matter, to all the carefully prepared, long-winded writing that University men may set forth. He jeers at Harvey's own lumbering style:

I talke of a great matter when I tell thee of a period, for I know two severall periods or full pointes, in this last epistle, at least fortie lines long a piece.[3]

Elsewhere he gives expression to his preference for nimble wit and spontaneity, as compared with more painstaking work:

Let other men . . . praise the mountaine that in seaven yeares brings foorth a mouse . . . give me the man, whose extemporal vaine in anie humor, will excell our greatest Art-masters deliberate thoughts.[4]

Thy soule hath no effects of a soule, thou canst not sprinkle i[t]

---

[1] *Strange Newes* (1592). *Works* (1958), I, 265, 272.
[2] Ibid., I, 314.
[3] Ibid., I, 329.
[4] Epistle prefixed to Greene, *Menaphon. Works*, ed. Grosart (1881–86) VI, 11.

into a sentence, & make everie line leape like a cup of neate wine new powred out, as an Orator must doe that lies aright in wait for mens affections.[1]

Harvey retorts with repudiation of Nashe's own style as reckless, fantastic, unnatural:

Right artificality... is not mad-brained, or ridiculous, or absurd... but deep-conceited, but pleasurable, but delicate ... not according to the fantastical mould of *Aretine* or *Rabelays*.[2]

The finest wittes preferre the loosest period in M. Ascham, or Sir Philip Sidncy, before the tricksiest page in Euphues, or Paphatchet.... Where is the polished and refined Eloquence, that was wont to bedeck, and embellish Humanity?[3]

Nashe's name, he admits, is 'blazed abroad'; but he is famous only in the opinion of the 'common rout', which 'never goes far currant'.[4] The best characterization of Nashe's own views is given in a passage placed in his mouth by Harvey, and intended as an ironical self-condemnation:

Till I see your finest humanitie bestow such a liberall exhibition of conceit, and courage, upon your neatest wittes; pardon me though I prefer one smart Pamflet of knavery, before ten blundring volumes of the nine Muses.... You may discourse of Hermes ... of Orpheus ... and I wott not what marvelous egges in mooneshine: but a flye for all your flying speculations, when one good fellow with his odd jestes, or one madd knave with his awke hibber-gibber, is able to putt downe twentye of your smuggest artificiall men, that simper it so nicely, and coylie in their curious pointes.... Penniles hath a certayne nimble and climbinge reach of Invention, as good as a long pole, and a hooke, that never fayleth at a pinch.... The Bookwoorme was never but a pick-goose.[5]

---

[1] *Strange Newes. Works* (1958), I, 307.
[2] *Foure Letters. Works* (1885), I, 218.
[3] *Pierces Supererogation. Works* (1885), II, 218.
[4] *The Trimming of Thomas Nashe. Works* (1885), III, 31.
[5] *Pierces Supererogation. Works* (1885), II, 62-4.

In the same way, the great stage-quarrel between Jonson, and Marston and Dekker, arose in part out of the critical attitude assumed by the former in regard to his opponents' literary work. Priding himself upon his careful 'art', his truth to nature, and his propriety of language, Jonson scornfully condemned Marston for bombastic, ranting diction, and blamed Dekker for his reckless want of art. In a realistic scene, which must have been irresistibly comic on the stage, he represented his enemies as forced to disgorge and spew out the hideous vocabulary with which they loaded themselves:

Crisp. O, I am sicke—
Horace. A bason, a bason, quickly, our physick works. Faint not, man.
Aris. O—*retrograde—reciprocall—incubus.*
Caesar. What's that, Horace?
Horace. Retrograde, reciprocall, and *incubus* are come up.
Gal. Thanks be to Jupiter.
Crisp. O—*glibbery—lubricall—defunct—*O—
Horace. Well said: here's some store.
Virgil. What are they?
Horace. Glibbery, lubricall, and *defunct.*
Gal. O, they came up easie.[1]

Marston and Dekker retaliated by making fun of his laborious, careful workmanship. They showed him on the stage sitting in his study, hammering out with infinite pains and much self-satisfaction his laboured rhymes:

O me thy Priest inspire
For I to thee and thine immortall name,
In—in—in golden tunes,
For I to thee and thine immortall name—
In—sacred raptures flowing, flowing, swimming, swimming:
In sacred raptures swimming,
Immortall name, game, dame, tame, lame, lame, lame. . . .[2]

[1] *The Poetaster*, V, iii. *Ben Jonson*, IV (1932), 312.
[2] *Satiromastix*, I, ii. *Dramatic Works* (1953), I, 316.

Each side despised the methods and aims of the other, and their quarrel was no mere trifle but the outcome of two antagonistic schools of literary thought.

It was a debate indeed of national importance. This was the age when the conflicting English dialects finally fused to become a Queen's English worthy of the realm: the language was in the melting pot. Issues were fiercely contested: the tradition of monosyllabics *versus* the elegance of Latinizations; the coining of neologisms *versus* the revival of archaisms; the importing of foreign words *versus* a nationalistic searching for Anglo-Saxon roots, and so on. In the battle the Courtly writer had a natural authority; as Sidney insisted—

Undoubtedly (at least to my opinion undoubtedly) I have found in divers smal learned Courtiers, a more sound stile, then in some professors of learning, of which I can gesse no other cause, but that the Courtier following that which by practise he findeth fittest to nature, therein (though he know it not) doth according to art, thogh not by art: where the other using art to show art and not to hide art (as in these casses he shuld do) flieth from nature, & indeed abuseth art.[1]

Or, as George Turberville has it, touching his cap:

> The courtier knows what best becomes,
>   in every kind of case:
> His nature is, what so he doth
>   to deck with gallant grace,
> The greatest clarkes in ither artes,
>   can hardly do the leeke:
> For learning sundry times is there
>   where judgement is to seeke.[2]

The difficulty was that neither Nashe nor Harvey, and neither Jonson nor Marston and Dekker, could claim this natural

[1] *The Defence of Poesie*, ed. A. Feuillerat: *Works of Sidney* (1923), III, 3.

[2] *Tragical Tales* (1587), ff. 198b–199.

authority: in fact, both camps claimed an authority they did not possess. Nashe would have agreed with Sidney's claims for the instinctive artist, and rested his case on this same principle. But in practice Sidney was scholarly, experimenting with quantitative measures and other classical examples, finding little to praise, for instance, in the drama of his own day, and on many issues Harvey would have found him a congenial ally.

The genuine literary issues were obscured by personalities, by theatrical rivalries, and by hostility towards certain stage-innovations (to which, for instance, Shakespeare alludes in his remarks in *Hamlet* about boy-players stealing the livelihood of older actors).[1] Jonson fell out with everyone in turn; even the dignified, peaceable Samuel Daniel was, he said, 'at jealousies with him'. Drayton seems to have become somewhat embittered by his long, unsuccessful struggle to obtain the Court favour which fell so much more easily to others. Acrimonious allusions to backbiting enemies are far from uncommon. As John Lyly suggests, 'Divers there are, not that they mislike the matter, but that they hate the man, that will not stick to teare Euphues, bicause they do envie Lyly.'[2] Dekker declared that envious opponents had tried to prevent the publication of one of his works. Chettle's unfortunate publication of the dying Greene's attack upon Shakespeare and others involved him in accusations of ill-will, from which he endeavoured to free himself by a full and frank apology. He declared himself a sorry 'as if the original fault had beene my fault, because mysel have seene his (Shakespeare's) demeanour no lesse civill than he excellent in the qualitie he professes'.[3]

There were, however, worse temptations than to professional enviousness. Authors, most of them, suffered severely

[1] II, ii.
[2] *Complete Works*, ed. R. W. Bond (1902), II, 11.
[3] *Kind-harts Dream* (New Shaks. Soc., 1874), 38.

from penury, as has been seen, and there was much temptation to literary fraud. Except in the case of the exceptionally lofty-minded, the standard of honour amongst them seems to have been fairly low. A great abuse was plagiarism, against which the law, then and for very long afterwards, afforded no protection, and which in any case was a common and legitimate practice in the Courtly circles of friends, where amicable competition on set themes and ideas was a popular exercise. To borrow the substance of a story, a poem, a drama, was then not only lawful, as now, but very much more common. Literary material was still thought of as common property; medieval habits died hard. In these circumstances, there are all kinds of echoes and parallels to which only the writer with thoroughly professional ambitions would attach any term as hard as plagiarism. Watson's and Breton's poems contain passages exactly alike. A whole sonnet and part of another, in Watson's *Tears of Fancy*, appears as scattered quatrains and couplets, alike word for word, in Breton's *Countess of Penbrooks Passion*. Passages from Gascoigne are appropriated by Watson, and passages from Watson's *Amyntas* appropriated by Fraunce. In Lyly's *Euphues* the greater part of the letter on education called *Euphues and Ephebus*, is a translation, unacknowledged, from Plutarch's περὶ παίδων ἀγωγῆς. Shakespeare was accused by Greene of being 'beautified with our feathers'. Certain sonnets by Spenser were published by translations of work by John Vandernoodt, the translator claiming, 'I have out of the Brabants spaeche turned them into the Englishe tongue.'[1] Dekker transferred wholesale passages from a forgotten book, Harman's *Caveat for Cursitors*, to his own pamphlet, *The Bel-man of London*.[2] The fault was general.

Some authors are quite ambivalent about the matter.

[1] Spenser, *Works*, ed. E. Greenlaw and others: *Minor Poems II* (1947), 612.
[2] Audley, *Fraternity of Vagabonds*, preface, (New Shaks. Soc., 1876–80), xvi.

Thomas Churchyard, after declaring that he 'never rob'd no writer', goes on to say

> Now must my Muse go borrow if I may
> My betters' works, to fill my matter full.[1]

John Taylor, the Water-poet, has some lines which possess interest here:

> There doth a strange, and true opinion runne,
> That Poets write much worse, then they have don. . . .
>
> And that their daily doings doe reveale,
> How they from one another filch and steale,
> As if amongst them 'twere a statute made,
> That they may freely use the theeving trade.
> And some there are that will not sticke to say,
> That many Poets living at this day,
> Who have the Hebrew, Latine, Greeke, at will,
> And in th'Italian and the French have skill,
> These are the greatest theeves they say, of all
> That use the Trade (or Art) Poeticall. . . .
>
> So whole bookes, and whole sentences have bin
> Stolne, and the stealers, great applause did win,
> And by their filching thought great men of fame,
> By those that knew not the right Authors name.
> For mine owne part. . . .
> Unto such robbery I could never reach,
> Because I understand no forreigne speach.
> Latin and French are heathen-Greeke to me. . . .
>
> Should I from English Authors, but purloyne
> It would be soone found counterfeited coyne.[2]

The unexceptionable practices of one age and one ethos were rapidly becoming the crimes of the next age and next ethos, as the professional principle begins to assert itself.

[1] *A Handful of Gladsome Verses* (1592), verses to readers.
[2] *A few lines against the scandalous Aspersions. Works* (Spenser Society, 1869), I, 26–7.

And, of course, side by side with plagiarisms and recrimina
tions go warm friendships between writers and genuine expressions of admiration. Jonson atones for many a carping criticism
by his whole-hearted tribute to Shakespeare: 'I lov'd the man,
and doe honour his memory (on this side Idolatry) as much as
any.'[1] Webster expressed generous admiration for his fellow-
dramatists, whose work he 'ever truly cherished'.[2] Drummond
wrote to Drayton in 1618: 'I long to see the rest of your
Polyolbion come forth, whiche is the only epic poem England,
in my judgment, hath to be proud of.'[3] Many more such
generous expressions might be quoted.

The custom of writing commendatory verses to be prefixed
to one another's works was a matter of fashion rather than
evidence of genuine literary approval. They served the purpose
nowadays fulfilled by excerpts from critical reviews appended
to dust jackets and advertisements. So common was the practice that the mere omission of such formal praises was apt to
be regarded as proof of the existence of ill-feeling; and one of
the first signs of the patching up of a quarrel between authors
was the appearance of verses by one of them commending the
other. Jonson declared that he was suspected of being no friend
to Drayton, simply

> Because, who make the question, have not seene
> Those ambling visits, passe in verse, betweene
> Thy Muse, and mine, as they expect.[4]

Some verses were mere empty compliments. Both Jonson and
Harvey, for instance, admitted that they sometimes praised
young writers beyond their deserts, with a view to encourag-

[1] *Discoveries. Ben Jonson*, VIII (1947), 583-4.
[2] *The White Devil* (1612), to the reader.
[3] David Masson, *Drummond of Hawthornden* (1873), 84.
[4] *The vision of Ben Jonson on the Muses of his Friend M. Drayton. Ben Jonson*, VIII (1947), 396.

ing them to greater efforts.[1] Jonson probably did himself some injustice here, for his eulogies suggest that he took a good deal of pains to confine his praise to points of real merit. In his lines of Breton, a second-rate writer whose value lay chiefly in unambitious truthfulness, he discriminatingly selected for commendation his avoidance of the fantastic and artificial.[2]

Writers also helped each other out by writing for publication prefaces or prefatory letters which absolved the published author from any stigma attached to appearing in print. George Turberville explains to the reader that Gascoigne's *Posies* was published at his insistence, and Barnabe Googe could blame his friend Blundeston for the publication of the *Eglogs*. It was genteel for the writer with social pretensions to seem reluctant to be interested in professional writing, either for the printed-book market or for the theatre, and friends cooperated in establishing this façade of gentility. 'Write for the Stage?' retorted Ovid Junior to Ovid Senior in *Poetaster*, 'Certainly not!'

> I am not knowne unto the open stage,
> Nor doe I traffique in their *theaters*.
> Indeede, I doe acknowledge, at request
> Of some neere friends, and honourable *Romanes*,
> I have begunne a *poeme* of that nature.[3]

In the small intimate world of letters of the day, it was inevitable that all classes of writer were affected by each passing popular fashion, no matter how lowly its origin. We shall see later how untrained was the taste of even the more aristocratic readers, as shown by their choice of extracts for their common-place-books, their manuscript books of 'selections'. Poor scribblers like Nicholas Breton, Thomas Churchyard, Christopher

[1] Jonson, '*An Epistle to Master John Selden*', *The Under-Wood. Ben Jonson*, VIII (1947), 158.

[2] *In Authorem* (1600). *Ben Jonson*, VIII (1947), 362.

[3] I, ii. *Ben Jonson*, IV (1932), 211.

Ocland and Samuel Rowlands, enjoyed an immense reputation. In fact, writers had virtually to educate their own public. Nashe warned his readers that there was a difference between the ballad-monger and the true poet, which they must learn to recognize:

If he love good Poets he must not countenance Ballad-makers; if he have learned Physicians, he must not favour horse-leeches and mountebanks.

And Jonson tried to bully his audiences into recognizing good work when they saw it: 'By —— 'tis good, and if you like't you may.'[1]

It was all very well. As far as the printed-book market was concerned, they knew that to the average reader printed work was all the same and that the worst scribblers were often accepted as representative of the whole profession. Daniel wearily laments that

> ... So many so confusedly sing,
> Whose diverse discords have the Musicke mar'd,
> And in contempt that mysterie doth bring,
> That he must sing alowd what will be heard:
> And the receiv'd opinion of the thing,
> For some unhallowed string that vildely jar'd,
> Hath so unseason'd now the eares of men,
> That who doth touch the tenour of that vaine,
> Is held but vaine; and his unreckned pen
> The title but of Levitie doth gaine.[2]

Writers themselves were not always free from blame. In their own estimates of each other, wilfully or unwittingly, they made erroneous and misleading comparisons. Harvey's wrongheaded parallel between Nashe and Elderton will be referred to later. In the same spirit of malice he called Robert Greene

---

[1] *Cynthia's Revels*, epilogue. *Ben Jonson*, IV (1932), 183.
[2] *Musophilus* (1599). *Complete Works* (1885), I, 227.

and Elderton the ballad-writer 'two notorious mates, & the very ringleaders of the riming, and scribbling crew'.[1] Jonson maliciously coupled Dekker with Edward Sharpham and John Day, calling them all three 'rogues', and he condemned Middleton, in company with Day and Gervase Markham, two quite inferior poets, as 'not of the faithful' (that is, true poets). And on the other hand they accepted into their fellowship men of talent so inferior as to be far unworthy. The quality of Thomas Churchyard's work may be guessed at from his own words:

Finding myself unfurnished of learning, and barely seen in the arts liberal, and far unfit to touch or treat of divinity . . . I saw me most able . . . to bring forth some acceptable work; not striving to shew anie rare invention (that passeth a meane man's capacity), but to utter and revive matter of some moment.[2]

Yet Nashe, who had some pretensions to critical insight, declared that he admired Churchyard's 'aged Muse', swearing that in *Shore's Wife* he would still live after death.[3]

The 'Grub Street' of the hacks and ballad-writers was no more popular than in Pope's day with those who had some sense of the dignity and value of English letters:

> These fellowes are the slaunderers of the time,
> Make ryming hateful through their bastard ryme.
> But were I made a judge in poetrie,
> They all should burne for theire vilde heresie.[4]

Martine Mar-Sixtus says

Every rednosed rimester is an author, every drunken man's dreame is a book, and he whose tallent of little wit is hardly worth a farthing yet layeth aboute him so outragiously as if all Helicon had run

[1] *Foure Letters. Works* (1885), I, 164.
[2] *A Sparke of Friendship. Harleian Miscellany*, III (1809), 262.
[3] *Strange Newes. Works* (1958), I, 309.
[4] I.C., *Epigrams* (n.d.) (New Shaks. Soc., 1874), 122.

through his pen. In a word, scarce a cat can look out of a gutter, but out starts a halfpenny chronicler, and presently 'a propper new ballet of a strange sight' is endited. What publishing of frivolous Prognostications! as if Will Sommers were againe revived! What counterfeiting and cogging of prodigious and fabulous monsters! as if they laboured to exceed the poet in his metamorphoses. What lascivious, unhonest, and amorous discourses . . . yet they shame not to subscribe, By a graduate in Cambridge. In Artibus Magister.[1]

It was not so much, then, the low origin of the hacks that disturbed more dedicated writers, but the cheapness of the literature, even if produced by a Greene or a Nashe. Nicholas Breton, no very great genius himself and having few social pretensions, expresses much the same feeling:

Ant.   Shall we speake of Poetrie?
Dina. What Ballades? why it is growne to such a passe, that the E. is taken out, and of Poetry, it is called pottry: why verses are so common, that they are nailed upon every poste: besides it is a poore profession.
Mean. . . . If there were a fall of rich men, there might be some worke for them about Epitaphs: for if they be too busie with Libels, they are put to silence for ever after.[2]

Men of talent and reputation were driven by the competition of scribblers to speak of them with bitterest indignation. They inveighed perpetually against 'red-nosed Elderton' and his tribe; at inferior self-styled scholars, who could 'scarcelie latinize their necke-verse',[3] and were mere 'excrementorie dishlickers of learning.'[4] They endeavoured to educate the public in discrimination by making fun of the poetaster's topics. The really clever thing in poetry, they ironically say, is to be able to write verses on 'nothing'—on a Mouse, on the Death of

[1] *Martine Mar-Sixtus* (anon, 1592), dedicatory epistle.
[2] *A dialogue full of pithe and pleasure* (1603). *Works* (1879), II, j, 6.
[3] Nashe, epistle prefixed to Greene, *Menaphon. Works* (1881-6), VI, 15.
[4] *Pierce Penilesse. Works* (1958), I, 240.

a Throstle, on Baldness, on the Lady Mayoress's French Hood and Scarlet Gown. They deride the ballad-maker's 'marvels', such as 'The Calf with Five Feet', 'The Raven sitting on top of a Newe Kitchin', 'Meeting the Devil in Conjure House Lane',[1] 'The witches bidding the Devill to dinner at Derbie'.[2] Jonson devoted a whole play to a merciless exposure of the unscrupulous and mendacious methods of the Chronigraphers, or writers of Newsletters and Pamphlets.[3] These are not only ignorant themselves; they mislead and delude the reader: 'They are so simple, they know what they do; they no sooner spy a new ballad, and his name to it that compiled it, but they put him in for one of the learned men of the time.' The wonder is that they do not thus spread the fame of the very serving-men and writing-masters out of employ, who advertise their qualifications on the pillars of St Paul's, and on the 'whipping-posts at the street corners'.[4] Dekker and Nashe skilfully tried to discredit their rivals, the makers of 'prognosticating almanacs', and to spoil the market by writing witty parodies of Prognostications themselves.[5]

Naturally, neither vituperation nor mockery destroyed the scribbling tribe. Ballads and pamphlets and prognostications continued to be the staple reading of the less educated. In 1635 George Wither complained bitterly of the hundreds of pounds spent yearly on 'vain songs and prophane ballads'; the stationers' warehouses contained then, he declared, thousands of them stored up.[6]

It will be noted that the battle was not between the men of the Court and the men of the streets: men of Courtly experience

[1] One of William Elderton's ballads.
[2] Jonson, *Newes from the New World* (1620). *Ben Jonson*, VII (1941), 515.
[3] *The Case is Altered* (1609) and *Newes from the New World* (1620).
[4] *Pierce Penilesse. Works* (1958), I, 194.
[5] Vide Nashe's *Prognostication* and Dekker's *Raven's Almanacke*.
[6] *Schollers Purgatory. Miscellaneous Works* (Spenser Society, 1872), I, 19.

worked in 'Grub Street', and some of their critics had very lowly status. Nor was it a battle between the educated and the uneducated: there were University men, and non-University men, in both camps. Nor was it a battle between the amateurs and the paid professionals: some of the amateurs had a better sense of literature than the writers who might have been expected to offer professional dedication. Fundamentally, it was a battle of standards and values, based on different conceptions of the function of literature, between those who 'entertained' by appealing to those common tastes which were predictable and exploitable, and those who 'entertained' by exploring a wider and deeper imaginative satisfaction. The only hope of the literary profession lay in the growth of a more discerning taste, not only among a few but also among a wide public. Writers had to wait until the late seventeenth and early eighteenth centuries before conditions radically changed in their favour. In the meantime, the fellowship of writers in London continued to present the complex and divided picture we have seen.

CHAPTER VII

Authors and Readers

> I have here set it downe whole: and doe heartily
> forgive their ignorance whom it chanceth not to
> please.
>
> JONSON[1]

> 'But wrote he like a Gentleman?'
> '... He was paid for it,
> Regarded, and rewarded: which few *Poets*
> Are now adaies'
> 'And why?'
> "Cause every Dabler
> In rime is thought the same.'
>
> JONSON[2]

THE foregoing pages have sketched in outline a somewhat dark picture of the life of the literary professional: harassed, suspected, poverty-stricken. Perhaps, it may be suggested, he derived some consolation and encouragement from living in an age of genuine literary interests? It is quite true that the Elizabethan and Jacobean period was an age not only of abundant and striking productiveness, but also of fashionable interest in literature. For reasons which we have discussed, it was the correct thing to take an interest in poetry. The Ordinary, where Gallants met together for social ends, was utilized almost as much as the bookseller's shop, for 'conference of the best Editions'.[3] At Court, in polite society everywhere, ladies and gentlemen discussed the latest sonnet and the current pamphlet, and they besprinkled their talk with quotations, to prove their literary tastes. Perhaps they tried to model their style of conversation upon *Euphues* or the *Arcadia*; or they even adopted

[1] *Hymenaei. Ben Jonson*, VII (1941), 225.
[2] *The Fortunate Isles*. Ibid., 717.
[3] *Lanthorne and Candle-light* (1609). *Non-dramatic works*, III (1885), 221.

the archaic vocabulary of Chaucer, as more striking and pictur-
esque than their own. The private records of the time reveal a
common habit of transcribing copies of verses: men kept
commonplace-books into which they entered verses that struck
their fancy. They exchanged with their private friends poems
and other works, both in manuscript and print. Poetry was
used to grace and comment on virtually every happening in
life, from birth to death, from the presentation of a gift to a
royal procession. For instance, the approved method of court-
ing a lady's favour was by sending her a sonnet,[1] and in time
this applied as much to the citizen's wife or the kitchen wench
as to the Courtly lady.

Shakespeare laid the scene of *Love's Labour's Lost* in Navarre,
but the king and his three companions, who show such facility
in devising sonnets for their mistresses, are Elizabethan
Courtiers; and the verse-making Spaniard, Don Armado, is
in this respect as genuinely English as the schoolmaster Holofernes, with his marvellous exploits in alliterative metre. And
as has been pointed out, Drayton's 'gatherings of shepherds
and shepherdesses who met for song and dance on Cotswold,
on the banks of the Trent and Avon, or on the Elizian plains,
were not just fictions of Drayton's muse, or echoes from Theocritus or Mantuan'.[2] Master Matthew, in *Every Man in his
Humour*, is an example of the would-be poetaster, driven for
lack of ability to reciting as his own odds and ends of verse
stolen from others. Dekker satirically advises the 'gull' for
whom his Horn Book is written, to 'hoard up the finest play-
scraps you can get, upon which your leane wit may most
favourly feede, for want of other stuffe, when the *Arcadians*

---

[1] A character in Jonson's *The New Inn*, I, i, describes 'a pretty riddling
way of wooing', with toys, verses, anagrams and trials of wit, the lady not
knowing whence they came.
[2] B. H. Newdigate, *Michael Drayton and his Circle* (1941), 40.

and *Euphuizd* gentlewomen have their tongues sharpened to set upon you'.[1]

Inevitably, Courtiers were unequal in inclination and ability. Although even senior statesmen followed the fashion and penned a poem or two, as did the monarchs themselves, their example seems to have been more important than their performance. Indeed, there were some like Languet, who reminded Sidney that the would-be statesman had to consider his prospects and would quickly have to abandon his 'literary use'.[2] There was even a reaction against the fashion for poetry, expressed by Jonson in one of his masques:

O, that Rime is a shrewish disease, and makes all suspected it would perswade. Leave it. . . . Rime will undoe you, and hinder your growth, and reputation in Court, more then any thing beside. . . . If you dable in Poetrie once, it is done of your being believ'd, or understood here.[3]

Daniel puts his finger on the reaction when he writes of all verse being considered mere levity.[4] As Puritanism strengthened its hold, all the arts came under fire. Most Courtiers were distinctly uneasy because an art, which they understood best as a medium of Courtly and private communication and conversation, was becoming more and more public, and meeting consequently fiercer and fiercer attention from those concerned with establishing higher standards of public morality. This was why in an age of golden poetry the poets, and especially the Courtly poets, were on the defensive: the very titles of the best Courtly essays of the day, like Sidney's *Apologie* or *Defence* indicate that there was a battle in progress. And though most Courtiers would have readily accepted the classical conception

[1] *Non-dramatic works*, II (1885), 254.

[2] H. R. Fox Bourne, *A Memoir of Sir Philip Sidney* (1862), 74.

[3] *Love's Welcome* (1634). *Ben Jonson*, VII (1941), 813; also vide *Bartholomew Fair*, III, i.

[4] *Civil Wars* (1609), preface.

of literature, as an art necessary to society both for its *utile* and its *dulce*, there were very few Spensers about who were actually engaged in writing literature which fitted the classical definition. The love sonnets, devoted to adultery as well as courtship (Sidney's Stella was, after all, another man's wife), took a great deal of defending, despite the fact that they were at the heart of the great poetry of the age.

There were limitations, then, on the free development of better taste and criticism. It must be admitted that discrimination was no strong point with most of the devotees of poetry. They took pains to transcribe into commonplace-books, or send to their friends, 'flashes of poetry' which prove to be the poorest trash. In a rough and ready way, they spotted some major poets; but they also made many mistakes (although perhaps every age is vulnerable in assessing its own literature). When Robert Allot published in 1600 his anthology of quotations, *England's Parnassus*, his top nine most popular choices were

Spenser	386
Drayton	225
Warner	171
Daniel	140
Harington	140
Sylvester	123
Lodge	119
Shakespeare	95
Chapman	80.[1]

Other anthologists fared less well. Scarcely any of the private records of the time contain poems of literary value. And some instances of manuscript circulation show very bad taste. The Earl of Shrewsbury is favoured by one devoted correspondent with two tasteless sonnets in which he enlarges on the topic:

[1] *England's Parnassus* (1600), ed. Charles Crawford (1913), xxix.

'Court hath me now transformed into a clock.'[1] James Howell is requested to write for a friend some verses upon 'his mistress black eyes, her becoming frowns, and upon her mask'; and he obligingly complies by sending some very ingenious but utterly valueless lines.[2]

It is the same with the printed literature exchanged. The dilettante, John Chamberlain, writes: 'For lacke of better matter I send you three or fowre toyes to passe away the time.' They are a letter on Squire's conspiracy, a 'ridiculous bable of an old imposturinge jugler',[3] some verses called *The Silkworme*, and Hayward's *Life of King Henrie IV*.[4] He thanks a friend for supplies of 'ballads, bookes and bables', and sends in return 'such pedlarie pamflets and threehalfpeny ware as we are served with', and certain epitaphs and epigrams that go under the name of 'pasquils'.[5] The only exceptions to this exchange of trashy wares are the works of learned writers, such as Camden and Holinshed, or works of theological controversy.

Drayton expressly ascribes the neglect of talented writers to the public taste for lower work:

> Base baladry is so belov'd and sought,
> And those brave numbers are put by for naught,
> Which rarely read, were able to awake
> Bodyes from graves. . . .
>   . . . . but I know, insuing ages shall,
> Raise her againe, who now is in her fall;
> And out of dust reduce our scattered rimes,
> Th' rejected jewels of these slothfull times.[6]

---

[1] John Lodge, *Illustrations of British History* (1838), III, 169–70.
[2] *Epistolae Ho-Elianae* (1629), V.
[3] About the astrologer, John Dee.
[4] 1 March 1599. *Letters*, ed. N. E. McClure (1939), I, 70.
[5] 17 September, 8 December 1598. Ibid., I, 45, 47.
[6] *To Master George Sandys. Works*, ed. J. W. Hebel, III (1932), 208

In the same spirit Jonson apologizes for the delay in the publication of *Neptune's Triumph*, on the ground that he preferred to wait till 'th' abortive, and extemporall dinne of balladry, were understood a sinne'.

> The Muses then might venter, undeterr'd,
> For they love, then, to sing, when they are heard.[1]

The literary titbits transcribed into private commonplace-books consist almost without exception of ballads, satirical verses, and brief pamphlets, the interest of which lies entirely in their bearing upon contemporary events and characters. Such verses as are, apparently, copied for their own sake are usually of a trivial kind.[2] Most men 'term all that is written

---

[1] Acted on Twelfth Night, 1624. *Ben Jonson*, VII (1941), 687.

[2] The following are specimens of verses found in contemporary commonplace-books:

(i) *Tempus* (1590-1603): verses on modern luxury—

> Now fye on facions fond
> That wastes both landes and see. . . .
> In gawdes the glory, but of fooles
> That leads the way to hell;

or a song of the rose beginning—

> The rose is from my garden gone. . . .

or a 'pleasant sweet song' beginning—

> In sommer tyme when Phebus rays. . . .

(ii) *Tempus* (James I MSS. of J. H. Gurney. *Hist. MSS. Comm.*, XII, App. ix, 161): Political ballad beginning—

> The Scotchmen are but beggars yet,
> Although their begginge was not small. . . .

(iii) *Tempus* (James I MSS. of Southwell Cathedral. *Hist. MSS. Comm.*, XII, App. iv, 545): Songs beginning—

> Here lyes he that once was poore. . . .

in verse poetry, and rather in scorn than in praise bestow the name of Poet on every base rymer and ballad-maker'.[1] It seems a matter of mere accident that occasionally in private records of the period one comes across more rewarding material. Nicholas Moore sends to John Fleming at Coniston 'a play-book printed this term and one of the newest, called Virgin Martin [sic]'.[2] And John Chamberlain records as a piece of Court gossip that 'yt seemes young Davison meanes to take another course (than that of Secretary to the Ambassador in Paris) and turne Poet, for he hath lately set out certain sonnets and epigrams'.[3]

Much interest in literature was the merest curiosity. Men liked to feel themselves abreast of the gossip of the day. 'I do boldly send these things,' says a correspondent to the Earl of Shrewsbury, referring to some enclosed verses 'compounded by Mr Secretary': 'I would not do so to anyone else, for I hear

---

> There was an ould laad roade on an ould jade. . . .

or a poem on Raleigh beginning—

> O, had thy name bene causer of thy death. . . .

or 'King James, his Verses on his Queene'—

> Anne, wilt thou goe and leave me here!
> O doe not soe, my dearest deare. . . .

or lines comparing Buckingham with the soldiers of Elizabeth's time—

> The noblest brave profession
> What ether is or hath bene
> Was for to be a souldier true
> And theire to live and die in. . . .

[1] Sir John Harington, *Orlando Furioso* (1591), preface.
[2] *Le Fleming MSS.*, *Hist. MSS. Comm.*, XII, App. vii, 16. Dating 8 March 1622: Massinger's *Virgin Martyr* was printed in 1621.
[3] *Letters*, ed. N. E. McClure (1939), I, 156.

they are very secret.'[1] There was gratification in the thought
of being in the inner circle: 'I think you will know the father,'
says the Duchess of Buckingham suggestively, enclosing some
anonymous lines.[2]

Another indication of the limitations of literary interests of
the day may be gathered, though but in scanty measure, from
extant family account books and inventories. Surprisingly,
these contain few references to books. In part this is due to the
incompleteness of the records relating to the period, and to
standard generalizations, like the 'residewe' and 'al other my
householde stuffe', even where particular records seem full and
detailed. But nevertheless it must be concluded that many
well-to-do households were piteously unprovided with books,
a fact which is illustrated in this amusing letter from an irate
private tutor whose services were about to be dispensed with:

Peter Mease to Sir John Coke: . . . I always complained of the want
of books. Your opinion was that a few books might perfect a
Divine. This was the difference between your genius and mine. . . .
Only let me admonish you that whereas your children have learned
on my books this two year and more, I shall not leave them behind
me, you are therefore withal to provide them such books as your
and the discretion of a provided tutor shall think fit. . . .[3]

And the proportion of English books in an average private
library appears to have been quite small. Inevitably there is a
preponderance of literary works in Latin, Italian or French;
but the scarcity of the English poets in particular suggests that
English literature still had to go a long way to establish itself:
Chaucer, Gower, Lydgate, Occleve, *Piers Plowman*, are conspicuous by their absence. The English books met with are
usually works of history, erudition and controversy. John,
Viscount Lisle and Earl of Warwick, possessed in 1551 about

[1] Letter by William Browne (not the poet), 18 September 1602.
[2] Letter to her son. J. S. Brewer, *Court of James I* (1839), 259.
[3] *Cowper MSS., Hist. MSS. Comm.*, XII. App. i, 117.

forty books, ten of which were English, but only four *belles-lettres*—four plays by John Heywood.[1] In the case of William Drummond of Hawthornden, himself a poet, the catalogue of his books taken in 1610 records only fifty English books as against 448 in other languages. It is true that his collection is more purely literary than most, and includes some of the best English writers—Sidney, Spenser, Drayton, Daniel, Fairfax and others, but even here there are very few English plays.[2] In the accounts of the Duke of Northumberland for October and December of 1601, there are fourteen items of expenditure on books, but not one of the purchases involves English *belles-lettres*.[3] The Duke spent very large sums on books, but there is scarcely a single English work of permanent literary interest to be found in any of his lists.[4] Notable exceptions are the *Shepheardes Calender* and the *Mirror for Magistrates*.[5] The library of William Whiteman contained a large number of standard literary works in Latin, Greek, French and Italian including Herodotus, Demosthenes, Aristotle, Marot, du Bartas, Rabelais, Guicciardini and others, but in English it contained only works on history, divinity and philosophy.[6] The solitary exception was Browne's *Religio Medici*, and one is tempted to wonder whether the worthy owner bought this as a work on divinity! Even if one makes allowance for

---

[1] *Hist. MSS. Comm.*, II, App., 102. This includes such as 'An English Testament', a book on *How to play at Christis*, and *A Declaration of the Crede*

[2] David Masson, *Drummond of Hawthornden* (1873), 19. Towards the close of the century private libraries must have been much larger: Pepys possessed 3,000 volumes.

[3] *Northumberland MSS., Hist. MSS. Comm.*, III, App., 44.

[4] *Bibliographica*, III (N.S.), 153–4.

[5] *Hist. MSS. Comm.*, VI, App., 226. These occur among 21 items, the only other English book of note being Holinshed's *Chronicle*.

[6] The date of this catalogue is uncertain, but it appears to have been drawn up some time before 1645, and must have been later than 1641, as *Religio Medici* was published in 1642. *Egerton MSS.* 784.

presentation copies, which would not be entered in a patron's list of purchases, the general total seems very meagre.

Car, Earl of Somerset, formed a striking exception in his literary predilections, for his library is said to have consisted of twenty play-books and romances. Such evidence of frivolous tastes drew down upon him sarcastic condemnation: 'a lord very likely to give good counsel'.[1]

It is worth repeating that the evidence of records has certain inadequacies which prevents us coming to firm conclusions. No books for instance are mentioned in the wills of Sir Thomas Walsingham, Sir Francis Drake, Sir Thomas Gresham, Sir Thomas White, the Earl of Southampton, or even William Shakespeare! Perhaps the secret is that English *belles-lettres* were still regarded as too ephemeral for special notice. The large numbers of books sold must have gone somewhere! Undoubtedly, gentlemen like Sir Thomas Bodley, the reviver of the University library at Oxford, regarded plays and similar works in English as *ephemera*:

I can see no good Reason, to alter my Opinion, for excluding such Books, as Almanacks, Plays, and an infinite Number, that are daily Printed. . . . Haply some Plays may be worthy the Keeping: But hardly one in Forty. For it is not alike in *English* Plays, and others of other Nations: Because they are most esteemed, for Learning the Languages, and many of them compiled, by Men of great Fame, for Wisdom and Learning: Which is seldom or never here among us. Were it so again, that some little profit might be reaped (which God knows is very little) out of some of our Play-Books, the benefit thereof, will nothing near Countervail, the harm that the Scandal will bring upon the Library, when it shall be given out, that we stuff'd it full of Baggage Books . . . the more I think upon it, the more it doth distaste me, that such kind of Books, should be vouchsafed a room, in so Noble a Library.[2]

[1] Sir E. Peyton, *Catastrophe of the House of Stuart* (1811), 353.
[2] *Reliquiae Bodleianae* (1703), 277–8.

The uncertainty of Courtly taste is manifest in a general obliviousness to the literary quality of the masques presented for the entertainment of the *élites*. In the correspondence of the time, allusions to masques are fairly frequent, but reference to the author is rare, and even then not highly appreciative. Writing in 1605, John Chamberlain remarks, 'The pastoral by S. Daniel was solemn and dull, but perhaps better to be read than presented.'[1] One of the most inspired passages of writing by Ben Jonson is the fine preface to *Hymenaei*, where he protests against the popular prejudice which rates the 'bodies' of masques higher than their 'souls'. Indeed, the total effect on the development of drama caused by the popularity of the masque was to turn the theatre away from what Yeats calls the 'sovereignty of words' towards the 'picture stage', where scenic illusion and spectacle reigned supreme.

By the later sixteenth century women provided a major literary audience. No doubt, women readers were still a minority. Spenser published, among the seventeen sonnets prefixed to the *Faerie Queene*, two addressed to Court ladies, and another to 'all the gratious and beautiful ladies in the Court'. At a lower level, there were the 'gentlewomen', to whom R. B. dedicated *A Pettite Palace of Pettie his Pleasure* (1576), and on whom Lyly relied with great success for popularity. And many citizens' wives could read, though probably fewer of them could write.[2] Nashe reckoned upon women readers for his *Anatomie of Absurditie*, crediting them, however, with little learning. He desired 'of the learned pardon, and of women patience'. His enemy Gabriel Harvey boasted of at least one lady reader of remarkable education, for she had read, if he is to be believed, Homer, Virgil, Plutarch, Polyen (?Politian),

[1] Quoted in *D.N.B.*
[2] In *Westward Hoe*, I, i, Dekker represents two city dames receiving private lessons from a writing-master.

Petrarch and Agrippa.[1] A few women were classically educated, but the greater number, of those with education, were
more familiar with Italian and French, and had a preference for
slighter works, love-poems and romances. Edward Hake
complains that men bring up their daughters unwisely:
either they are 'altogether kept from the exercise of good
learning and knowledge of good letters, or else . . . nousled in
amorous books, vain stories, and fond, trifling fancies'.[2] No
wonder that Drayton should fear lest the 'unusual tract' of
his long-winded *Polyolbion* 'may perhaps seem difficult to the
female sex'.[3] According to William Harrison, the taste of the
Court ladies was apt to grow more serious with the years. He
describes the elderly ladies as reading scripture, or history,
writing works of their own, translating into Latin or English.[4]
But the younger women could not have been so entirely given
up to the reading of frivolous romances as Hake would lead us
to believe. Daniel reckoned confidently upon their reading his
Civil Wars, and apologized to youthful ladies for want of
success in the drawing of Queen Isabel, in 'not suiting her
passions to her years'.[5] As might be expected, the evidence of
women's reading habits is tentative and varied; and records
help very little—one makes what one can of entries, like the
purchase of two books by a Court lady in 1603: 'ane French
Nou Testement, with ane uder French bouk, 6/-'.[6]

Thanks to the elementary and grammar schools, the means
of learning, and instruction in writing and the classics, were
available for the middle and lower classes. It is not unusual to
meet, in the records of Corporation Free Schools, with the

[1] *Pierces Supererogation. Works* (1885), II, 320.
[2] *A Touchstone* (1574).
[3] 1613, to the general reader.
[4] *Description of England* (New Shaks. Soc., 1877), II, 272.
[5] *Civil Wars* (1609), dedication.
[6] *Eglinton MSS., Hist. MSS. Comm.*, X, App. i, 32.

complaint that children throng to be taught in such numbers that the schoolmaster cannot deal with them. Literacy is more and more widely extended through the fifteenth and sixteenth centuries, and printed books took over from manuscripts large lower-class audiences. Heminge and Condell address their 1623 folio edition of Shakespeare's works to readers 'from the most able to him that can but spell'. Dekker's *Bel-man* is described on the title-page as 'Profitable for Gentlemen, Lawyers, Merchants, Citizens, Farmers, Masters of Households, and all sorts of servants, and delightful for all men to read'. Jonson, in the 'Address to the Reader' prefixed to his *New Inn*, says, 'If thou can'st but spell, and join my sense, there is more hope of thee than of a hundred fastidious impertinents.' Country carters carried home broadsides and pamphlets to be read by the way, and citizens' apprentices stole moments from their work to bestow on the delectable reading of ballads and old romances. As Dekker advertises in his *Wonderful Yeare*, reading has become an established pleasure "to shorten the lives of long winters' nights, that lie watching in the dark for us'.

These lower-class readers would necessarily be confined to works in English. Thus, we find that the library of Captain Cox, the celebrated mason of Kenilworth, consisted entirely of old English romances, ballads, broadsheets and almanacs, with one or two more literary works like the *Shepheardes Calender*, the *Ship of Fools*, and *Hick Scorner*.[1]

A school practice which should have contributed to training an educated class of readers was that of teaching the boys to act plays, sometimes in Latin, sometimes in English, plays like *Ralph Roister Doister*.[2] But the literary quality of such plays

---

[1] *Laneham's Letter*, ed. F. J. Furnivall (1907), 28–30. It is amusing to note that Laneham credits Captain Cox with a knowledge of astronomy, apparently on the strength of his possession of the *Shepheardes Calender*.

[2] Either at Eton or Westminster.

is not known, in general, and there was a good deal of opposition to the practice, as Jonson's character, Censure, suggests:

... And there were no wiser then I, I would have ne'er a cunning *Schoole-master* in *England*. I meane a *Cunning-Man*, a *Schoole- master*; that is, a *Conjurour*, or a *Poet*, or that had any acquaintance with a *Poet*. They make all their schollers *Play-boyes*! Is't not a fine sight, to see all our children made *Enterluders*? Doe wee pay our money for this? wee send them to learne their *Grammar*, and their *Terence*, and they learn their *play-books*?[1]

The Puritan reaction was strong here too. Indeed, on one occasion the Lords in Council intervened to stop the reading of classical dramatists and authors, on moral grounds, although on literary grounds the humanism of the Renaissance committed them to this very study. Instead of the 'heathen poets from the whiche the youthe of the Realme receyve rather infectyon in manners and education than advancement in vertue', they substituted for a time more innocuous modern Latin poems, written by the schoolmaster, Christopher Ocland, in praise of the Queen![2]

With contradictions of this kind at the highest level, and the whole field of criticism bedevilled by an instability of conflicting values, it is no wonder that general taste should have appeared so ignorant and undiscriminating. Perhaps the public could discern the difference between poetry and doggerel, between the racy pamphlets of Nashe and Dekker and the humdrum descriptions of Tom Coryat, but the distinction was little understood. It was not seldom wilfully ignored. Harvey probably knew he was doing Nashe an injustice in the following words, but he certainly reckoned upon many readers accepting it in full faith:

He disdaineth Thomas Delone, Philip Stubs, Robert Armin, and the common Pamfletters of London, even the painfullest Chroniclers,

[1] *The Staple of Newes. Ben Jonson*, VI (1938), 344–5.
[2] 21 April 1582. *Acts of the Privy Council*, ed. Sir John Dasent, XIII, 389.

tooe; bicause they stand in his way, hinder his scribling traffique . . .
or have not Chronicled him in their Catalogues of the renowned
moderne Autors. . . . But may not Thomas Delone, Philip Stubs,
Robert Armin, and the rest of those misused persons, more disdainfully disdaine him; bicause he is so much vayner, so little learneder,
so nothing eleganter, then they; and they so much honester, so little
obscurer, so nothing contemptibler, then he?[1]

Added to all these frailties in the Elizabethan public, there
is also the major difficulty, that, though he read him, the gentleman of the day despised the poet who went beyond manuscript
circulation to the printed-book market. While, up to a point,
writers of learned or controversial work were excusable, if
they appeared in print, because such books were skilled and
useful, to 'live by verses' was a disgrace. Partly the gentleman
resented *belles-lettres* being associated with the very different
world of almanacs and broadsheets; but more fundamentally,
the gentleman regarded it as degrading to sell the products of
one's labour, whether of hands or brain. 'Thou call'st me *Poet*,
as a terme of shame,' says Jonson.[2] The word is used 'as if it
were a most contemptible *Nick-name*'.[3] Nashe finds more
galling than any other of Harvey's gibes the assertion that he
relies on the printing-press to provide him with apparel and
maintenance.[4]

Despite the fact, then, that poetry was a major art necessary
to Courtly culture, there was both a social and a moral stigma
devaluing any kind of professional poetry. Jonson complains
that readers regard poets as little better than cooks, compound-
ing tasty dishes to please the palate. The poet is 'the most un-
profitable of his (Majesty's) servants. . . . A kind of a *Christmas*
ingine; one, that is used, at least once a yeare, for a trifling

[1] *Pierces Supererogation. Works* (1885), II, 280–1.
[2] *Epigrammes*, X. *Ben Jonson*, VIII (1947), 29.
[3] *Discoveries. Ben Jonson*, ibid., 572.
[4] *Pierces Supererogation. Works* (1885), II, 243.

instrument, of wit, or so.'[1] 'Great men in this age,' remarks
Sir William Alexander to William Drummond, 'either respect
not our toys at all, or if they do, because they are toys, esteem
them only worthy the kiss of their hand'.[2] According to Daniel
there had been an overthrowing of

> . . . that holy reverent bound
> That parted learning and the Laiety

that had cheapened the estimate of literary genius.[3]

Poets were perhaps no worse off than professional painters.
Note the horror with which Balthazar Gerbier, writing to the
Duke of Buckingham, a great collector of pictures, repudiates
the charge of being himself an artist:

I swear to God that I was never a painter till I placed myself under
your patronage, leaving the Prince of Orange; and come what will,
I will never be one; poverty shall change neither my blood nor my
courage.[4]

In extenuation, it must be confessed he was living amongst a
people so blind to the value of great works of art, that they
scoffed at Buckingham when he bought masterpieces, for
throwing away money on 'bobles and shadows'.[5]

If possible, the dramatist was in even worse case than poet
or painter. Some playwrights were actors, and players still
had to emerge from a tradition of being regarded as rogues
and vagabonds. Again, there is a dualism: the player who fulfilled an essential duty at Court nevertheless carried a social
stigma as a professional. As has been shown already, Shakespeare betrays a bitter consciousness of a humiliating social

---

[1] *Neptunes Triumph. Ben Jonson*, VII (1941), 682–3.
[2] David Masson, *Drummond of Hawthornden* (1838), 120.
[3] *Musophilus*, 689 ff.
[4] J. S. Brewer, *Court of James I* (1839), II, 392. Gerbier was in Buckingham's service, 1616–28.
[5] Ibid., II, 370–1.

position, describing himself as 'in disgrace with fortune and men's eyes', and grieving that the goddess has placed him in a profession from which his 'name receives a brand'.[1] In vain the choicer spirits among playwrights, such as Chapman, himself a Courtly satellite and a classical scholar of note, protest that

> The stage and actors are not so contemptfull
> As every innovating puritan. . . .
> Would have the world imagine.[2]

Some of the blame for public odium must rest with the writers themselves, who presented a public image of licentiousness and dissipation. They were commonly guilty of the vice of the age, excessive drinking: the charge is reiterated again and again, even by the friendly. Drayton is expressly singled out as an exception: he 'wants one true note of a Poet of our times, and that is this, hee cannot swagger it well in a Taverne, nor dominere in a hot-house'.[3] For the rest: 'A passing potman, a passing Poet.'[4] Poets are regarded as 'drunken parasites'.[5] The general public made no fine distinctions: they judged the whole class by the most conspicuous examples, so that to the average man poets were associated with the beggarly wretches he met who would 'hang upon a young heyre like a horseleech',[6] or who, with 'slovinly tatterd sleeves' could be seen wandering and selling 'Ballets in the streetes'.[7]

The general contempt for professional writers was not a class distinction. Only a very small number of the poets whose

---

[1] Sonnets XXIX, CXI.
[2] *Revenge of Bussy d'Ambois*, I, i.
[3] *2 Return from Parnassus*, I, ii. *Three Parnassus Plays* (1949), 240.
[4] Nashe, *Anatomie of Absurditie. Works* (1958), I, 31.
[5] Nashe, *Summers Last Will and Testament. Works* (1958), III, 273.
[6] Jonson, *Staple of Newes*, I, vi. *Ben Jonson*, VI (1938), 302.
[7] *Summers Last Will and Testament. Works* (1958), III, 276.

names have come down to us are known to have been of really humble origin. Among those who appear to have made the writing of *belles-lettres* an important part of their life, we find that there is a large majority drawn from the ranks of the country gentry, the professions and the rich merchant class. Perhaps among dramatists the proportion is lower: out of twenty-nine, eleven may be regarded as belonging to the 'gentry', fourteen were the sons of citizens, rich or poor, or of lower class still; the rest are of unknown origin. But even with the lowliest, the opportunities of University education and Courtly promotion transformed them during their careers, and it is likely that over four-fifths of the writers of the period finished up as 'nobiles', as defined by the Elizabethan social commentator, Thomas Wilson.[1]

And writers were very apt to call attention to their gentility. Quite apart from sturdy self-respecters like Ben Jonson, Spenser, for instance, was humbly proud of the acquaintance of Sir Philip Sidney and Sir Edward Dyer: 'They have me, I thank them, in some use of familiarity.'[2] George Wither openly admits the 'despisedness' of his 'person and quality', but maintains that this does not render him less fit than Sternhold and Hopkins (grooms of the Privy Chamber) to write hymns.[3] Nicholas Breton and many, many others are scrupulously described as 'gentleman' on title-pages and in dedications. Nashe's *Pierce Penilesse* is announced as by 'Tho. Nash, Gent.', and though Harvey inquires sneeringly what special cause 'the Pennilesse Gentleman hath, to bragge of his birth', he does not deny him the title.[4] Moreover, Nashe himself, while calling it 'vaine', vindicates his right to it. Drayton makes a point of

[1] *The State of England* (1600), ed. F. J. Fisher (*Camden Miscellany*, XVI, 1936).
[2] *Letters between Edmund Spenser and Gabriel Harvey. Works* (1885), I, 7.
[3] *A Schollers Purgatory. Miscellaneous Works* (1872), 40, 53.
[4] *Foure Letters. Works* (1885), I, 206.

using his title *Esquire*, and is in consequence derided by bluff Jonson: 'Every Poet writes Squire now'.[1]

The real difficulty was that, while gentry, the writers were engaged in ungenteel practices. In *The Puritan* scant work is made of the pretensions of a poet to be regarded as a gentleman: 'You a gentleman! That's a good jest, i'faith. Can a scholar be a gentleman, when a gentleman will not be a scholar?'[2] That the Courtly amateur was far from being flattered when classed with professionals is evident from the words of Nicholas Ling's *Address to the Reader*, prefixed to the anthology called *England's Helicon* (1600). Ling asserts boldly that no man ought to 'take it in scorn that a far meaner man in the eye of the world shall be placed by him', for the names of poets can be fitly placed side by side with those of the greatest princes of the world. 'If any man take exception to this', he declares him 'unworthy to be placed by the meanest that is but graced with the title of a poet'. Though elsewhere Ling shows scant respect for the rights of professional authors, here at least he has his eye on a professional distinction well in advance of his age.

It was to avoid the suspicion of living by his pen that the gentleman-poet refrained from publishing. The learned Selden says

It is ridiculous for a lord to print verses; 'tis well enough to make them to please himself, but to make them public is foolish. If a man in a private chamber twirls his band-string, or plays with a rush to please himself, it is well enough; but if he should go into Fleet Street, and sit upon a stool and twirl a band-string, or play with a rush, then all the boys in the street would laugh at him.[3]

---

[1] *The Magnetic Lady*, induction. The application may be questioned because the play is generally held to have been first performed in October 1632, and Drayton died in December 1631. But the play is mentioned, in a letter dated January 1629, by James Howell.

[2] *The Puritan* (anon., n.d.), II, iv.

[3] *Discourse of John Selden Esq.*, ed. S. H. Reynolds (1892), 135-6.

Even the best writers, lacking the sense of professional dignity that did not properly arrive until the eighteenth century, had to defer to this judgment, and make excuses and apologies for publishing. John Donne experimented with print during the years of his poverty, but he thought it a serious fault 'to have descended to print anything in verse'. He wonders how he declined to it, and cannot pardon himself.[1] Two years later, in 1614, we find him again about to publish, and again ashamed of it. He says to Sir Henry Goodyere:

One thing more I must tell you, but so softly that . . . if that good Lady (Lady Goodyere) were in the room with you and this letter, she might not hear. It is that I am brought to a necessity of printing my poems. . . . I am at an end of much considering.[2]

Nashe, when sneered at for earning his livelihood by publishing, regards it as a disgraceful accusation, and clears himself by retorting that he has earned nothing by publishing for three years![3] Though Daniel published willingly enough, he preferred the genteel means of private editions and subscriptions, and he did not like his dramas to be regarded as acting plays. He would not have put *Philotas* on the stage, had not his necessities 'overmastered' him.[4]

And in an infuriating sense the Courtly amateurs, who so despised the professionals, were serious competitors. The Sidneys and Dyers set the best standards of the day. A natural prestige was attached to the work of gentlemen of distinction. A natural curiosity built up interest in manuscripts which were secretly handed about, transcribed and talked about. There was a catchpenny value about this work when it finally reached print, with authority or without it. Even the poetasters, writing rubbish, caught some of the glow and prestige of amateur

[1] Edmund Gosse, *Life and Letters of John Donne* (1899), I, 303–4.
[2] Ibid., II, 68.
[3] *Have with you to Saffron-Walden. Works* (1958), III, 128.
[4] Letter to Earl of Devonshire, 1604.

status. 'Men that should employ such as I am,' Nashe grumbles, 'are enamoured of their own wits, and thinke what ever they do is excellent, though it be never so scurvie'.[1] Drayton, few of whose poems sold well, complains when bringing out his *Polyolbion*: 'There is this great disadvantage against me; that it commeth out at this time, when Verses are wholly deduc't to Chambers, and nothing esteem'd in this lunatique Age, but what is kept in Cabinets and must only passe by Transcription.'[2] When passing in review the poets of the day, he reveals all his professional antagonism when he expressly excludes the writers of 'private pieces' from his notice:

> (I) only my selfe to those few doe tye
> Whose workes oft printed, set on every post,
> To public censure subject have bin most:
> For such whose poems, be they nere so rare,
> in private chambers, that incloistered are,
> And by transcription daintyly must goe;
> As though the world unworthy were to know
> Their rich composures. . . .
>   . . . . let such Peeces bee
> Spoke of by those that shall come after me,
> I pass not for them.[3]

The leading Court poets genuinely avoided print: Sidney, Dyer, Greville, Raleigh, the Earl of Oxford, Wotton. Others published only those works specially deemed of dignity and value: Sir John Harington, Sir Edward Fairfax, Sir Henry Constable, Sir William Alexander, Sir John Davies. But lesser gentry found ways and means of circumventing the stigma of print.[4] Indeed, Lyly considered that printers ought to think

---

[1] *Pierce Penilesse. Works* (1958), I, 158.

[2] To the general reader. *Works*, ed. J. W. Hebel (1933), IV, v.

[3] *Epistle to Henry Reynolds*. Ibid., III, 230–1.

[4] Vide J. W. Saunders, 'The Stigma of Print' (*Essays in Criticism*, I, April 1951).

themselves greatly indebted to gentlemen, because they provided 'so many fantasies to print'.[1] Hence it is not surprising to find a hostile spirit shown by many professional writers towards the more fashionable part of their public. Feeling the contempt of the expert for the dilettante, he could at least ridicule by innuendo, as Jonson insists about his gentleman verse-maker in the *Staple of Newes*: 'He writes like a *Gentleman*. Pox o' your scholler.'[2] The measure of Spenser's bravado and pioneering courage may be gauged from his quite extraordinary *volte-face* in 1589, turning his back on the whole Courtly tradition and deliberately seeking out a new kind of professional dignity through print.[3] It was not until Milton and the Augustans that this dignity was properly recognized.

In the meantime, poets hit back as they could. Finding that his most popular writings were those which raised a malicious laugh, he was tempted to make epigram, satire, and unscrupulous libel his chief employment. Publishers who would not look at a new manuscript changed their tone if offered something spicily scandalous.[4] Hence the popularity of Nashe, who raised 'railing' to the level of a fine art. Hence the immense sales of Dekker's racy, reckless exposures of social vice. Hence the development of the epigram by Jonson and Donne. As in the later seventeenth century, satire was the professional writer's surest means of enforcing respect even from the most contemptuous.

In this period satire had not attained the artistic dignity it was to gain from Dryden. It tended to be either personal and malicious, or vaguely general and academic. Tempted by the comparative smallness of the society for which they wrote,

[1] *Euphues*, to the Gentlemen Readers. *Complete Works*, ed. R. W. Bond (1902), I, 182.
[2] IV, ii. *Ben Jonson*, VI (1938), 352.
[3] Vide J. W. Saunders, *The Profession of English Letters* (1964), 81–3.
[4] *2 Return from Parnassus*, I, iii. *Three Parnassus Plays* (1949), 248.

knowing that every personal stroke would be recognized; writers wasted their strength fencing with individuals, avenging a personal insult, the neglect of a patron, the condescension of a lord, the superciliousness of a lackey, with epigrams and satiric pamphlets. They even threatened beforehand. Nashe is firm:

If I be evill intreated, or sent away with a Flea in mine eare, let him looke that I will raile on him soundly: not for an houre or a day . . . but in some elaborate, pollished Poem, which I will leave to the world . . . to be a living Image to all ages, of his beggerly parsimony and ignoble illiberalitie . . . I have tearmes . . . laid in steepe in *Aquafortis*, & Gunpowder, that shall rattle through the Skyes, and make an Earthquake in a Pesants eares.[1]

Even a churlish serving-man would be threatened with a lampoon:

> Answerr not a man of art so churleshlye againe while thou
> livest. Why man, I am able to make a pamphlet of thy
> blew coate and the button in thy capp.

Scholars were both hated and feared for their epigrams: 'they are pestilent fellowes, they speake nothing but bodkins'. Moreover, they had an instrument of vengeance even more potent than epigram or pamphlet, the public stage. Even the very sheriff's sergeants dreaded their dramatic gibes: ''Ti natural in us,' says one of them, 'to hate scholars—natural besides they will publishe our imperfections, knaveries, and conveyances upon scaffolds and stages.'[3] 'Bables & Comedies,' says Harvey, 'are parlous fellowes to *decipher, and discourage men.* You . . . were best to please Pap-hatchet . . . for feare lesse he be mooved . . . to make a Playe of you; and then i

[1] *Pierce Penilesse. Works* (1958), I, 195.

[2] *1 Return from Parnassus*, I, i; *2 Return from Parnassus*, III, ii. *Three Parnassus Plays* (1949), 148, 297.

[3] *The Puritan* (anon., n.d.), II, iv.

your credit quite un-done for ever.'[1] The satirist justified himself by professing to regard his writings as a kind of moral police-work, and possibly sometimes they were inspired by genuine moral indignation. But at any rate Nashe boasts of their efficacy: 'Those that care neither for God nor the divell, by their quills are kept in awe.'[2]

In spite, however, of his dreaded skill in retaliation, the literary man suffered much from the hostile public. Fashion exacted from its adherents a readiness to criticize; and criticism, often born of ignorant vanity, usually guided by no principles of art, and unrelated to any definite ideal, was inevitably capricious and perverse. The few genuine critics, such as Sidney, or the pedant William Webbe, who had at least some criterion, were lost in the multitude of ignorant chatterers who represented unorganized public opinion. These men took the easiest road to gain a critic's reputation, capricious fault-finding. On the stage, especially, the writer's reputation was at the mercy of men who asserted their critical superiority by such elementary means as would nowadays be regarded as plain bad manners. The spectators came, suggests Jonson,

To . . . possesse the Stage, against the Play. To dislike all, but marke nothing. And by their confidence of rising between the Actes, in oblique lines, make *affidavit* to the whole house, of their not understanding one Scene.[3]

Fitzdottrel, in *The Divell is an Asse*, cannot bear to miss the play—but all he cares for is to sit through one act, in order to have earned the chance of rising and going away, 'to vex the Players, and to punish their Poet—keepe him in awe'.[4] Some poets were indeed kept in awe by such methods. Chapman's

[1] *Pierces Supererogation. Works* (1885), II, 213.
[2] *Pierce Penilesse. Works* (1958), I, 193.
[3] *The New Inn*, dedication to the reader. *Ben Jonson*, VI (1938), 397.
[4] III, v. *Ben Jonson*, ibid., 224.

appeal to the fashionable audience to hear him through is
positively plaintive:

> If our other audience see
> You on the stage depart before we end
> Our wits go with you all, and we are fools.[1]

According to the evidence of *The Guls Horn-Booke*, such
merely silent censure was not sufficient for many fashionable
critics. This is the advice given to the full-fledged gallant:

It shall crowne you with rich commendation, to laugh alowd in
the middest of the most serious and saddest scene of the terribles
Tragedy: and to let that clapper (your tongue) be tost so high, that
all the house may ring of it . . . for by talking and laughing . . . you
heap *Pelion* upon *Ossa*, glory upon glory. . . . Thirdly, you mightily
. . . disgrace the Author: marry, you take up . . . a strong opinion
of your own judgement, and inforce the Poet to take pity of youre
weaknesse, and, by some dedicated sonnet, to bring you into a
better paradice, onely to stop your mouth.[2]

Similar methods were employed to gain the reputation of a
critic at the bookstalls:

You stand sometimes at a Stationers stal, looking scurvily . .
on the face of a new Booke bee it never so worthy: & goe (as il
favouredly) mewing away.[3]

Truly a public difficult to please, when the chief title to critica
judgment was ability to look bored and to sneer! No wonder
Jonson, for all his learning and fastidiousness, yearned sometimes for the reader that can 'but spell'.

Some of the criticism of the day *was* based upon definite
principles. There were indeed two chief standards at work
one very commonly accepted by the general public and based
upon moral criteria, and the other, the classical, based upon
literary concepts, and adopted only by a cultivated few. From

[1] *All Fools* (1605), prologue.
[2] Dekker, *Non-dramatic works*, II (1885), 251-2.
[3] *Seven Deadly Sinnes*. Ibid., 5.

those who adopted the former, the literary artist could hope
but little: though well-meaning, it was narrowing, stultifying,
ignorantly hostile. Of the latter, writers rarely complain.
Either they implicitly acknowledged it themselves, or they
regarded classical reference as ineffective and not worth contest-
ing. These classical critics do not seem to have induced the
general reader to accept their judgments in the least, and a
discussion of their dicta is therefore not relevant here. Neo-
classicism was to become important in a later age; for the time
being, if it exerted any influence at all, it encouraged the conception of poetry as concerned with the imaginative and
fictitious, and this merely added strength to the forces arrayed
against literature upon grounds of moral prejudice.

Ethical criticism of poetry and drama was based largely on
the idea of its 'falsity' and 'frivolity', for such were the terms
into which the Puritan translated 'imaginative fiction' and
'artistic beauty'. Poets they regarded as 'fantasticall fooles',[1]
if not worse. Whereas Bacon asserted no moral inferiority in
poetry when he described it as 'submitting the shows of things
to the desires of the mind',[2] it was precisely such a 'turning
aside from the truth of things' which aroused censure in the
mind of the average Puritan. For one thing, such purely fanci-
ful work, they held, required no honest labour and no skill.
As Nashe puts it,

The enemies of Poetrie . . . tearme our best Writers but babling
Ballat-makers. . . . Some dul-headed Divines . . . deeme it no more
cunning to wryte an exquisite Poem, then to preach pure *Calvin*,
or to distill the juice of a Commentary in a quarter Sermon. . . .
You shall finde there goes more exquisite paines and puritie of
witte, to the writing of one such rare poem as *Rosamond*, than to a
hundred of your dunsticall Sermons.[3]

[1] *Pierce Penilesse. Works* (1958), I, 192.
[2] *Advancement of Learning*, II, iv (2).
[3] *Pierce Penilesse. Works* (1958), I, 192.

These charges were reinforced by the occasional maliciousness and immorality of the poets. 'Take heed of Poetry,' was the saying, 'for it hath commonly one of these three properties, belibelling the wicked, abusing the honest, or pleasing the foolish.'[1]

Sober Englishmen regarded poetry, if not actually immoral, as at least harmful because wanting in seriousness, and alluring to vain delights. Spenser had this kind of criticism in mind when he prefixed to the fourth book of the *Faerie Queene* these lines:

> The rugged forhead that with grave foresight
> Welds kingdomes causes, and affaires of state,
> My looser rimes (I wote) doth sharply wite,
> For praising love, as I have done of late,
> And magnifying lovers deare debate;
> By which fraile youth is oft to follie led,
> Through false allurement of that pleasing baite,
> That better were in vertues discipled,
> Then with vaine poemes weeds to have their fancies fed.

'To such,' says the poet, 'I do not sing at all', and he turns with dignity from those who are incapable of understanding the sacred mysteries of poetry, to appeal to a more kindly audience. Yet even Spenser had to bow to the hostile force of moral criticism.[2] For instance, he acquiesced humbly in the judgment which condemned his beautiful and innocent poems on Love and Beauty, writing in atonement, though rather perfunctorily, two other hymns on Heavenly Love and Heavenly Beauty.

In the case of drama, there were further causes for reprobation, based on the very real disorders attendant upon public performances. In *Kind-harts Dream* (1592), Chettle, a friendly writer, makes the ghost of Tarlton the player entreat

[1] Breton, *A Poste with a packet of mad letters.Works* (1879), II, h, 37.
[2] Vide, J. W. Saunders, 'The Façade of Morality', in D. C. Allen and W. R. Mueller, *That Soueraine Light* (1952).

playgoers to 'use themselves after a more quiet order', reminding them that 'it is far from manhood to make so public a
place their field to fight in'. The character of many plays also
exposed authors and actors, justly, to the charge of grossness,
and in later times, of immorality. Still, had this not been the
case, it would have been impossible for playwrights to comply
with the demands of the stern moralist. Nothing less would
satisfy him than the subordination of all artistic purpose to the
aim of conveying moral stimulus and instruction. Had the
Elizabethan Puritan gained his point, he would have stifled
the drama, as indeed happened in the late seventeenth century
after Jeremy Collier. Paradoxically, the playwrights had too
great a sense of the reality of the world to listen to the Puritan,
who, for all his distrust of fiction, in the last analysis required
playwrights to use their imagination not on the world as it was,
but on the world as it ought to be.

In spite of heroic efforts to be impartial, the Puritan writer,
Philip Stubbes, shows that the stern moralist was unable to
regard the drama with any feeling but abhorrence. Stubbes
admits that 'there is nothing so good but it may be abused', and
declares himself not so precise that he would have the thing
removed for the abuse. He wishes simply to have the abuse
taken away:

Some kind of playes . . . containe matter . . . both of doctrine,
erudition, good example, and wholesome instruction . . . so that
when honest & chast playes . . . are used to these ends . . . than are
they very tollerable exercyses.

But he is unable to help himself falling into wholesale condemnation:

If they be of divine matter, than are they most intollerable, or rather
Sacrilegious . . . if their playes be of prophane matters, than tend
they to the dishonor of God, and norishing of vice. . . . I have hard

some hold opinion . . . that many a good Example may be learned out of them. . . . O blasphemie intollerable![1]

Gosson sums up the whole matter in one trenchant phrase: 'Thus have I set down of the abuses of poets, pipers and players, which bring us to pleasure, slouth, sleepe, sinne, and without repentaunce to death and the devill.'[2] Even the more genial Harrison becomes intolerant when it is a question of theatres: 'Would to god,' he cries, 'these common plays were exiled . . . as semenaries of impiety . . . & their theaters pulled downe.'[3]

More exalted personages shared these views, supporting their strictures by citations from the Fathers of the Church. Thus, Bishop Babington complains:

These prophane & wanton stage playes or interludes: what an occasion they are of adulterie and uncleanenesse . . . the world knoweth with too much hurt by long experience. . . . These players behaviour polluteth all thinges. And of their playes he (Chrysostom) saith, they are the feasts of Sathan, the inventions of the devill, &c . . . polluted bodies by these filthie occasions have on their death beddes confessed the daunger of them.[4]

And Grindal, Bishop of London, writes to Cecil in 1562:

In my judgment ye should do very well to be a mean, that a proclamation was set forth to inhibit all plays for one whole year (if it were for ever it were not amiss), within the city or three miles compass.[5]

The distrust of moral fanatics like Stubbes was based upon hostility to all pleasure, regarded as tending to withdraw the

[1] *Anatomy of Abuses* (New Shaks. Soc., 1877–9), preface and 140–3.

[2] *Schoole of Abuse* (Shakes. Soc., 1841), 32.

[3] *Chronologie. Description of England* (New Shaks. Soc., 1877), I, liv.

[4] '*On the Ten Commandments*', *Anatomy of Abuses* (New Shaks. Soc., 1877–9), 83.

[5] Vide T. Wright, *Elizabeth and her Times* (1838), I, 167.

mind from contemplation of things spiritual, and thus endangering the salvation of the soul. This attitude towards all the more humane instincts, as prompting towards undue indulgence of oneself or of others, cannot be better illustrated than by a passage from the life of Katherine Stubbes, the wife of the moralist. It is written by her husband, not long after her early death, to enshrine her memory as an example of piety to others. In quaint language he relates how earnestly she sought to deny herself all earthly pleasures, even caresses towards her favourite dog. As she lay on her death-bed, she espied lying at her feet 'a little puppy or bitch (which in her lifetime she loved well)'. She beat her away, 'and calling her husband to her, said: "Good husband, you and I have offended God grievously in receiving this bitch many a time into our bed; the Lord give me grace to repent it and all other vanities."'[1] Minds of such a temper were not likely to tolerate poetry or plays.[2] It was in vain that Sir John Harington, in the preface to his translation of *Orlando Furioso*, took pains to propitiate the reader who might have 'this scruple, that it may be hurtful for his soul or conscience, to read a book of poetry'. It was a hopeless effort to gain over the goodwill of a body of men growing day by day more unfriendly.

Gosson rejoices in proofs of the spread of his way of thinking, applauding the 'Gentlewomen, Citizens of London' for having schooled themselves, and of their own accord abhorred plays.[3] Already, by 1615, the author of the *Refutation of the Apology for Actors* is able to assert that one never sees now at a theatre 'an ancient citizen, a chaste matron, a modest maid, a grave

---

[1] *A Chrystal Glasse for Christian Women* (1591), f. B.

[2] Thomas Wilcox says (9 December 1576): 'The cause of plague is sin, the cause of sin is plays, hence plays cause plague. All sin is taught in these schools of vice.' Vide H. S. Symmes, *Débuts de la critique dramatique en Angleterre* (1903), 71.

[3] In a letter to them at the end of *Schoole of Abuse* (1579).

177

senator, a wise magistrate, a just judge, a godly preacher, a religious man not blinded in ignorance'.[1] They have left for their audience profane gallants, City dames, country clowns, and evil characters. 'Magistrates, throughout almost every city in the land, by their authority . . . do prohibit them (the players) from entering their precincts to exercise their craft.' On the other side, Jonson bears unwilling witness to the hostile faction

> . . . scandaliz'd at toyes,
> As Babies, Hobby-horses, Puppet-playes,[2]

and deplores the success of the 'sowrer sort' in putting down innocent pastimes.[3]

The strict Puritan, with his ideal of a life spent in devotion to religious duties and contemplation, could not but abhor all pleasurable diversions. Everything beautiful, to the more austere and narrow-minded zealot, was *ipso facto* evil. The human body itself was to be sacrificed to the needs of the soul, and that this might the more readily be accomplished men were bidden to loathe and revile it: 'O what a filthy, unclean, and ugglesome carcase do I bear about with me, that for very shame had need to be covered with garments!'[4] And yet this was the very time when many Englishmen were learning from Renaissance Italy to regard this same human body as a miracle of beauty, worthy of all reverence!

The kind of life inculcated, and followed out, as far as possible, by the sincere Puritan, is to be found exemplified in the diary kept by Lady Margaret Hoby, a niece by marriage to Lord Burghley. She devoted herself to private prayer regularly four times a day. She read and annotated her Bible constantly.

[1] J.G. (1615), 58.
[2] *Bartholomew Fair*, prologue to the Kings Majesty.
[3] *The Sad Shepherd*, I, iv.
[4] Philip Stubbes, *The Perfect Pathway* (New Shaks. Soc., 1877-9), 219.

Every sermon attended she made a practice of writing out by heart. And all this in addition to the family Bible reading and worship conducted by the chaplain! As she also had to super-intend the household, working with her own hands, to look after the ploughing and sowing on the estate, and to act as general nurse, it may be believed that there was little time to spare. Yet such leisure moments as could be found were religiously devoted to reading or listening to 'a sermon book', 'Cartwright's book': 'a good man's book who proveth against M. Bilson that Christ suffered in soul the wrath of God'.[1] Had England been peopled entirely with Puritans, the outlook for the professional writer who happened not to be a divine would have been poor indeed.

But the moralists had to fight hard to make their views prevail. Many are the complaints they raised about the attempts of the pleasure-loving populace to retain or regain their old diversions. The Corporation of Kendal, wishing to put down the old Corpus Christi play, met with great opposition from 'many of the common inhabitants of the borough', whom they accused of 'preferring their own private commodities and the customs of usage to the benefits and common wealth of all others'.[2] The folk of Coventry grudged sorely the loss of their old Hock Tuesday play, 'of late laid down, they knew no cause why, unless it were by the zeal of certain of their preachers, men very commendable for their behaviour and learning ... but somewhat too sour in preaching away their pastimes'.[3]

Nor was it only the uneducated who clung to the old dramatic sports. For instance, the schoolmaster of the Grammar School of Wells fell into disgrace with the authorities for hav-ing taken his boys to Axebridge 'to playe in the parish church

[1] *Diary. Egerton MSS.*, 2614F.

[2] *MSS. of Corporation of Kendal*, 22 September 1586. *Hist. MSS. Comm.*, X, App. iv, 314.

[3] *Laneham's Letter*, ed. F. J. Furnivall (1907), 27–8.

theare'.[1] And there are records of the punishment of more than one cleric for taking part in forbidden diversions. Thus, William Gale was reprimanded because he 'did openlie in disguised order . . . goe in a maske with a visarde on his face into the parish of Pilton . . . to the evil example of others'.[2]

The rising tide of asceticism could not be stemmed. Even the royal authority could only injure its own prestige by the attempt. James I, in his character of liberal-minded patron of the arts and innocent sports, endeavoured personally to secure some sort of toleration. In 1617, upon an appeal made to him, he issued a Declaration of Sports, granting the public the right of enjoying their old amusements, now everywhere proscribed by the local authorities. But when he tried in 1618 to get the Declaration read from the pulpits, a most determined opposition forced him to give way. Arthur Wilson, in his *Life and Reign of James I*, voices the horror with which men greeted the 'frightful apparition' of this 'dancing book'. Not only was James's general order a failure; in individual instances the royal authority was even openly defied. On 5 July 1630, 'the puppet-players craved leave to play here in this town (? Dorchester), and had a warrant under the king's hand, and ye were refused!'[3] There was indeed an irreconcilable division between the values of the Court, and the values of the Puritans and this was shortly to reveal itself in the civil war, and in the complete triumph of the moralists, sweeping away not only immoral sports and plays, but art in all its forms.

Meanwhile, what were the men of letters doing? They tried all means of defence, but it was difficult to get a hearing. Too many of the authorities were on the side of the aggressors and when, for instance, Thomas Lodge wrote a *Defence o*

[1] *MSS. of Wells Cathedral*, 20 February 1582. *Hist. MSS. Comm.*, X, App iii, 243.

[2] Ibid., 244.

[3] *Egerton MSS.*, 784.

Music, Poetry, and Stage Plays, it was refused a licence, on the
ground of its subject, though an answer to it, based by Stephen
Gosson upon a 'private and imperfect copy' was readily
allowed publication.[1] The simplest method of defence was
that adopted by George Whetstone, in his preface to *Promus
and Cassandra*: he attributed the discrediting of drama to the
'tryfels of yong unadvised and rash witted youngsters'.[2] But
this was giving the case away. A stronger line of defence was
the endeavour to meet the moralists on their own ground, and
prove the ethical usefulness of poetry and plays. This was
indeed the commonest defence, because even the learned and
artistic were committed, after the classical precept of Horace,
to the notion that literature should inspire (some said teach)
morality. It was simply a matter of bringing the *utile* into
prominence above the *dulce*.

The apologist, then, accepted with as good grace as possible
the position thrust upon him, and set out to demonstrate the
ethical teaching of poetry and plays. It must be confessed that
it was a task fundamentally impossible. Thus, William Webbe,
pointing out that 'good lessons ... pithie and wise sentences'
might be gathered from the least serious writings by those
minded to observe them, went so far as to declare that in
English poetry he knew of no such 'perilous peeces' as were to
be found in the Latin poets.[3] It must be surmised that the
worthy tutor was but scantily read in the English poets. Gosson
was ready with the obvious retort to the earlier assertion. In
quaintly Euphuistic language he argued:

... the calmest seas hide dangerous rockes: the woolfe jets in
weathers felles. Manie good sentences are ... written by poets as
ornamentes to beautifie their woorkes, and sette their trumperie to

[1] Lodge, *Alarum for Usurers* (1584), preface.
[2] *Débuts de la critique dramatique en Angleterre* (1903), 76–7.
[3] *A Discourse of English Poetrie* (1586), ed. E. Arber (1870), 43–5.

sale without suspect ... pul off the visard that poets maske in, you shall disclose their reproch.[1]

Thomas Heywood, abandoning reliance upon scattered moral 'sentences', asserted morality to be the general *aim* of many plays. They reprove vice, he says, by showing its loathsome deformity,[2] an argument revived later against another Puritan onslaught by Sir John Vanbrugh. Nashe went further, boldly declaring that plays were 'a rare exercise of vertue'. They reprove evil, he says, under cover of delighting: they do not corrupt, they warn.[3] A most valiant defender is Philip Massinger, whose play, *The Roman Actor*, is entirely devoted to the vindication and eulogy of the stage. In a speech made before the assembled Roman senate, the actor Paris thus eloquently pleads his cause:

> ... If to enflame
> The noble youth with an ambitious heat
> To endure the frosts of danger, nay, of death.
> To be thought worthy the triumphal wreath,
> By glorious undertakings, may deserve
> Reward or favour from the commonwealth;
> Actors may put in for as large a share
> As all the sects of the philosophers.[4]

Sidney had taken the same standpoint in his *Apologie for Poetrie*. He could not use the Courtly justification of poetry as a necessary imaginative pleasure, and, accepting the position laid down by the moralist, he asserted the positive ethical value of poetry to be greater than that of either Philosophy or History. He was too wise to admit moral teaching to be the aim of literary art, but he showed in effect that by appealing

[1] *Schoole of Abuse* (New Shaks. Soc., 1841), 10.
[2] 'Apology for Actors' (1612). *Somer's Tracts*, series ii, I, 197–8.
[3] *Pierce Penilesse. Works* (1958), I, 211–14.
[4] (1629), I, iii.

to the emotions by the presentation of noble example, art provided the strongest possible stimulus to virtue.

Men of narrower range tried to prove the definite teaching function of literature, and for this purpose, they found, as medieval scholars had found before them, the great usefulness of the plan of 'allegorical interpretation'. Sir John Harington painfully evolved a moral allegory from almost every canto of *Orlando Furioso*. For instance:

In the beginning of this booke (book XV) was an excellent morall (if you observed it) showing how hurtfull it is for a captaine to be prodigall of his men, and rash or headlong in his attempts.

Again, with reference to Canto i:

For the allegorie in this Canto I find not much to be said ... yet an allegory may not unfitly be gathered of Bayardo's following Angelica, which may thus be taken. Bayardo, a strong horse, without rider or governor, is likened to the desire of man, that runs furiously after pleasure or honour, or whatever man doth most curiously affect.

Harington is careful not to interfere with latitude of interpretation! Moreover, whenever a general reflection of a moral character occurs, the translator calls attention to it by the word *sentence* in the margin. There was really no excuse for the reader if he failed to gather for himself moral teaching out of this work!

Writers took pains to propitiate opinion, and advertised their wares on the title-pages as 'profitable'. Dekker announced that he described villainy 'only to have others shun it'. Others made more definite and real concessions to Puritan opinion: even Jonson confessed that he gave an ending not happy to *Volpone* in order to 'put the snaffle in their mouths, that cried out, we never punish vice in our *enterludes*'.[1] Greene made the

---

[1] *Volpone* (1605), dedication. *Ben Jonson*, V (1937), 20.

most wholesale attempts to conciliate public opinion. Several of his pamphlets, evidently intended as bids for the favour of the sober citizen, were devoted entirely to the discussion of moral aphorisms, enlivened by a few illustrative stories.[1]

It must, however, be confessed that in many cases the professions of moral intention were extremely perfunctory. Nashe, who made no concessions to the Puritan, abuses other writers for their hollow pretences: 'Are they not ashamed,' he asks, 'in their prefixed posies, to adorne a pretence of profit mixt with pleasure, whenas . . . there is scarce to be found one precept pertaining to vertue?'[2] It is to be observed that he also seems to be of those who confine their notions of ethical value to that which directly teaches.

Not much more effective were the efforts made by some apologists to defend their art by distinguishing between the use and abuse of poetry. Most thinking men tried to make this distinction, Gosson and Stubbes among them. But in application, like most other attempts at moderation in times of strong passion, it broke down entirely, and Nashe was left lamenting the suicidal futility of extending 'invectives so farre against the abuse, that almost the things remaines not whereof they admitte anie lawfull use'.[3]

Another kind of defence was the endeavour to bring discredit upon the opposition by suggesting that it was based upon motives of self-interest. Thus, for example, the defenders of the drama urged that its real opponents were not honest respectable citizens, but vintners, alewives, proprietors and frequenters of dicing-houses, bowling-alleys and the like. They argued that plays ought to be regarded by sober-minded folk with favour, as providing a fairly harmless entertainment for

[1] Vide The Royal Exchange and Farewell to Follie. His Mourning Garmen and Never Too Late are definitely moral in tone.
[2] Anatomie of Absurditie. Works (1958), I, 10.
[3] Ibid., I, 20

those who would otherwise seek amusement in evil haunts.[1]
But this argument was generally felt to have even less force
than the preceding: the apologists were uncomfortably conscious that the bulk of the opposition arose in fact from a pious
asceticism, entirely unmixed with interested motives.

One weapon, however, found the Puritan party more
vulnerable. It was difficult for them to clear themselves as a
class from the charge of hypocrisy and insincerity: charges at
all times difficult to disprove. And the defenders of the literary
profession made the most of the popular prejudice against
excessive scrupulousness. They drew pictures of unctuous
hypocrites seeking a reputation for godliness by the use of
cant phraseology, and by captious prohibition of innocent
pastimes, while themselves indulging in sins of avarice, malice,
and all unrighteousness. They are

> . . . such, whose faces are all zeale,
> . . . that will not smell of sinne,
> But seemes as they were made of sanctitie!
> Religion in their garments, and their haire
> Cut shorter than their eye-browes.[2]

They have no sincerity. Their lives are ruled by words, not
ideas; they may not swear, but they may lie, will not steal but
will 'nym'.[3] They have a convenient cloak for all manner of
vices: 'A sermon's a fine short cloak of an hour long, and will
hide the upper part of a dissembler.' Dekker sketches in clear
colours the 'sober *Perpetuana* suited Puritane', with his open
affectation of righteousness, and his secret indulgence in
oathsome vice.[4]

[1] Chettle, *Kind-harts Dream*. Nashe, *Pierce Penilesse*, *Works* (1958), I,
212.
[2] *Every Man out of his Humour* (1600), prologue. *Ben Jonson*, III (1927),
429.
[3] *The Puritan* (anon., n.d.), II, i.
[4] *Seven Deadly Sinnes. Non-dramatic works* (1885), II, 44.

Most striking, among representations of the kind, are those by Spenser, Jonson and Shakespeare. Spenser contents himself with bewailing, in the spirit of the lover of beauty, the ravages committed by sacrilegious intolerance, typified by the Blatant Beast, in churches and monasteries.[1] Jonson in *The Alchemist* has drawn convincingly cruel pictures of the baser natures among the Puritan party: Ananias, the ignorant, prating, fanatical zealot; and the more despicable Tribulation, plausible, cunning, and unscrupulously devoted to his own avaricious ends. Shakespeare's attitude is marked by none of Jonson's relentless bitterness. He ridicules in Malvolio some of the minor foibles specially characteristic of the Puritans; and in Angelo in *Measure for Measure*, he shows the pitfalls that beset the self-righteous man, implacably bent on ignoring or uprooting human frailty. But in each case he refrains from narrowing the scope of the satire to an attack against Puritans as a class. Their faults and vices, as he represents them, are only an exaggeration of those common to all men. Shakespeare is no mere special pleader, holding a brief for the artist's liberty as against the moralist censor; he urges the cause of freedom, sincerity and sympathy for all humanity.

Writers of less seriousness than Jonson and Shakespeare content themselves with simply pouring ridicule upon their opponents. Chapman suggests in one of his masques that the Puritan is fitly represented with a pair of bellows on his head to typify his inflated self-opinionatedness.[2] Middleton makes fun of the Puritan fustian-weaver, who swears that he will swoon if forced to sit through the performance of a play. Not very effective as argument, this; but it served its purpose of turning the laugh against the enemy.

The artist conscious of the dignity of his art did not scruple

[1] *Faerie Queene*, VI, xii, 24–5.
[2] *Masque of the Middle Temple and Lincoln's Inn* (1613).
[3] *The Mayor of Quinborough*, V, i.

at times, to turn the tables and hold up to derision one of the chief weaknesses of his antagonist, an ignorant incapacity to comprehend literary beauty. He had no hesitation in accusing his enemies of crass dullness, of absorption in material pursuits, of incapacity for admiring beauty or greatness in any form. Show such men, said Nashe, a magnificent image in a historical play of the greatness of their fatherland: 'I, but (will they say) what do we get by it?'[1] That drastic satire, *The Pilgrimage to Parnassus*, represents Stupido counselling the would-be scholars, out of the depths of his wisdom, to 'follow noe longer these profane artes, that are the raggs and parings of learning':

Sell all these bookes, and buye a good Martin, and twoo or three hundreth of chatechismes of Jenevas printe, and I warrant you will have learning enoughe.[2]

'Soul blinded sots', Drayton angrily calls such folk

... that creepe
In durt, and never saw the wonders of the Deepe.[3]

Only Sidney and Daniel go to the roots of the matter, the main theme of the justification of poetry, daring to assert that poetry is valuable and socially justifiable in its own right. Sidney does not say so in so many words, but the famous passage in which he enthusiastically extols poetry, above and beyond Nature, is based upon this conception:

Nature never set foorth the earth in so rich Tapistry as diverse Poets have done, neither with so pleasaunt rivers, fruitfull trees, sweete smelling flowers, nor whatsoever els may make the too much loved earth more lovely: her world is brasen, the Poets only deliver a golden.... With the force of a divine breath he (man) bringeth things foorth surpassing her doings.... But these arguments wil by few be understood, and by fewer graunted.[4]

[1] *Pierce Penilesse. Works* (1958), I, 213.
[2] III. *Three Parnassus Plays* (1949), 113–14.
[3] *Polyolbion*, VI, 303 ff. *Works*, ed. J. W. Hebel (1933), IV, 199.
[4] *Defence of Poesie*, ed. A. Feuillerat (1923), 8–9.

Neither Sidney nor Daniel wasted words in idle recrimination against opponents. They made no accusations of stupidity, ignorance, hypocrisy and the like. Daniel simply asserted with dignity, as if unquestioned, the supreme worth of poetry; showing in eloquent, cogent and thoughtful words the great need for learning and literary art, and the evils which must ensue upon contempt for them. He is jealous for the honour or England, in face of the nations of Europe, and pleads that she may be allowed, as she well can, to take her place worthily among them:

> Should we this ornament of Glory then
> As th' unmateriall fruits of shades, neglect?
> Or should we carelesse, come behinde the rest
> In powres of words, that goe before in worth,
> Whenas our accents equall to the best,
> Is able greater wonders to bring forth:
> When all that ever hotter spirits exprest
> Comes bettred by the patience of the North.
> And who, in time, knowes whither we may vent
> The treasure of our tongue, to what strange shores
> This gaine of our best glory shall be sent,
> T' inrich unknowing Nations with our stores?

For himself he cares nothing. His art brings its own reward. Though his audience be few, 'that few, is all the world'. One understanding reader is to him 'a Theater large enow'. No matter if men 'neglect, distaste, uncomprehend, disdain'. No public neglect can undo, says he,

> The love I beare unto this holy skill:
> This is the thing that I was borne to doo,
> This is my Scene, this part must I fulfill.[1]

Alas, this kind of defence, based upon a truly professional dedication to literature, was rarely heard: professionalism of

---

[1] *Musophilus* (1599), 949–60, 556–79.

this intensity had had neither time nor context in which to develop.

On the other hand, discouraging as were the effects of ignorance, bad taste and narrow hostility, it must be recognized that there was much in the public life of the day to stimulate literary production. Without entering into a full discussion of the characteristics of public life, it is nevertheless possible to outline certain facts which help to explain why so much of the energy of the time was manifest in literary activity.

One particular Elizabethan taste which found its gratification most easily in imaginative literature was an abundant love of the strange and marvellous. The Elizabethan lived in an age of expansion and discovery, and in addition he had fed his mind for some time upon newly-revived medieval romances. Innumerable references to Sir Dagonet, the Twelve Peers of France, Sir Lancelot, the Round Table, the Four Sons of Aymon, Bevis of Hampton, Guy of Warwick, William of Cloudesley, Sir Gawayn and other legendary heroes, prove that Elizabethan writers could depend with certainty upon a widespread familiarity with these old stories.[1] Doubtless, they owed to Caxton, and other early printers, for their revival of medieval romance, a debt greater than they knew. Such records as we possess of the libraries of the middle and lower classes reveal a great preponderance of books of this class. The country gentry had a particular taste for them. In the *Dialogue between the English Courtier and the Countrey-Gentleman* (1579), the latter thus vaunts the pleasures of rural society:

Wee want not also pleasant mad headed knaves, that bee properly learned, and will reade in diverse pleasant bookes and good Authors: such as Sir Guy of Warwicke, the foure Sonnes of Amon, the Ship of Fooles, the Budget of Demaundes, the Hundreth merry Tales,

[1] Dekker's pamphlets abound in such references. Vide also the list of Captain Cox's books in *Laneham's Letter*, ed. F. J. Furnivall (1907), xiv, 29–30.

the Booke of Ryddles, and many other excellent writers both witty and pleasaunt.[1]

Readers who esteemed themselves too genteel for old-fashioned English romance read *Amadis of Gaul*, *Palmerin d'Oliva*, and other foreign tales.[2]

Later on, when taste was changing, and the familiar and realistic coming into vogue, Samuel Rowlands described in somewhat unsympathetic vein the supposed effects of over-much reading of romance, in the character of *The Melancholy Knight* (1615). The Knight had read Sir Lancelot, The Knight of the Sun, Sir Triamour, Sir Bevis, Sir Guy, The Four Sons of Aymon and 'all the old world's worthy men at armes', with the result that he dreamed perpetually of woods, wildernesses, groves and castles, and was almost ready to combat the Terrible Dragon at Horsham.[3] There was thus great encouragement for the production of new works of invention and imagination: readers, if not highly cultivated, were at any rate not limited in mental range.

This kind of public taste, however, proved a snare to the mediocre writer unfurnished with material from real life. He was tempted to rely upon the facile invention of marvels. Joseph Hall, with the contempt of a satirist, scoffs at the unlucky tragic poet, grounded for lack of matter and driven to make up

> his hard-betaken tale
> With strange enchantments, fetcht from darksom vale.[4]

Hence the preference long displayed in drama—until Ben

---

[1] *Inedited Tracts*, ed. W. C. Hazlitt (1868), 56–7.

[2] Anthony Munday catered for this class. He published between 1588 and 1619 translations of more than seven popular romances, including *Amadis de Gaule*, *Palmerin d'Oliva* and *Palmerin of England* (which ran through five editions).

[3] A translation of *Don Quixote* had been licensed for publication in January 1612.

[4] *Virgidemiarum*, I, iv. *Collected Poems* (1949), 16.

Jonson, and Beaumont and Fletcher, dethroned it to make way for the study of contemporary social types—for the romantic. The imaginative public loved to admire the adventures of a Perdita or a Rosalind, and to gape at the magic exploits of a Faustus or a Friar Bacon. The author of *The Four Prentises*, carrying his scene to Jerusalem, appealed with confidence to his audience:

Had ye not rather, for noveltie's sake, see Jerusalem ye never saw, than London that ye see hourly?[1]

And Jonson thus scoffingly describes the taste of the 'people':

If a Child could be borne, in a *Play*, and grow up to a man, i' the first Scene, before hee went off the Stage: and then after to come forth a Squire, and bee made a Knight: and that Knight to travell betweene the Acts, and doe wonders i' the holy land, or else where; kill Paynims, wild Boores, dun Cowes, and other Monsters; beget him a reputation, and marry an Emperours Daughter for his Mistris; convert her Fathers Countrey; and at last come home, lame, and all to be laden with miracles. . . . These miracles would please, I assure you . . . for there be of the *People*, that will expect miracles.[2]

In the same way Nashe waged war against the romantic prose story, scoffing at

. . . the fantasticall dreames of those exiled Abbie-lubbers, from whose idle pens proceeded those worne out impressions of the feyned no where acts, of Arthur of the rounde table, Arthur of litle Brittaine, Sir Tristram, Hewon of Burdeaux, the Squire of low degree, the foure sons of Amon, with infinite others.[3]

Readers will be reminded of that excellent witty satire upon the taste of the middle classes, Beaumont and Fletcher's

[1] (1615), prologue.
[2] *The Magnetic Lady*, I, vii. *Ben Jonson*, VI (1938), 527–8.
[3] *Anatomie of Absurditie*. *Works* (1958), I, 11.

Knight of the Burning Pestle (c. 1611), where the grocer's wife in the audience insists on their prentice being allowed to play a part on the stage, and as a result a very ordinary drama of citizen life is shot through and through with wild impossible scenes of adventure.

The public fancy was fed not only by reading, but also by the marvellous reports of travellers and discoverers, many of which were put into print. Everyone had heard stories of the fabulous treasures and uncanny creatures to be found, for instance, in unexplored American forests. Caliban, half-human, half-beast, was suggested by such a report. Spenser humorously appealed for belief in his faery land, on the strength of other recent marvellous discoveries.[1]

There is, however, a dark side to this indulgence in the fantastic and imaginative. Among the ignorant, imagination readily turns to credulity and superstition: the Elizabethan was haunted by superstitious fears of devils, spirits, ghosts, witchcraft and evil omens. Gentle and simple alike believed in possession by the devil. When Dr John Dee's maidservant was afflicted with melancholia, he recorded in his private diary her sad 'temptation' and 'possession' 'by a wicked spirit', and related how, in spite of prayer and anointing with holy oil, the evil one at length prevailed upon her to destroy herself.[2] The death of the Earl of Derby in 1594 was generally believed to have been brought about by witchcraft.[3] Many strange stories of devils, ghosts, haunting spirits and wizardry were related, with full credence, by Thomas Heywood in his *Hierarchie of Angels*, and the whole subject of the miraculous powers of witches, their leagues with the evil one, and their malicious practices, was dealt with at length by no less a person than

[1] *Faerie Queene*, IV, proem.

[2] August 1590–December 1591. *Diary of D. John Dee* (Camden Society, 1842).

[3] John Lodge, *Illustrations of British History* (1838), III, 47–9.

King James in his *Demonologie*.[1] Such was the public terror that the notorious wizard, Dr Lambe, was beaten to death in London streets by the boys and apprentices in 1628.[2] Even so enlightened and humane a thinker as Sir Thomas Browne declared, and unhappily acted upon, his conviction that 'there are Witches' and that 'the Devill doth really possesse some men'.[3]

Hence an inexhaustible fund of material for imaginative and emotional treatment lay ready to hand for the writer: material offering opportunities for stirring and immediate effect such as can be obtained from few other subjects. Authors availed themselves largely of it. They differ in their representation of the supernatural, from Shakespeare, whose ghosts are nearly always solemn, awe-inspiring visionary beings, and whose witches are unearthly incarnations of evil, to Chapman, whose Umbra Friar[4] is a mere piece of 'stage business', and Dekker, whose *Witch of Edmonton* is a poor, downtrodden old woman, tempted, incongruously enough, by a vulgar demon in the shape of a black dog. One and all, employing the supernatural whether for purposes of tragedy or of comedy, or as mere 'machinery', rely upon a belief in its perfect credibility. Some of the representations are broadly and crudely comic, as for example when the devil strikes consternation into the heart of the naughty Friar by carrying on to the scene, on his back, the said Friar's crony, the hostess with her shoulder of mutton and spit.[5] But to the Elizabethan the situation, whatever its comic points, was enhanced by a thrilling belief in its possibility. The scene in which Faustus is dragged off to Hell by demons,

---

[1] Reginald Scot published in 1584 *The Discovery of Witchcraft*, a most exhaustive discussion of witchcraft, and all the beliefs relating to it.

[2] *Egerton MSS.*, 784.

[3] *Religio Medici*, 30. *Works*, ed. G. Keynes (1928), 40–1.

[4] In *Bussy d'Ambois*.

[5] In Greene's *Friar Bacon and Friar Bungay* (1594).

in spite of the 'squibs and fireworks' of the stage production,[1] must have struck terror into the hearts of the audience.

The same awesome attraction surrounded narratives of the doings of alchemists and astrologers. In this case writers usually preferred to make capital out of them by jesting rather than by serious treatment. Elizabethans were ambivalent about astrology and alchemy: on the one hand, they found much excellent matter for jesting and satire, and were quick to suspect charlatanry; on the other hand, especially in the lower and middle classes, the astrologer regulated, with his almanacs and horoscopes, the minutest details of life, prescribing, to adopt Nashe's jesting description, 'unfallible rules' as to, for instance, the days when it is 'good to clyp and shave haires, and to clyp sheepe', or when it is good 'to fyshe in rivers, and to bathe in baths'.

Prognosticating almanacs[2] were for the bookseller and author 'readier money than Ale and cakes'.[3] The lover in the *Magnetic Lady* is represented as making love to 'notes and prognostics'.[4] Dekker and Nashe both wrote witty *Prognostications* for the year, after the manner of Rabelais, prescribing the 'best time to breed love-lockes in ... as also under what Planet a man maye with least danger picke his teeth'.[5] The witty exposure of the impostures and frauds of alchemists by Jonson in 1610 probably did little more to convince the public mind than Chaucer's sarcasm had done two centuries earlier.[6] Philip Stubbes, with his usual sobriety, discusses astrology seriously. He refuses to believe that a man's fortune can be told by the

[1] Vide Dekker, *Worke for Armourours· Non-dramatic works*, IV (1884), 154-5.

[2] Vide *inter alia*, in the Bodleian Library, an Almanac for 1579, by Alexander Mounslowe.

[3] *Have with you to Saffron-Walden*. Works (1958), III, 72.

[4] IV, i.

[5] Nashe, *Have with you to Saffron-Walden*. Works (1958), III, 9.

[6] To judge from the career of the notorious William Lilly, in the middle of the seventeenth century, astrology even gained renewed credence.

stars, but confesses that he holds that they 'have effects and operations', and that 'it pleaseth the majestie of God to worke by them, as by his instruments'. Finally he adds, 'I neither condemne astronomie nor astrologie, nor yet the makers of prognostications, or almanacks for the yeere. But yet I condemne the abuse in them.'[1]

But however little most writers shared in these public errors, the less scrupulous were willing enough to make their profit out of them. 'That greedy seagull ignorance is apt to devoure any thing,' says Nashe,[2] and the cheap press of the day supplied their readers abundantly with such narratives as 'the witches bidding the Devill to dinner at Derbie',[3] or 'the strange and wonderful judgment of God upon a false swearer'.[4]

They talke of an Oxe that tolde the bell at *Wolwitch*, & howe from an Oxe hee trans-formed himselfe to an olde man, and from an old man to an infant, & from an infant to a young man. Strange propheticall reports . . . they mutter he gave out, when in trueth they are nought els but cleanly coyned lyes.[5]

The standard 'prodigy' was the famous 'serpent of Sussex', described at length in a pamphlet of 1614, signed by three eye-witnesses. It lurked in a forest near Horsham, was a dragon nine feet long, casting venom to the distance of four rods, and had already slain a man, a woman, and four mastiffs.[6] It is a far cry from the Dragon of Horsham to Caliban and the Witches of *Macbeth*, but the public feeling aroused by the one

[1] *Anatomy of Abuses* (New Shaks. Soc., 1877–9), II, 66.
[2] *Nashes Lenten Stuffe. Works* (1958), III, 212.
[3] *News from the New World. Ben Jonson*, VII (1941), 515.
[4] Stubbes tells of a blasphemer who became rooted to the spot so that he could not be dragged thence by horses, and remained there till that day. This extraordinary event took place in Germany, he says, on 4 July 1580, and he was writing in 1583 (*Anatomy of Abuses*, op. cit., 114).
[5] Nashe, *Christs Teares. Works* (1958), II, 172.
[6] *Harleian Miscellany*, I, iii (1809).

was ready to welcome the other, a stimulus missing in more sophisticated times.

Another common taste of the day indulged in richness, luxuriance, elaboration. Seeking for beauty, many Elizabethans were misled by the gaudy and pretentious: this is notable in architecture, in dress, in pageants, as well as in literature. Writers endeavoured to please both their readers and themselves by inventing new artificial forms of diction, of verse rhythm, and of ingenious adornment. At one time the elaborately beautiful mechanism of the sonnet attracted public taste; at another the demand was all for lyrical stanzas. At one time the Euphuistic fashion of similes and alliterative decoration was in vogue; at another the Arcadian metaphorical style held the field: in Jonson's words—

Now nothing is good that is naturall: Right and naturall language seeme(s) to have least of the wit in it; that which is writh'd and tortur'd, is counted the more exquisite. Cloath of Bodkin, or Tissue, must be imbrodered; as if no face were faire, that were not pouldred, or painted? No beauty to be had, but in wresting, and writhing our owne tongue? Nothing is fashionable, till it bee deform'd; and this is to write like a *Gentleman*. All must bee ... affected, and preposterous.[1]

Daniel sighs for an age of greater simplicity, free from 'wanton and superfluous bravery'.[2] For the delectation of the fashionably educated, classical allusions decorated every page: 'Take anie of our play-bookes without a *Cupid*, or a *Mercury* in it, and burne it for an heretique in *Poetrie*.'[3] For a lower class, puns and coarse jests, ingenious playing with words, supplied the place of the classical allusions.

The superficiality of much Elizabethan refinement is obvious in the writings of the time. Just as an interest in poetry was

[1] *Discoveries. Ben Jonson*, VIII (1947), 581.
[2] *A Panegyricke Congratulatory* (1603), stanza 55.
[3] Jonson, *Cynthia's Revels*, induction. *Ben Jonson*, IV (1932), 36.

quite compatible with a strange inability to discern good from bad, so in manners elaborate elegance coexisted with a lack of dignity, of consideration, even of decency. Queen Elizabeth boxed the ears of the Earl of Essex in the Council Chamber. She punished 'both with bloes and yevill wordes' a gentlewoman who had offended her.[1] She rebuffed a suitor by complaining of his stinking boots, and he retorted, 'Tut, tut, Madame, 'tis my sute that stinkes.'[2] Philip Stubbes thinks it remarkable about his dead wife that 'there was never one filthy, uncleane, undecent, or unseemly word heard to come forth of her mouth, nor ever once to curse or ban, to sweare or blaspheme God'.[3]

One can feel no surprise, then, at the coarseness of language in representations of the conversation of high life: Shakespeare's Beatrice was doubtless no more outspoken than Elizabeth's own gentlewomen. There was plenty of justification for Peele's Queen Elinor, who gives a cuff on the ears to King Edward I,[4] Marston's Rossaline, who offers to spit at her lover as a favour to him,[5] or for Chapman's picture of an intoxicated Court lady.[6] At the entertainment which James I offered in 1606 to the King of Denmark, several of the principal personages were too drunk to stand. One lady, representing the Queen of Sheba and carrying rich gifts to the royal guest, fell sprawling in front of him and spilled her gifts in his lap. His Danish Majesty himself fell down while attempting to dance, and was carried off to bed 'not a little defiled with the presents of the Queen'. The narrator of this story says that it

---

[1] *Rutland Papers*, Hist. MSS. Comm., XII, App. iv, I, 107.

[2] *Anecdotes and Traditions*, ed. W. J. Thoms (Camden Society, 1839), 47 (*L'Estrange*, 357).

[3] *A Chrystal Glasse* (1626), f. A3. *Anatomy of Abuses* (New Shaks. Soc., 1877–9), 199.

[4] *Edward I*, scene 6. ed. F. S. Hook and J. Yoklavich (1961), 111.

[5] *Antonio and Mellida*, II, i: 'Paugh, servant, rub out my rheum, it soils the presence. . . . I'll spit in thy mouth, and thou wilt, to grace thee.'

[6] *The Gentleman Usher*, III, i.

reminded him 'of what passed of this sort in our Queen's days', but he adds, 'I ne'er did see such lack of good order, discretion, and sobriety as I now have done.'[1]

There seems to have been a general decline of manners at the Court of James, with general foolery, horseplay and low revelry. Perhaps the writers reflect this decline, carrying bad taste beyond the limits of decency, combining lack of refinement with a finikin elaboration of style.[2] Even Nicholas Breton can suggest the following as an example of 'A Letter of Scorne to a coy Dame':

Mistress Fubs, if you were but a little faire, I see you would bee mighty proud, and had you but the wit of a Goose, you would surely hisse at the Gander. . . . It is not your holyday face put on after the ill favoured fashion, can make your half nose but ugly in a true light. . . .[3]

There is worse outrageousness in this vein in Donne's eighth elegy, *The Comparison*. Nashe's controversy with Harvey affords other examples of this witty grossness. He compares Harvey's writing to vomit, constantly alludes to lousiness, and pictures Harvey taming a flea and carrying it about with him on a chain. The terms of abuse hurled at detractors include 'mongrel cur', 'tyke' and 'fool'. Readers enjoyed this kind of robustness. 'That same vein of railing is become,' says Chapman,

[1] Letter from Sir John Harington to Secretary Barlow, 1606: *Nugae Antiquae* (1804), I, 348.

[2] Vide Jonson's evidence:

> Play-wright me reades, and still my verses damnes,
> He sayes, I want the tongue of *Epigrammes*;
> I have no salt: no bawdrie he doth meane.
> For wittie, in his language, is obscene.
> > (*Epigrammes*, XLIX. *Ben Jonson*, VIII (1947), 42).

[3] But note this is from *A Poste with a packet of mad letters*: *Works* (1879), II, h, 11.

Now most applausive; your best poet is
He that rails grossest.[1]

Here is the influence of another characteristic of the typical
Elizabethan: he fed his emotional nature upon a devouring
love of the audacious, successful and great, a lure that never
failed to blind him to all other qualities. The finest shape assumed by this sentiment was the spirit of patriotic pride, an
admiration for the audacious manliness and fortitude of
Englishmen, including the daring buccaneers, defiant in the
face of a hostile Europe. In Thomas Heywood's *Fair Maid of
the West*, the adventurous heroine, invited by the Emperor of
Morocco to ask from him some great gift, disdainfully replies:
'Our country breeds no beggars.' Roused to admiration by
the unshaken demeanour of the hero, in the power of his
Spanish enemies, one of them exclaims:

> These Englishmen,
> Nothing can daunt them. Even in misery,
> They'll not regard their masters.[2]

Even condemned criminals earned public admiration for
their bearing in sight of death. Harrison boasts that they

doo go so cheerefullie to their deths, for our nation is free, stout,
hautie, prodigall of life and bloud . . . and therefore cannot in anie
wise digest to be used as villanes and slaves.[3]

No characteristic is more constantly exhibited in drama than
this of courage and audacity in danger: Vittoria Corombona,
Iago, Britomart, Tamburlaine, the Roman Actor, and many
more, had this kind of heroism and glory. Even the laments
stress the same quality. Harrison fears that Englishmen are
losing their greatness through self-indulgence:

When our houses were builded of willow, then had we oken men;
but now that our houses are come to be made of oke, our men are

[1] *All Fools*, II, i.   [2] V, i; IV, i.
[3] *Description of England* (New Shaks. Soc., 1877), 221–2.

not onlie become willow, but a great manie (through Persian delicacie crept in among us) altogither of straw.[1]

This was the key to the enthusiastic admiration of Queen Elizabeth. John Lyly testifies to her audacious courage and success in *Euphues*:

What hath this chast Virgin *Elizabeth* don, who by the space of twenty and odde yeares with continuall peace against all policies, with sundry myracles, contrary to all hope, hath governed that noble Island. Against whome neyther forren force, nor civill fraude, neyther discorde at home, nor conspirices abroad, could prevaile. What greater merveile hath happened since the beginning of the world, then for a young and tender Maiden, to govern strong and valiaunt menne, then for a Virgin to make the whole worlde, if not to stand in awe of hir, yet to honour hir, yea and to live in spight of all those that spight hir, with hir sword in the sheth, with hir armour in the Tower, with hir souldiers in their gownes. . . .[2]

On the one hand, this kind of patriotism expresses itself in Shakespeare's devoted hyperboles about 'This other Eden, demi-paradise':

This blessed plot, this earth, this realm, this England,
This nurse, this teeming womb of royal kings
Fear'd by their breed, and famous for their birth. . . .
This land of such dear souls, this dear, dear land,
Dear for her reputation through the world.[3]

On the other hand, and less creditably, there is the exhibition of an insular contempt for other nations, when Shakespeare deliberately represents the French in *Henry V* as bragging coxcombs.

Perhaps the spirit of contempt is not common: Elizabethans were generally ready to acknowledge greatness wherever

[1] *Description of England*, 237–8.
[2] *Complete Works*, ed. R. W. Bond (1902), II, 209.
[3] *Richard II*, II, i.

found. One of the most striking passages in all Elizabethan literature is Raleigh's magnanimous tribute to the daring of his lifelong enemy the Spaniard:

Here (in writing of a sea disaster of the Romans) I cannot forbeare to commend the patient vertue of the Spaniards. We seldome or never finde, that any Nation hath endured so many misadventures and miseries, as the Spaniards have done, in their *Indian discoveries*. Yet persisting in their enterprises, with an invincible constancie, they have annexed to their Kingdome so many goodly Provinces, as burie the remembrance of all dangers past. Tempests and shipwracks, famine, overthrowes, mutinies, heat and cold, pestilence, and all manner of diseases, both old and new, together with extreme povertie, and want of all things needfull, have beene the enemies, wherewith every one of their most noble Discoverers, at one time or other, hath encountred. Many yeeres have passed over some of their heads, in the search of not so many leagues: yea more than one or two, have spent their labour, their wealth, and their lives, in search of a golden Kingdome, without getting further notice of it, than what they had at their first setting forth. All which notwithstanding, the third, fourth, and fift undertakers, have not beene disheartened. Surely, they are worthily rewarded with those Treasuries, and Paradises, which they enjoy; and well they deserve to hold them quietly, if they hinder not the like vertue in others, which (perhaps) will not be found.[1]

Even the equable-minded Daniel could be set afire by the thought of enterprise calling for high courage:

> The mounting venter for a high delight,
> Did make the honour of the fall the more,
> For who gets wealth that puts not from the shore?
> Danger hath honor, great designes their fame,
> Glory doth follow, courage goes before.
> And though th' event oft answers not the same,
> Suffice that high attempts have never shame.

[1] *History of the World* (1628), V, i, para 10., 312.

The meane observer (whom base safety keeps)
Lives without honour, dies without a name,
And in eternal darknesse ever sleeps.[1]

Hence arose that interest in the past history of their beloved
country, which called forth a flood of chronicles, history plays
long historical poems, topographical poems, and many somewhat weary historical passages in poems of more purely poetic
interest. In fact, writers seem at times to have over-estimated
the taste of the public for heavy historical diet: Daniel's *Civi*
Wars did not quite suit popular reading as he had expected,
and Drayton complained that whereas he had hoped that many
would read his lengthy *Polyolbion*, because 'it contained all the
Delicacies, Delights, and Rarities of this renowned Isle', it had
fallen out otherwise. It seems indeed to have promoted some
reaction, for, he adds, 'Some of our outlandish, unnatural
English' have even gone so far as to say that 'there is nothing
in this Island worth studying for', and they pride themselves
thus in ignorance, with the result that the poem has not sold
nearly so well as other 'beastly and abominable Trash (a shame
both to our Language and Nation)'.[3]

In his enthusiasm the Elizabethan made many errors of
judgment. Even so deep a thinker as Bacon held that 'a man
may truly make a judgment that the principal point of greatness in any state is to have a race of military men'.[4] Mere
violence, brutality and riotousness were constantly admired
mistaken for heroism. In literary expression, similarly, declam-
ation and rant too often passed muster for true exaltation. To
a people familiarized with violence and bloodshed, by the
perils of street life and travel, and by the spectacle of sanguinar

---

[1] *To Delia*, sonnet XXXV.

[2] At any rate, there are few editions of it, though he kept enlarging it.

[3] Second Part, introduction. *Works*, ed. J. W. Hebel (1933), IV, 391.

[4] 'Of the true greatness of kingdoms and estates': *Essays*, ed. S. F
Reynolds (1890), 204.

public whippings and executions, there was nothing revolting, but rather something boldly great, in the excesses shown at times upon the stage. The law against treason could, and did, afford them sights quite as horrible as that of Bajazet beating out his brains at the side of his cage,[1] or that of Giovanni with the heart of his sister impaled upon his sword.[2] Tastes among writers varied: only in one instance, the scene of the plucking out of Gloucester's eyes, did Shakespeare descend to picturing physical barbarity, though he never shrinks, it must be said, from wholesale bloodshed. On the other hand, Marston had no scruples about bloody spectacles rivalling those of real life. In *Antonio and Mellida*, the hero tortures his helpless enemy by plucking out his tongue and exclaiming exultantly:

> I have't, Pandulpho; the veins panting bleed,
> Trickling fresh gore about my fist.

Then he displays (V, ii) to the agonizing wretch a dish containing the limbs of his murdered child!

Horrible though they were, the barbaric penalties exacted by Elizabethan penal law were yet often treated as subjects for jest. Thomas Norton, who caused torture to be applied to a priest, Alexander Briant, boasted that he had 'stretcht him on the rack a foot longer than God had made him'.[3] And the somewhat prosaic Harrison has his joke upon the hanging of highwaymen. They commonly, he says, 'get trussed up in a Tyburn tippet' before they come to middle age, 'whereby it appeareth that some sort of youth will have its swing, though it be in a halter'.[4] Similarly, the Elizabethan viewed madness with habitual jocoseness.

It is in keeping, then, that noise and clamour were the

[1] Marlowe, *Tamburlaine*, V, ii.
[2] Ford, *'Tis Pity She's a Whore*, V, vi.
[3] *D.N.B.*
[4] *Description of England* (New Shaks. Soc., 1877), I, 221.

regular accompaniments of all forms of entertainment. Though some writers object to the ill-manners and filth of playhouses, all assume noise to be quite in place. All the stage-manager had to do was to provide plenty of it. In Greene's *Alphonsus of Arragon*, there are twenty-five separate directions for the sounding of drums and trumpets, besides some half-dozen marching entries of soldiery, accompanied of course by military music. Plenty of fighting and rough violence were also essential to a play. *Hamlet* derived a large part of its popularity from the 'mad' scenes. Webster, Middleton and others inserted scenes of riotous madness to meet the same taste.[1] Thomas Heywood shows how completely he shares in the common error of mistaking noise and violence for 'greatness':

To see, as I have seene, Hercules in his own shape hunting the boare, knocking down the Bull . . . pashing the Lion, squeezing the Dragon, dragging Cerberus in chains. . . . O, these were sights to make an Alexander . . . so bewitching a thing is lively and well spirited action.[2]

Hamlet's objection to seeing 'a robustious periwig-pated fellow tear a passion to tatters' was not commonly held.

In language, similarly, vigorousness of expression was demanded more constantly than elevation of thought. 'The multitude commend Writers', says Jonson, 'as they doe Fencers, or Wrastlers; who if they come in robustiously, and put for it, with a deale of violence, are received for the *braver-fellowes*.'[3]

---

[1] Ibid., I, 337-8, vide *The Duchess of Malfi, the Changeling*, and elsewhere.
[2] *Apology for Actors, Somer's Tracts*, series ii, I, 178.
[3] *Discoveries*. VIII (1947), 583. Vide also Hall's *Virgidemiarum*, I, vi:

> If *Jove* speake English in a thundring cloud,
> *Thwick thwack* and *rif raf*, rores he out aloud.
> Fie on the forged mint that did create
> New coyne of words never articulate.
>
> (*Collected Poems* (1949), 17).

The representation of the comic was marked, especially during the earlier part of the period, by similar features of violence and crudity. Rough practical jokes, ridiculous gestures and buffoonery, coarsely plain-spoken allusions, formed the staple comic materials. The old morality comedy of the Vice belabouring the Devil, and the Devil carrying off the Vice to Hell on his back, was good enough, even as late as 1616, for many of the audience, and popular enough for Jonson to caricature in *The Divell is an Asse*.[1] *Doctor Faustus* affords examples of this comedy of violence: Faustus boxing the ears of His Holiness the Pope, and snatching food from his hands; Faustus ordering the horse-courser to pull at his leg, and laughing at the consternation with which he sees it come off in his hands. The Clowns, even such leading comic actors as Tarlton and Kempe, provided comic gesture of the coarsest kind. Witness Joseph Hall's description of the tricks by which the audiences were entertained in the midst of a tragedy:

> Now, least such frightfull showes of Fortunes fall,
> And bloody Tyrants rage, should chance appall
> The dead stroke audience, mids the silent rout,
> Comes leaping in a selfe-misformed lout,
> And laughes, and grins, and frames his Mimik face,
> And justles straight into the Princes place.
> Then doth the *Theatre Eccho* all aloud,
> With gladsome noyse of that applauding croud.
> A goodly *hoch-poch*, when vile *Russettings*,
> Are match't with monarchs, & with mighty kings.
> A goodly grace to sober *tragike Muse*,
> When each base clown, his clumbsie fist doth bruise,
> And show his teeth in double rotten-row,
> For laughter at his selfe-resembled show.[2]

[1] Dekker confesses, however, that it was 'out a fashion to bring a Divell upon the Stage' (*Newes from Hell*, 1606: *Non-dramatic works*, II (1885), 95).
[2] *Virgidemiarum*, I, iii. *Collected Poems* (1949), 15.

It was customary for the comic actors to dance jigs, to the accompaniment of comic songs, before, after, and sometimes in the middle of plays of all kinds. Sometimes this comic play pokes fun at well-known personages. When Martin Marprelate was arousing the anger of the actors, they brought Divinity on the stage 'wyth a scratcht face, holding of her hart as if she were sicke'.[1] Nashe threatens the Usurer with being held up to public scorn, 'in a merriment of the Usurer and the Divel'.[2] Jonson scoffed at the taste of the groundlings for seeing on the stage 'tooth-drawers', 'clever apes', 'Servant-monsters', and 'Jigges and Dances'.[3] 'If thou canst but drawe thy mouth awrye, laye thy legg over thy staffe . . . lape up drinke on the earth, I warrant thee, theile laughe mightilie,' says a character in the *Pilgrimage to Parnassus*.[4] 'Goe ae Theater, and heare a Queenes Fice,' says Will Summers the Clown, imitating the speech of a Welshman, 'and he make hur laugh, and laugh hur belly-full.'[5] Even at the Court entertainments, if the evidence is to be believed, the opinion of an anti-masque was: 'De more absurd it be, and vrom de purpose, it be ever all de better.'[6] No wonder that the better writer should have reproached his audience, as 'fitter *Spectators* for the *Beares* . . . or the Puppets' than for a well-thought-out play.[7] Frequently, the comic business was left by the dramatist for the improvization of the actors. On the other hand, as with Shakespeare's Caliban, a taste for rough low comedy had sometimes its dramatic appropriateness.

Writers at times expressly draw a contrast between the crude taste of the 'groundlings' and that of the more cultivated part

[1] Nashe, *The Returne of Pasquill*. *Works* (1958), I, 92.

[2] *Pierce Penilesse*. *Works* (1958), I, 213.

[3] *Bartholomew Fair*, induction.

[4] V. *Three Parnassus Plays* (1949), 129.

[5] Nashe, *Summers Last Will and Testament*. *Works* (1958), III, 244.

[6] Jonson, *Masque of Augurs*. *Ben Jonson*, VII (1941), 638.

[7] Jonson, *The Magnetic Lady*, II, vii. *Ben Jonson*, VI (1938), 546.

of the audience. In the prologue of a play written for the private, Blackfriars Theatre, but presented at the public, Globe Theatre, the author insolently apologizes for his inability to meet the wishes of the lower ranks: 'No shews, no dance . . . no target-fighting upon the stage . . . no bawdry, nor no ballads . . . no clown, no squibs, no devil in't. Oh now, you squirrels that crack nuts, what will you do?'[1] But the truly judicious spectator, to use Hamlet's adjective, was very rare: in general, the Court loved the grotesque and ridiculous as well as the ground-lings, and the Tarltons, Kempes and Lanams were popular with all classes. Tarlton, who was famed for his jig-dancing and at whom people roared with laughter the moment he 'peept out his head', was a great favourite with the Queen. And Will Kempe, a member of the Lord Chamberlain's company, along with Shakespeare, a jig-dancer and a 'merriment' maker, dedicated to a Court lady the account of his famous dance, for a wager, from London to Norwich. Jonson took it upon himself to elevate public taste by weaning part of his audience from a taste for jigs and antics to the study of social types or 'humours'. But his followers misused the example set by replacing the earlier coarse buffoonery by a more sophisticated licentious-ness.

Thus, it has been seen how closely, in spite of much con-tempt and hostility, Elizabethan writers were in touch with the general spirit of a public, who little realized what faithful reflection of their habits, thoughts and sentiments was being handed down to posterity. With so many discouragements and hindrances of every kind, their perseverance has something of the spirit which also animated statesmen, adventurers, mer-chant princes and highwaymen of the day. Bold in conception, reckless, often tasteless in execution, their work is stamped with the striking inconsistencies of the age. Coarseness and finikin artificiality, lofty nobility and sordidness, ideal purity

[1] Shirley, *The Doubtful Heir*, prologue.

and debased sensuality: these contradictions meet us at every turn in the work of men who sought faithfully to 'hold up the mirror to life'. Some, while responding to the motley ideals of their public, idealized and ennobled them. Others pandered to their grossest feelings. But all gave to their generation that for which they asked.

APPENDIX I

The following are the *Complete Works* referred to in abbreviated form in the footnotes:

BRETON, Nicholas *Works in Verse and Prose*, ed. A. B. Grosart (1879).

CHAMBERLAIN, John *Letters*, ed. N. E. McClure (1939).

DANIEL, Samuel *Complete Works*, ed. A. B. Grosart (1885).

DEKKER, Thomas *Dramatic Works*, ed. Fredson Bowers (1953). *Non-dramatic Works*, ed. A. B. Grosart (1884–1886).

DRAYTON, Michael *Complete Works*, ed. J. W. Hebel and others (1931–41).

GREENE, Robert *Life and Complete Works in Prose and Verse*, ed. A. B. Grosart (1881–6).

HALL, Joseph *Collected Poems*, ed. A. Davenport (1949).

HARVEY, Gabriel *Works of Gabriel Harvey*, ed. A. B. Grosart (1885).

JONSON, Ben *Ben Jonson*, ed. C. H. Herford, and P. and E. Simpson (1925–52).

LYLY, John *Complete Works*, ed. R. W. Bond (1902).

NASHE, Thomas *Works of Thomas Nashe*, ed. R. B. McKerrow, revised F. P. Wilson (1958).

PARNASSUS plays *Three Parnassus Plays*, ed. J. B. Leishman (1949).

SIDNEY, Sir Philip *Works of Sidney*, ed. A. Feuillerat (1923).

SPENSER, Edmund *Works*, ed. E. Greenlaw and others (1932–49).

STATIONERS Register E. Arber, *A Transcript of the Registers of the Company of Stationers of London, 1554–1640* (1875 ff.).

APPENDIX II

An Analysis of the Social Status of
200 Renaissance Poets

Poets are selected for this list according to three quite arbitrary qualifications:

(i) They were alive at some time in the century between 152 and 1625.

(ii) Enough had to be known about their careers to enable an estimate of their social status.

(iii) They were important enough to be named in one or more of the following standard works:

    (a) C. S. Lewis, *English Literature in the Sixteenth Century excluding Drama* (Oxford History of English Literature, 1954).

    (b) Douglas Bush, *English Literature in the Earlier Seventeenth Century* (Oxford History of English Literature, 1945).

    (c) *Poetry of the English Renaissance 1509–1660*, ed. J. William Hebel and Hoyt H. Hudson (New York, 1947).

Scottish poets were excluded unless, after the accession of James to the throne of England, they contributed to English poetry.

It must be emphasized that this list does not attempt a complete record of the poets of the day (of whom at least 500 are known by name). It represents merely a reasonably full cross-section of the poets. If the list had been enlarged, or the method of selection varied, the result would have been the same.

The list records the following details:

(i) The name of the poet.

(ii) His dates of birth and death, as given in the *Dictionary of National Biography*, or as conjectured by the latest scholarship to hand. Where these dates are not known and may not be conjectured, an estimate is given of the date at which the poet *floruit*.

(iii) His final title or rank, *as given by himself or by his friends or publisher*. In some instances where no rank is given, one might well conjecture the title of *generosus* or *gentleman*, but I have resisted the temptation and demanded contemporary evidence.

(iv) The occupation by which he chiefly earned his living. It is not always easy to decide which of two alternatives provides the poet's chief occupation. John Donne, for instance, was a Churchman from 1615 onwards, that is to say, for 16 years of his life; but for the greater portion of his adult life he earned his living by other means. In other instances the answer is plain enough: Edmund Spenser, for instance, for all his published books, earned next to nothing as a professional writer; his main support came from the various appointments held in Ireland. The term 'Courtly Satellite' is used to describe any man who served the Court in one or more of a group of associated occupations: groom, secretary, tutor, musician, Revels assistant, agent, envoy, 'poet laureate', antiquary, solicitor, jester, etc., etc. The term 'Country Gentleman' is used to describe the poet of independent means with a private estate in the country. 'Journalist' and 'Writer' are terms which merge into one another; the former should be understood to signify a pamphleteer, a man engaged in writing about current controversy and news; the latter is reserved for the man who writes books for print. In some instances a hairline separates the two categories and the term finally adopted is one of *ad hoc* convenience. The terms 'Military Service' and 'Military Commander' are also close, the latter conveying a rather higher professional aptitude for things military.

(v) Attendance at one or more Universities, if the information is available (often it is not).

(vi) Residence at an Inn of Court, if known.

(vii) Other occupations attempted during his career. Many of these poets were extremely versatile, and in such instances the list confines itself to the more important occupations, representative of the whole career.

	Name	Dates	Title at death	Occupation	Univ.	Inn of Court	Other Occupations
1	Alexander, Sir William	c. 1567–1640	Earl of Stirling	Courtier	Yes		Attached to Earl of Argyll, Tutor to Prince Henry, Secretary for Scotland
2	Audley, John	fl. 1559–1577		Printer and Stationer			
3	Aytoun, Sir Robert	1570–1638	Knight	Courtier and Diplomat	Yes		Secretary to Anne of Denmark and Queen Henrietta Maria
4	Bacon, Sir Francis	1561–1626	Visct. St Albans	Courtier (Lord Chancellor)	Yes	Yes	Barrister, M.P., Solicitor-General, Attorney-General, Privy Councillor, Lord Keeper
5	Baldwin, William	fl. 1547	Gent.	Courtly Satellite	Yes		Printer's corrector, Court Revels assistant, Minister, Schoolmaster
6	Bale, John	1495–1563	Bishop of Ossory	Churchman	Yes		Lecturer, Antiquarian, Chaplain to Bishop Ridley
7	Barclay, Alexander	?1475–1552	Minister	Churchman	Yes		Chaplain of College of St Mary Ottery, Monk

8	Barnes, Barnabe	1570–1609	Gent.	Country Gentleman	Yes		
9	Barnfield, Richard	1574–1627	Gent.	Country Gentleman	Yes	Yes?	
10	Basse, William	c. 1583–c. 1653		Courtly Satellite			Attached to Lord Wenman, Theatre Shareholder
11	Bastard, Thomas	1566–1618	Minister	Churchman	Yes		University Fellow, Chaplain to Earl of Suffolk
12	Beaumont, Francis	1584–1616	Gent.	Country Gentleman	Yes	Yes	Playwright
13	Benlowes, Edward	1603–1676	Gent.	Country Gentleman	Yes	Yes	
14	Berkeley, Sir William	c. 1605–1677	Knight	Courtier	Yes	Yes	Governor of Virginia
15	Best, Charles	fl. 1592		Attorney		Yes	
16	Blenerhasset, Thomas	?1550–?1625	Gent.	Country Gentleman	Yes		Military service
17	Bodenham, John	?1558–1610	Gent.	Grocer			Literary compiler
18	Boleyn, George	?–1536	Visct. Rochford	Member of Royal Family			
19	Bolton, Edmund	?1575–?1633		Writer	Yes	Yes	Antiquarian

	Name	Dates	Title at death	Occupation	Univ.	Inn of Court	Other Occupations
20	Braithwaite, Richard	?1588–1673	Gent.	Country Gentleman	Yes		
21	Breton, Nicholas	?1545–1626	Gent.	Writer	Yes		Courtly Satellite (Attached to Countess of Pembroke)
22	Brinkelow, Henry	?–1546		Mercer			Friar
23	Browne, William	c. 1591–?1643	Gent.	Courtly Satellite	Yes	Yes	Attached to Earl of Pembroke, Tutor
24	Bryan, Sir Francis	?–1550	Knight	Courtier (Lord Marshal of Ireland)	Yes		King's Cup-Bearer, Sheriff of Essex and Herts, Privy Councillor, Ambassador to France
25	Bryskett, Sir Lodowick	fl. 1571–1611	Knight	Courtly Satellite	Yes		Attached to Lord Grey and Sir P. Sidney, Clerk to Munster Council
26	Campion, Thomas	1567–1620	Gent.	Physician	Yes		Musician
27	Carew, Richard	1555–1620	Esq.	Courtly Satellite	Yes	Yes	High Sheriff, Cornwall, J.P., M.P., Deputy Lieut., Cornwall

	Name	Dates					
28	Carew, Thomas	?1594–?1639	Gent.	Courtly Satellite	Yes	Yes	Attached to Lord Herbert, Secretary to Sir Dudley Carleton, Gent. of the Privy Chamber, Sewer to Charles I
29	Cartwright, William	1611–1643		University Reader	Yes		
30	Cary, Lucius	?1610–1643	Visct. Falkland	Courtier (Secretary of State)	Yes		Diplomat and Privy Councillor, M.P.
31	Cavendish, George	1500–?1561	Gent.	Courtly Satellite			Gentleman-Usher to Wolsey
32	Cavendish, Margaret	?1623–1674	Duchess of Newcastle	Courtier			
33	Cecil, William	1520–1598	Lord Burghley	Courtier (Chief Secretary of State)	Yes	Yes	Secretary to Somerset, M.P., Chancellor of the Garter, Privy Councillor, Lord High Treasurer
34	Chaloner, Sir Thomas (the Elder)	1521–1565	Knight	Courtier (Clerk to the Privy Council)	Yes		Military service, Attached to Somerset and Burghley, Ambassador to Spain
35	Chapman, George	?1559–1634	Gent.	Playwright	Yes		Courtly Satellite, Attached to Raleigh, Sewer to Prince Henry

P

	Name	Dates	Title at death	Occupation	Univ.	Inn of Court	Other Occupations
36	Cheke, Sir John	1514–1557	Knight	Courtier (Secretary of State)	Yes		University Professor and Provost, M.P., Gentleman of the Privy Chamber
37	Chettle, Henry	?–1607		Printer and Stationer			Playwright and Journalist
38	Churchyard, Thomas	1520–1604	Gent.	Courtly Satellite (professional soldier)			Attached to Surrey, Somerset and Leicester, Professional writer
39	Cleveland, John	1613–1658		University Fellow and Reader	Yes		Courtly Satellite (Royalist soldier), M.P.
40	Constable, Sir Henry	1562–1613	Knight	Courtly Satellite (Pensioner, French Court)	Yes		
41	Copland, Robert	fl. 1508–1547		Printer and Stationer	Yes		

			Gent.	Courtly Satellite (Parma and Spain)	Yes	Secret Agent
42	Copley, Anthony	15/?–1607				
43	Corbet, Richard	1582–1635	Bishop of Oxford and Norwich	Churchman	Yes	University Dean
44	Coverdale, Miles	1488–1568	(Bishop of Exeter)	Churchman	Yes	Chaplain to Henry VIII
45	Cowley, Abraham	1618–1667	Gent.	Courtly Satellite (Secretary to Queen Henrietta Maria)	Yes	Attached to Jermyn and Buckingham, Secret Agent
46	Crashaw, Richard	1612–1649	Canon (Loretto)	Churchman	Yes	University Fellow
47	Crowley, Robert	?1518–1588	Archdeacon of Hereford	Printer and Stationer	Yes	Churchman
48	Daniel, Samuel	1562–1619	Gent.	Courtly Satellite (Gentleman of the Chamber)	Yes	Private tutor, Attached to the Cliffords, Wriothesleys, Herberts, Master of the Revels, Groom to Queen Anne

	Name	Dates	Title at death	Occupation	Univ.	Inn of Court	Other Occupations
49	Davenant, Sir William	1606–1668	Knight	Courtier ('Poet Laureate')	Yes		Attached to Duchess of Richmond, and Greville, Playhouse Manager
50	Davies, John (of Hereford)	c. 1565–1618		Writing-master			Attached to Herberts, Egertons, etc., Tutor to Prince Henry
51	Davies, Sir John	1569–1626	Knight	Courtier (Lord Chief Justice)	Yes	Yes	Barrister, M.P., Solicitor-General for Ireland
52	Davison, Francis	1575–c. 1619	Gent.	Courtly Satellite		Yes	Secretary to Sir Thomas Parry
53	Dekker, Thomas	c. 1570–c. 1641		Playwright and Journalist			Tailor
54	Deloney, Thomas	?1543–?1607		Silk weaver			Journalist
55	Denham, Sir John	1615–1669	Knight	Courtier (Surveyor Gen. of Works)	Yes	Yes	Royalist soldier

No.	Name	Dates					
56	Devereux, Robert	1566-1601	Earl of Essex	Courtier (Earl Marshal)	Yes		Privy Councillor, Diplomat, Chancellor of Cambridge
57	Donne, John	1573-1631	Dean of St Paul's	Courtly Satellite (Secretary to Sir Thos. Egerton)	Yes	Yes	M.P., Chaplain to James I, Reader to Benchers of Lincoln's Inn
58	Dowland, John	fl. 1600		Courtly Satellite (Musician)			Lutenist to King of Denmark
59	Drant, Thomas	?-?1578	Archdeacon of Lewes	University Fellow	Yes		Churchman
60	Drayton, Michael	1563-1631	Esq.	Courtly Satellite			Attached to Sir Henry Goodyere and Sir Walter Aston, Playwright
61	Drummond, William (of Hawthornden)	1585-1649	Laird	Country Gentleman	Yes		
62	Dyer, Sir Edward	?-1607	Knight	Courtier (Chancellor of the Garter)	Yes		Secretary to Leicester, Steward of Woodstock, Diplomat
63	Earle, hn	?1600-1665	Bishop of Salisbury	Churchman	Yes		Tutor to Prince Charles, Dean of Westminster

	Name	Dates	Title at death	Occupation	Univ.	Inn of Court	Other Occupations
64	Edwards, Richard	?1523–1566	Gent.	Courtly Satellite (Musician)	Yes		Master of Children of Chapel Royal
65	Elizabeth I	1533–1603	Queen				
66	Fairfax, Edward	?–1635	Gent.	Country Gentleman			
67	Fane, Mildmay	1602–1666	Earl of Westmorland	Courtier (Lord Lieut. of Norhants)	Yes		M.P., K.B.
68	Fanshawe, Sir Richard	1608–1666	Knight	Courtier (Privy Councillor)	Yes	Yes	Secretary to Lord Aston, Attached to Prince Charles, M.P., Ambassador to Spain and Portugal
69	Feltham, Owen	?1602–1668	Gent.	Courtly Satellite			Secretary to Earl of Thomond
70	Ferrers, George	?1500–1579	Gent.	Courtly Satellite	Yes	Yes	Page of the Chamber to Henry VIII, Master of the King's Pastimes to Edward VI, M.P., Country Gentleman

No.	Name	Dates	Status	Role			Notes
71	Fletcher, Giles (The Elder)	?1549–1611	Gent.	Courtier (Ambassador to Moscow)	Yes		University Deputy Orator, Attached to Essex, M.P., Treasurer of St Paul's
72	Fletcher, Giles (The Younger)	c. 1588–1623	Minister	University Fellow and Reader	Yes		Churchman
73	Fletcher, John	1579–1625	Gent.	Playwright	Yes		
74	Fletcher, Phineas	1582–1650	Minister	Churchman	Yes		Chaplain to Sir Henry Willoughby, Fellow
75	Ford, John	1586–post 1640	Gent.	Playwright	Yes	Yes	Attorney
76	Fraunce, Abraham	fl. 1587–1633	Gent.	Courtly Satellite	Yes	Yes	Attached to Sidney and Herberts, Queen's Solicitor
77	Gascoigne, George	?1525–1577	Esq.	Courtly Satellite	Yes	Yes	Professional soldier, Attached to Lord Grey, M.P., writer
78	Gifford, Humphrey	?–1589	Gent.	Headmaster Barnstaple G.S.	Yes		
79	Godolphin, Sidney	1610–1643	Gent.	Courtly Satellite	Yes	Yes	M.P., Country Gentleman, Royalist soldier
80	Goffe, Thomas	1591–1629	Minister	University Fellow	Yes		Churchman

	Name	Dates	Title at death	Occupation	Univ.	Inn of Court	Other Occupations
81	Golding, Arthur	1536–?1606	Gent.	Country Gentleman	Yes	Yes	Courtly Satellite, Attached to Leicester, Oxford, etc., Antiquary
82	Googe, Barnabe	1540–1594	Esq.	Courtly Satellite (Gentleman-Pensioner)	Yes	Yes	Attached to Sir William Cecil, Provost-Marshal in Connaught
83	Gorges, Sir Arthur	?–1625	Knight	Courtly Satellite (Gentleman-Pensioner)			Attached to Raleigh, M.P., Professional soldier
84	Gosson, Stephen	1554–1624		Private Tutor	Yes		Actor and playwright, Writer, Minister
85	Graham, James	1612–1650	Marquis of Montrose	Courtier (Lieutenant General)			Lieut.-Governor to Charles II, Field Marshal to Emperor Ferdinand III
86	Grey, William (of Reading)	?–1551	Esq.	Courtly Satellite			Attached to Somerset, Writer, Chamberlain in Court of General Surveyors, M.P., Country Gentleman

No.	Name	Dates	Rank	Occupation			Career Notes
87	Greene, Robert	?1558–1592		Playwright and Journalist	Yes		
88	Greville, Fulke	1554–1628	Lord Brooke	Courtier (Chancellor of the Exchequer)	Yes		M.P., Country Gentleman, Treasurer of the Wars and Marine Causes, Secretary for Wales, K.B., Gentleman of the Bedchamber, Privy Councillor
89	Griffin, Bartholomew	fl. 1596	Gent.	Attorney		Yes	
90	Grimald, Nicholas	?1519–?1562	Minister	Churchman	Yes		University Lecturer, Chaplain to Bishop Ridley
91	Habington, William	1605–1654	Gent.	Country Gentleman	Yes		
92	Hall, Arthur	fl. 1563–1604	Esq.	Country Gentleman	Yes		Attached to Cecils, M.P.
93	Hall, Joseph	1574–1656	Bishop of Norwich	Churchman	Yes		Chaplain to Prince Henry
94	Harington, John (the Elder)	fl. 1550	Esq.	Courtly Satellite			Confidential Servant to Henry VIII and Princess Elizabeth

	Name	Dates	Title at death	Occupation	Univ.	Inn of Court	Other Occupations
95	Harington, Sir John	c. 1561–1612	Knight	Courtier (High Sheriff of Somerset)	Yes	Yes	Military service
96	Harvey, Gabriel	?1545–1630	Gent.	University Lecturer and College Head	Yes		Courtly Satellite, Secretary to Leicester
97	Henry VIII	1491–1547	King				
98	Herbert, Edward	1583–1648	Lord Herbert of Cherbury	Courtier and Diplomat	Yes		Military service, Ambassador to France
99	Herbert, George	1593–1633	Minister	University Fellow and Public Orator	Yes		Churchman
100	Herbert, Mary	1561–1621	Countess of Pembroke				
101	Herrick, Robert	1591–1674	Minister	Churchman	Yes		Courtly Satellite, Chaplain to Buckingham
102	Heywood, Jasper	1535–1598	Jesuit Priest	Churchman	Yes	Yes	University Fellow and Professor, Attached to Duke of Bavaria

	Name	Dates	Status	Occupation			Notes
103	Heywood, John	c. 1497–c. 1580	Gent.	Courtly Satellite (Musician)	Yes		Sewer of the Chamber to Henry VIII, Edward VI, and Mary, Mercer, Actor and playwright, Country Gentleman
104	Heywood, Thomas	?1574–?1650		Actor and playwright	Yes		Attached to Earls of Southampton and Worcester
105	Hopkins, John	?–1570	Minister	Churchman	Yes		Schoolmaster
106	Hoskyns, John	1566–1638	Gent.	Barrister (Sergeant-at-Law)	Yes	Yes	Schoolmaster, M.P., University Fellow
107	Howard, Henry	?1517–1547	Earl of Surrey	Courtier (Lieutenant General)			Companion of Duke of Richmond
108	Howell, James	1594–1666	Gent.	Courtly Satellite (Historiographer Royal)	Yes		University Fellow, Glass factor, Secretary to Lord Scrope, M.P., Envoy
109	Howell, Thomas	fl. 1568–1581	Gent.	Courtly Satellite			Attached to Earl of Shrewsbury and Countess of Pembroke

	Name	Dates	Title at death	Occupation	Univ.	Inn of Court	Other Occupations
110	Hunnis, William	c. 1530–1597	Esq.	Courtly Satellite (Master of the Chapel Royal)			Attached to the Herberts, Grocer, Writer
111	James I	1566–1625	King				
112	Jonson, Ben	1572–1637	Gent.	Courtly Satellite (Pension as 'King's Poet')			Apprentice bricklayer, Actor and playwright, Attached to Raleigh, Secret Agent, City of London Chronologer
113	Kethe, William	?–?1608	Minister	Churchman			Journalist
114	Kindlemarsh, Francis	fl. 1570	Esq.	Country Gentleman		Yes	M.P.
115	King, Henry	1592–1669	Bishop of Chichester	Churchman	Yes		Canon of Christ Church, Dean of Rochester
116	Kynaston, Sir Francis	1587–1642	Knight	Country Gentleman	Yes	Yes	Founder of the Museum Minervae

117	Leland, John	?-1552	Canon	Courtly Satellite ('Regius Antiquarius')	Yes		Chaplain to Henry VIII, Tutor to the Howards, Librarian
118	Lluelyn, Martin	1616-1682	Gent.	Physician	Yes		Royalist soldier, University Principal, Mayor, High Wycombe
119	Lodge, Thomas	c. 1558-1625	Gent.	Physician	Yes	Yes	Playwright and writer, Military service, Attached to Earl of Derby
120	Lok, Henry	c. 1553-c. 1608	Gent.	Courtly Satellite	Yes		Attached to Sir Robert Cecil, Secret Agent
121	Lovelace, Richard	1618-1658	Esq.	Country Gentleman	Yes		Courtier and Royalist soldier
122	Lyly, John	c. 1554-1606	Gent.	Courtly Satellite (Vice-master of St Paul's and Savoy children's companies)	Yes		Secretary to Oxford, Actor, M.P., clerk controller at Revels Office

	Name	Dates	Title at death	Occupation	Univ.	Inn of Court	Other Occupations
123	Markham, Gervase	?1568–1637	Gent.	Country Gentleman (Horse-breeder)			Military service (attached to Essex), Writer
124	Marlowe, Christopher	1564–1593	Gent.	Courtly Satellite	Yes		Attached to Sir Francis Walsingham, Secret Agent, Playwright
125	Marmion, Shakerley	1603–1639	Esq.	Country Gentleman	Yes		Military service, Playwright
126	Marston, John	1576–1634	Minister	Playwright	Yes	Yes	Churchman, Theatrical shareholder, Writer
127	Marvell, Andrew	1621–1678	Gent.	Courtly Satellite	Yes		Clerk, Attached to Fairfax and Cromwell as Tutor, Asst. Secretary to Council of State, M.P.
128	Massinger, Philip	1583–1640	Gent.	Playwright	Yes		Attached to Earl of Pembroke
129	May, Thomas	1595–1650		Playwright and writer	Yes	Yes	Attorney

No.	Name	Dates	Rank				
130	Mennes, Sir John	1599–1671	Knight	Courtier (seaman)		Yes	Admiral, Commander and Comptroller of Navy, Governor North Wales
131	Middleton, Thomas	?1570–1627	Gent.	Playwright and writer	Yes		City of London Chronologer
132	Milton, John	1608–1674	Gent.	Country Gentleman	Yes		Tutor, Secretary of Foreign Tongues to the Council of State, Journalist
133	More, Henry	1614–1687		University Fellow and College Head	Yes		
134	More, Sir Thomas	1478–1535	Knight	Courtier (Lord Chancellor)	Yes	Yes	M.P., Speaker of Commons, Privy Councillor, Chancellor of Duchy of Lancaster
135	Morton, Sir Albertus	?1581–1625	Knight	Courtier (Secretary of State)	Yes		M.P., Privy Councillor, Attached to Elizabeth of Bohemia
136	Munday, Anthony	1553–1633	Gent.	Courtly Satellite (Queen's Messenger of Bedchamber)			Apprentice printer, Attached to Oxford, Writer
137	Nashe, Thomas	1567–1601		Playwright and Journalist	Yes		

	Name	Dates	Title at death	Occupation	Univ.	Inn of Court	Other Occupations
138	Newton, Thomas	?1542–1607	Minister	Churchman	Yes		Schoolmaster, Physician, Attached to Essex
139	Norton, Thomas	1532–1584	Gent.	Attorney	Yes	Yes	M.P., Leader of Commons, Counsel to Stationers, Solicitor to Merchant Tailors, Licenser of the Press, Remembrancer of the City
140	Parker, Henry	1476–1556	Lord Morley	Courtier (Privy Councillor)	Yes		Gentleman Usher, Ambassador, Commissioner in Essex and Herts
141	Parker, Matthew	1504–1575	Archbishop of Canterbury	Churchman	Yes		Chaplain to Henry VIII, Anne Boleyn, Edward VI, Dean of Lincoln
142	Peele, George	c. 1558–c. 1597	Gent.	Actor and Playwright	Yes		Writer (for City, etc.)
143	Peend, Thomas	fl. 1565	Gent.	Attorney	Yes	Yes	
144	Percy, William	1575–1648	Esq.	Country Gentleman	Yes		

145	Pestell, Thomas	?1584–?1659	Minister	Churchman	Yes		Chaplain to Essex
146	Pettie, George	1548–1589	Gent.	Professional Soldier	Yes		Writer
147	Phaer, Thomas	?1510–1560	Esq.	Attorney (King's and Queen's Solicitor in Marches of Wales)	Yes	Yes?	Physician
148	Proctor, Thomas	fl. 1578		Printer and Stationer			
149	Pullain, John	1517–1565	Archdeacon of Colchester	Churchman	Yes		Senior Student Christ Church, Chaplain to Duchess of Suffolk, Prebendary of St Paul's
150	Puttenham, George	?1530–1590	Gent.	Courtly Satellite (Gentleman-Pensioner)	Yes	Yes	
151	Quarles, Francis	1592–1644	Gent.	Courtly Satellite	Yes	Yes	Attached to Elizabeth of Bohemia, Arundel, Secretary to Archbishop Usher, Journalist

	Name	Dates	Title at death	Occupation	Univ.	Inn of Court	Other Occupations
152	Raleigh, Sir Walter	c. 1552–1618	Knight	Courtier (Military and Naval Commander)	Yes	Yes	Privy Councillor, Lord Warden of the Stanneries, Lieutenant of Cornwall, Governor of Jersey, Antiquary, Chemist
153	Randolph, Thomas	1605–1635	Gent.	University Fellow	Yes		
154	Roydon, Matthew	fl. 1580–1622	Gent.	Courtly Satellite	Yes		Attached to Earl of Sussex
155	Sackville, Thomas	1536–1608	Earl of Dorset	Courtier (Lord Treasurer)	Yes	Yes	M.P., Privy Councillor, K.G., Lord High Steward, Ambassador, Chancellor of Oxford
156	St Leger, Sir Anthony	1496–1559	Knight	Courtier (Lord Deputy of Ireland)	Yes	Yes	Privy Councillor, K.G.
157	Sandys, Sir Edwin	1561–1629	Knight	Company Treasurer (Virginia)	Yes	Yes	University Fellow, M.P., official of East India Company

	Name	Dates			Role		
158	Sandys, George	1578–1644	Gent.	Yes	Company Agent (Virginia)		Attached to Falkland
159	Seymour, Edward	?1506–1552	Duke of Somerset	Yes	Courtier (Protector of the Realm)		Privy Councillor, K.G.
160	Shakespeare, William	1564–1616	Esq.	Yes	Actor, Playwright and theatrical shareholder		Attached to Southampton
161	Sherburne, Sir Edward	1618–1702	Knight	Yes	Clerk of the Ordnance	Yes	Royalist soldier
162	Shirley, James	1596–1666	Gent.	Yes	Schoolmaster		Minister, Playwright
163	Sidney, Sir Philip	1554–1586	Knight	Yes	Courtier (Joint Master of Ordnance)		Military Commander, M.P., Ambassador
164	Skelton, John	c. 1460–1529	Minister	Yes	Courtly Satellite ('Regius Orator')		Churchman, Tutor to Henry VIII
165	Smith, James	1605–1667	Archdeacon of Barnstaple	Yes	Churchman		Chaplain to Earl of Holland
166	Southwell, Robert	c. 1561–1595	Priest	Yes	Churchman		Chaplain to Arundel

	Name	Dates	Title at death	Occupation	Univ.	Inn of Court	Other Occupations
167	Spenser, Edmund	1552–1599	Gent.	Courtly Satellite (attached to Leicester, Grey, Raleigh, Essex)	Yes		Secretary to Grey, Clerk of the Irish Court of Chancery, Clerk of the Munster Council, Sheriff of Cork
168	Stanley, Thomas	1625–1678	Gent.	Scholar	Yes	Yes	
169	Stanyhurst, Richard	1547–1618	Priest	Churchman	Yes	Yes	Chaplain to Archduke Albert of Austria
170	Sternhold, Thomas	?–1549	Gent.	Courtly Satellite (Groom of the Robes to Henry VIII and Edward VI)	Yes		M.P.
171	Stevenson, William	1546–1575	Minister	Churchman	Yes		University Fellow, Prebendary of Durham
172	Storer, Thomas	1571–1604	Gent.	University Fellow	Yes		

No.	Name	Dates	Rank	Category			Occupation
173	Strode, William	1602–1645	Minister	University Fellow	Yes		Chaplain to Bishop Corbet
174	Studley, John	?1545–?1590	Minister	University Fellow	Yes		Churchman
175	Suckling, Sir John	1609–1642	Knight	Courtier (Military Commander)	Yes	Yes	Attached to Gustavus Adolphus, M.P.
176	Sylvester, Joshua	1563–1618	Gent.	Courtly Satellite (Groom of the Chamber to Prince Henry)			Under-clerk of the Parliament, Tutor to the Devereux, Mercer's factor
177	Tarlton, Richard	?–1588		Courtly Satellite (Jester)			Innkeeper, Actor, Fencer
178	Taylor, John (The Water Poet)	1580–1653		Waterman			Duty-collector on Thames
179	Tourneur, Cyril	?–1626	Gent.	Courtly Satellite (Secretary to Sir Edward Cecil)			Professional soldier, Secret Agent, Playwright
180	Townshend, Aurelian	?1583–?1651	Gent.	Courtly Satellite			Attached to the Cecils, Lord Herbert, Dorset

	Name	Dates	Title at death	Occupation	Univ.	Inn of Court	Other Occupations
181	Turberville, George	c. 1540–c. 1610	Gent.	Courtly Satellite (Secretary to Thomas Randolph)	Yes	Yes	Military service, Writer
182	Tusser, Thomas	c. 1524–1580	Gent.	Farmer	Yes		Court musician, attached to Lord Paget, Schoolmaster, Lay-clerk at Norwich, College servant
183	Udall, Nicholas	1505–1556	Minister	Headmaster	Yes		Prebendary of Windsor, Actor, Writer, Private Tutor
184	Vaughan, Henry	1622–1695	Gent.	Physician	Yes		Military service
185	Vaux, Thomas	1510–1556	Lord Vaux	Courtier (Privy Councillor)	Yes		Governor of Jersey, K.B., Diplomat
186	de Vere, Edward	1550–1604	Earl of Oxford	Courtier (Lord Great Chamberlain)	Yes		Privy Councillor, Commissioner for State trials
187	Waller, Edmund	1606–1687	Esq.	Country Gentleman	Yes		M.P., Dramatic Censor, Commissioner for Trade

							Attached to Hunsdon
188	Warner, William	?1558–1609	Gent.	Attorney of Common Pleas	Yes	Yes	
189	Watson, Thomas	c. 1557–1592	Gent.	Courtly Satellite	Yes	Yes	Attached to William Cornwallis and Sir Francis Walsingham
190	Webbe, William	fl. 1568–1591		Private Tutor	Yes		Writer
191	Webster, John	c. 1580–?1634	Gent.	Playwright			Apprentice Tailor, Courtly Satellite
192	Whetstone, George	c. 1544–1587	Gent.	Professional soldier	Yes		Courtly Satellite, Writer
193	Whiting, Nathaniel	c. 1612–post 1662	Minister	Churchman	Yes		
194	Whitney, Geoffrey	?1548–?1601	Gent.	Country Gentleman	Yes		Attached to Leicester, Underbailiff of Great Yarmouth
195	Whittingham, William	?1524–1579	Dean of Durham	Churchman	Yes		Chaplain under Earl of Warwick
196	Wisdom, Robert	?–1568	Archdeacon of Ely	Churchman	Yes		
197	Wither, George	1588–1667		Journalist and writer	Yes	**Yes**	Parliamentary soldier

	Name	Dates	Title at death	Occupation	Univ.	Inn of Court	Other Occupations
198	Wotton, Sir Henry	1568–1639	Knight	Courtier (Ambassador to Venice)	Yes	Yes	Headmaster, Diplomat, M.P.
199	Wyatt, Sir Thomas	1503–1542	Knight	Courtier (Ambassador to Spain)	Yes		Esquire of the Body to Henry VIII, Clerk of the King's Jewels, Marshal of Calais, Diplomat, M.P., Vice-Admiral of the Fleet, Privy Councillor
200	Young, Bartholomew	fl. 1577–1598	Gent.	Attorney		Yes	

Index

This index is restricted to names, the titles of anonymous works, and the major topics discussed in the book. Post-1650 writers, classical and foreign writers, and titles are given in *italics*. Major references are given in **bold** type. Editors of works frequently referred to are given only the one reference (to the full title of the work in Appendix I). Since subject-divisions under writers tend to be arbitrary, idiosyncratic, and not very useful, I have eliminated them from this edition. (J. W. S.)

Acheson, Arthur: 121
Agrippa: 159
Alexander, Sir William, Earl of Stirling: 67, 163, 168, **212**
Alexandria: 8
Alfonso, of Naples: 9
Alfred, King: 9
Allen, D. C.: 110, 174
Alleyn, Edward: 89, 96, 97, 98
Allot, Robert: 151
Alvarez, A.: 131
Andrewes, Bishop Lancelot: 126
Anne, Queen: 217
Arber, Edward: ix, 181, **209**
Aretino: 23, 31, 79, 135
Argyll, Earls of: 212
Ariosto: 79
Aristotle: 156
Armin, Robert: 97, 105, 161
Arundel, Earls of: 36, 227, 231, 233
Ascham, Roger: 12, 15, 110, 135
Ashbee, J. E.: 9
Aston, Sir Thomas: 219, 220
Athens: 8
Aubigny, Esme Stuart, Lord d': 18
Aubrey, John: 31
Audley, John: 139, **212**
Augustus: 8, 9
Aylmer, Bishop John: 42, 133
Aytoun, Sir Robert: **212**

Baber, John: 112

Babington, Bishop: 176
Babington Plot: 42
Bacon, Sir Francis, Viscount St Albans: 33, 60, 84, 87, 128, 173, 202, **212**
Baldwin, William: 156, **212**
Bale, John: **212**
Ball, Thomas: 102–3
Bancroft, Bishop (later Archbishop) Richard: 45, 48
Barclay, Alexander: 160, **212**
Barker, Christopher, publisher: 65, 71, 74
Barker, Richard, publisher, 65
Barksted, William: 97
Barlow, Secretary: 198
Barnes, Barnabe: 16, **213**
Barnes, Joseph, printer: 83, 85
Barnfield, Richard: **213**
Bartas, du: 156
Basse, William: 97, **213**
Bastard, Thomas: **213**
Baxter, William: 120
Beale, James, printer: 84
Beaumont, Francis: 16, 130, 131, 191, 192, **213**
Bedford, Lucy, Countess of: **17,** 32
Benlowes, Edward: **213**
Berkeley, Sir William, **213**
Best, Charles: **213**
Bible, authorized translation of: 72
Bibliographica: 65, 66, 156

Binneman, Henry, publisher: 65
Bird, William: 97
Bishop, George, publisher: 66, 72
Blenerhasset, Thomas: **213**
Blount, Edward, publisher: 37, 66, **67,** 69
Boas, F. S.: 130
Bodenham, John: 71, **213**
Bodley, Sir Thomas: 16, 157
Boleyn, George, Viscount Rochford: **213**
Boleyn, Queen Anne: 230
Bolton, Edmund: **213**
Bond, R. W.: **209**
Bookselling: viii, **64 ff.**
Bourne, H. R. Fox: 150
Bowers, Fredson: **209**
Braithwaite, Richard: 16, **214**
Brandon, Samuel: 68
Breton, Nicholas: 13, 14, 32, 52, 57, 68, 74, 80, 82, 105, 106, 108, 109, 139, 142, 145, 165, 174, 198, 209, **214**
Brewer, J. S.: 155, 163
Briant, Alexander: 58, 203
Brinkelow, Henry: **214**
Brougham, Henry: 114
Browne, Sir Thomas: 193
Browne, William: 155
Browne, William, the poet: 14, 120, 156, **214**
Bryan, Sir Francis: **214**
Bryskett, Sir Lodowick: 132, **214**
Bullough, G.: 85
Burbage, James: 91, 94, 96, 97, 98
Burby, Cuthbert, publisher: 67, 69, 87
Burn, J. S.: 41, 44, 45, 60, 120
Bush, Douglas: 210

C., (I.): 144
Caesar, Sir Julius: 24
Cambridge University Press: 42, 65, 107, 108

Camden, William: 31, 67, 116, 121, 152
Campion, Edmund: 42, 50
Campion, Thomas: **214**
Carew, Richard: 132, **214**
Carew, Thomas: **215**
Carey, Elizabeth, and family: 17, 18, 21, 24
Carleton, Sir Dudley, Viscount Dorchester: 215
Cartwright, Thomas: 15, 44, 61, 179
Cartwright, William: **215**
Cary, Lucius, Viscount Falkland: **215,** 233
Castiglione: 9
Cavendish, George: **215**
Cavendish, Margaret, Duchess of Newcastle: **215**
Caxton, William, printer: 189
Cecil, Sir Edward, Viscount Wimbledon: 235
Cecil, Sir Robert, Earl of Salisbury: 227
Cecil, Sir William, Lord Burghley, and Lady Cecil: 31, 40, 46–7, 70, 107, 108, 110, 118, 176, 178, **215,** 222, 223, 235
Censorship: **39 ff.**
Cervantes: 67, 190
Chaloner, Sir Thomas: **215**
Chamberlain, John: 3, 28, 58, 112, 152, 158, 209
Chapman, George: 14, 17, 36, 59, 61, 68, 80, 94, 121, 128, 151, 164, 171–172, 186, 193, 197, 198–9, **215**
Charles I, King: 17, 29–30, 125, 215
Charles II, King: 219, 220, 222
Chaucer, Geoffrey: 12, 22–3, 25, 149, 155, 194
Cheke, Sir John: **216**
Chesterfield, Philip Stanhope, Earl of: 38
Chettle, Henry: 133, 138, 174–5, 185, **216**

Church, career in: **109 ff., 121 ff.**
Churchyard, Thomas: 33, 36, 140, 144, **216**
Cicero: 119
Cleaton, Ralph: 124
Cleveland, John: **216**
Clifford, Lady Anne: 17, 217
Coke, John: 114
Coke, Sir John: 155
Colet, Dean John: 113, 116
Collier, Jeremy: 175
Collier, J. P.: 92, 95
Collins, J. C.: 28
Commonplace-books: 149, 153-4
Condell, Henry, publisher: 160
Constable, Sir Henry: 168, **216**
Cooper, C. H.: 114
Copland, Robert, printer: **216**
Copley, Anthony: **217**
Coppey, Roger: 120
Corbet, Bishop Richard: **217**, 235
Cornwallis, Sir William: 67, 237
Corporation of London: **39 ff.**
Coryat, Thomas: 128, 161
Cotton, William: 75
Court of High Commission: **39 ff.**
Court, power of: viii, 2, **9 ff., 39 ff., 89 ff., 127 ff.,** 148 ff.
Coverdale, Bishop Miles: **217**
Cowley, Abraham: **217**
Cox, Captain, of Kenilworth: 160, 189
Crashaw, Richard: **217**
Crawford, C.: 151
Creede, Thomas, publisher: 69
Cromwell, Oliver: 228
Cross, T. P.: 132
Crowley, Robert, printer: **217**
Cumberland, Margaret, Duchess of: 17
Cunningham, P.: 95

Daborne, Francis: 92
Daniel, Samuel: 12, 13, 14, 16, 17, 18, 20, 26, 28-9, 31, 32, 36, 46, 57, 67, 76, 78, 85, 86, 89, 95, 120, 128, 129, 131, 138, 143, 150, 151, 156, 158, 159, 163, 167, 187, 188, 196, 201-2, 209, **217**
Danter, John, publisher: **68-9**, 72, 87
Dasent, Sir John: 48, 58, 118, 161
Davenant, Sir William: **218**
Davenport, A.: **209**
Davies, John, of Hereford: 17, 47, 121, **218**
Davies, Sir John: 19, 108, 128, 131, 168, **218**
Davison, Francis: 14, 154, **218**
Day, John, publisher: 66, 104, 144
Dearmer, P.: 133
Dedications: **23 ff.**
Dee, John: 152, 192
Dekker, Thomas: 6, 34, 36-7, 61, 64, 68, 73, 74-5, 93, 98-9, 104, 105, 123, 128, 129, 130, 136, 137, 138, 139, 144, 146, 148, 149-50, 158, 160, 161, 169, 172, 183, 185, 189, 193, 194, 205, 209, **218**
Deloney, Thomas: 105, 161, **218**
Demosthenes: 156
Denham, Sir John: **218**
Derby, Earls of: 192, 227
Devereux: *vide* Essex
Devonshire, Earls of: 28-9, 36, 167
Dialogue between the English Courtier and the Country Gentleman: 189-190
Digby, John, Earl of Bristol, and Lady Digby, 26
Donne, John: 14, 17, 18, 22, 23, 126, 128, 131, 167, 169, 198, 211, **219**
Dowland, John: **219**
Drake, Sir Francis: 157
Drant, Thomas: 103, **219**
Drayton, Michael: 6, 17, 18, 43, 44, 61, 71, 81-2, 94, 104, 128, 129, 138, 140, 149, 151, 152, 156, 159, 164, 165-6, 168, 187, 202, 209, **219**

Drummond, William, of Hawthornden: 32, 94, 140, 156, 163, **219**
Drury, Sir Robert: 18, 22
Dryden, John: 72, 169
Dyer, Sir Edward: 100, 128, 165, 167, 168, **219**

Earle, Bishop John: 67, **219**
Edward VI, King: 116, 220, 225, 230
Edwards, Richard: **220**
Egerton, Sir Thomas, and family: 13, 17, 36, 218, 219
Elderton, William: 105, 128, 143, 144, 145, 146
Elizabeth, of Bohemia: 229, 231
Elizabeth I, Queen: 9, 12, 18, 27–8, 30, 42, 45, 60, 89 ff., 197, 200, 207, 220, 223
Ellis, Sir H.: 25, 47, 110, 113, 118
Elwaie, Sir Gervase: 14
English, Queen's: 137–8
Essex, Earl of (Robert Devereux): 11, 16, **27–8**, 46, 114, 128, 197, **219**, 221, 228, 230, 231, 234, 235
Evans, Henry: 95

Fairfax, Sir Edward: 156, 168, **220,** 228
Famous Victories of Henry the Fifth: 83–4
Fane, Mildmay, Earl of Westmoreland: **220**
Fanshawe, Sir Richard: **220**
Felltham, Owen: **220**
Ferrers, George: **220**
Feuillerat, A: **209**
Field, John: 54
Field, Nathaniel: 25, 96
Fisher, F. J.: 165
Fleming, Abraham: 126
Fleming, Sir Daniel le: 120
Fleming, John: 154
Fletcher, Giles, the elder: 47, 61, **221**
Fletcher, Giles, the younger: 108, **221**

Fletcher, John: 130, 131, 191, 192, **221**
Fletcher, Phineas: 108, **221**
Florio, John: 14, 15, 16, 20, 67, 103, 115, 121, 133
Foakes, R. A.: 92
Ford, John: 130, 203, **221**
Four Prentises, The: 191
Foxe, John: 6, 44, 85, 104, 112, 120
Fraunce, Abraham: 14, 19, 128, 139, **221**
Frere, W. H.: 121
Frizer, Ingram: 62
Fulke, Dr: 66, 72
Fuller, Bishop Thomas: 129, 130–1
Furnivall, F. J.: 160, 179, 189

G. (J.): 177–8
Gager, William: 90
Gale, William: 180
Gascoigne, George: 139, 142, **221**
Gellibrand, Professor Henry: 44
Geraldi: 79
Gerbier, Balthazar: 163
Germany: 38
Gibson, E.: 31
Gifford, Humphrey: 132, **221**
Godolphin, Sidney: **221**
Goffe, Thomas: **221**
Golding, Arthur: 76–7, **222**
Goldsmith, Oliver: 87
Goodman, Bishop: 31, 60
Goodyere, Sir Henry: 131, 167, 219
Googe, Barnabe: 142, **222**
Gorges, Sir Arthur: **222**
Gosse, Edmund: 167
Gosson, Stephen: 34, 36, 96, 120, 176, 177, 181, 182, 184, **222**
Gower, John: 12, 155
Grafton, Richard: 71
Graham, James, Marquis of Montrose: **222**
Greene, Robert: 15, 24, 49, 68, 72, 73, 84, 87, 89, 93, 96, 105, 128,

129–30, 132, 134, 138, 139, 143–4, 145, 183–4, 191, 193, 204, 209, **223**

Greenlaw, E.: **209**

Gresham, Sir Thomas: 157

Greville, Fulke, Lord Brooke: 31, 85, 100, 128, 168, 218, **223**

Grey, Thomas, Lord Grey of Wilton: 16, 214, 221, 234

Grey, William: 18–19, **222**

Griffin, Bartholomew: **223**

Grimald, Nicholas: 90, **223**

Grindal, Edmund, Bishop, later Archbishop: 121, 176

Grosart, A. B.: ix, **209**

Guicciardini: 67, 156

Guilpin, Edward (or Everard): 47

Habington, William: **223**

Hake, Edward: 15, 27, 73, 104, 159

Hakluyt, Richard: 126

Hall, Arthur: **223**

Hall, Joseph: 8, 47, 73, 98, 104, 124, 126, 190, 204, 205, 209, **223**

Halliwell, J. O.: 55, 116

Harding, George, Lord Berkeley: 36

Harington, John, the elder: **223**

Harington, Sir John: 17, 103, 151, 153–4, 168, 177, 183, 198, **224**

Hariot, Thomas: 31

Harman, Thomas: 139

Harrison, John: 40

Harrison, William: 2, 3, 108, 122, 123, 124, 126, 159, 199–200, 203

Harvey, Brilliana: 114, 125

Harvey, Gabriel: 5, 47, 48, 50, 68, 74, 75, 86, 87, 105, 106, 113, 125, 128, 132, 133–5, 137, 138, 141, 143–4, 158, 161–2, 165, 170–1, 198, 209, **224**

Harvey, Richard: 125

Hayward, Sir John: 28, 46, 61, 152

Hazlitt, W. C.: 190

Hebel, J. W.: **209,** 210

Heminge, John, publisher: 160

Henrietta Maria, Queen: 212, 217

Henry Frederick, Prince of Wales (son of James I): 18, 91, 212, 215, 218, 223, 235

Henry I, King: 9

Henry VIII, King: viii, 9, 217, 220, 223, 224, 225, 227, 230, 233, 238

Henslowe, Philip: 75, 91, **92 ff.**

Herbert, Edward, Lord Herbert of Cherbury: 215, 217, **224,** 235

Herbert, George: 14, **224**

Herbert, Henry, and William, Earls of Pembroke, and Lord Charles Herbert: 13, **14,** 23, 214, **2**18, 221, 226, 228

Herbert, Philip, Earl of Montgomery: 14

Herford, C. H.: x, **209**

Herodotus: 156

Herrick, Robert: 19, 126, 131, **224**

Hesiod: 119

Heywood, Jasper: **224**

Heywood, John: 90, 156, **225**

Heywood, Thomas: 34, 69, 71–2, 74, 78, 79, 83, 92, 96, 97, 112, 129–130, 182, 192, 199, 204, **225**

Hoby, Lady Margaret: 178–9

Hoby, Thomas: 9

Hodgets, bookseller: 69

Hollinshed, Raphael: 45, 60, 61, 71, 152, 156

Holland, Earls of: 233

Holland, Philemon: 103

Homer: 119, 158

Hook, F. S.: 197

Hooker, Richard: 6

Hopkins, John: viii, 165, **225**

Horace: 119, 181

Horror stories: 189 ff.

Hoskyns, John: 131, **225**

Howard, Charles, Lord Howard of Effingham, Earl of Nottingham: 91

Howard, Henry, Earl of Surrey: 216, **225**

Howard, Philip, and Thomas: *vide* Arundel

Howell, James: 2, 14, 152, 166, **225**

Howell, Thomas: **225**

Hudson, Hoyt H.: 210

Hunnis, William: 18, **226**

Hunsdon, Henry Carey, Lord: 19, 46, 91, 237

Inflation: **2–4**

Isocrates: 119

Italy: 9, 79

Jaggard, John, publisher: 69, 84

Jaggard, William, publisher: 69

James I, King: 2, 33–4, 45, 54, 91, 111, 129, 154, 180, 192–3, 197–8, 219, 226

Jermyn, Sir Robert: 217

Johnson, Samuel: 38

Jones, Inigo: 95

Jones, Richard, publisher: 80, 86

Jonson, Ben: x, 1, 5, 6, 12, 14, 15, 17, 18, 26, 29–30, 32, 45, 56, 57, 58, 59, 61, 62, 67, 68, 73, 75, 80, 89, 92–3, 94–5, 96, 99, 100, 102, 104, 127, 128, 129, 130, 131, 133, 136, 137, 138, 141, 142, 143, 144, 146, 148, 149, 150, 153, 158, 160, 161, 162, 163, 164, 165, 166, 169, 171, 172, 178, 183, 185, 186, 190–1, 194, 196, 198, 204, 205, 206, 207, 209, **226**

Juvenal: 119

Kempe, William: 205, 207

Kethe, William: **226**

Keynes, G.: 193

Kindlemarsh, Francis: **226**

King, Bishop Henry: **226**

Knolles, Richard: 121

Kyd, Thomas: 61, 62–3, 130, 131

Kynaston, Sir Francis: **226**

Lambe, Dr: 193

Lanam, actor: 207

Langland, William: 155

Languet, Hubert: 150

Laud, Archbishop William: 125

Law, T. G.: 45, 58

Lawe, M., publisher: 52

Leach, A. F.: 106, 115, 117

Lee, S.: 45, 55

Leicester, Robert Dudley, Earl of: **15–16,** 18, 27, 44, 53–4, 90, 103, 216, 219, 222, 224, 234, 237

Leishman, J. B.: ix, **209**

Leland, John: **227**

Lewis, C. S.: 210

Licensers: **43 ff.**

Lilly, William: 194

Ling, Nicholas, publisher: 67, 81, 166

Livy, 77

Lluelyn, Martin: **227**

Lodge, John: 74, 124, 125, 152, 192

Lodge, Thomas: 8, 12, 27, 61, 78, 105, 128, 151, 180–1, **227**

Lok, Henry: 16, **227**

Lovelace, Richard: **227**

Lydgate, John: 155

Lyly, John: 24, 30–1, 67, 108, 113, 135, 138, 139, 148, 158, 168–9, 196, 200, 209, **227**

McClure, N. E.: **209**

McKerrow, R. B.: ix, 72, 103, **209**

Madan, F.: 108

Maecenas: 9, 20, 35

Markham, Gervase: 16, 144, **228**

Marlowe, Christopher: 11, 19, 38, 47, 61, 62–3, 67, 89, 100, 106, 128, 129, 130, 131, 191, 192–3, 199, 203, 205, 228

Marmion, Shakerley: **228**

Marot: 156

INDEX

Marprelate, Martin, controversy: 43–4, 133, 206

Marsh, Thomas, publisher: 65

Marston, John: 17, 47, 59, 61, 68, 100, 126, 136, 137, 197, 203, **228**

Martine Mar-sixtus: 144–5

Marvell, Andrew: **228**

Mary, Queen: 225

Mary, Queen of Scots: 42

Massinger, Arthur: 23

Massinger, Philip: 12, 14, 23, 33, 74, 80, 94, 100, 154, 182, **228**

Masson, David: 14, 140, 156, 163

May, Thomas: 130, **228**

Mayne, Jasper: 93–4

Mease, Peter: 155

Medici, Lorenzo de: 9

Mennes, Sir John: **229**

Merchants, power of: 2–3, 53 ff., 177–8

Meres, Francis: 110, 121, 126

Messala: 9

Middleton, Thomas: 61, 74, 80, 89, 95, 100, 102, 105, 130, 144, 186, 204, **229**

Millington, Thomas, publisher: 52

Milton, John: 17, 86, 102, 169, **229**

Minshew, John: 16

Montemayor: 82

Moore, Nicholas: 154

More, Henry: **229**

More, Sir Thomas: 71, **229**

Morrice, pamphleteer: 41

Morton, Sir Albertus: **229**

Mounslowe, Alexander: 194

Mueller, W. R.: 174

Mullinger, J. Bass: 106, 109, 111, 113, 114

Munday, Anthony: 61, 96, 128, 133, 190, **229**

Nashe, Thomas: ix, 1, 5, 6, 12, 13, 14, 16, 17, 18, 19–20, 21, 24, 31, 35, 36, 37, 38, 39, 47, 48, 50, 56, 57, 58–9, 60–1, 68, 72, 73, 74, 75, 77–8, 80, 82, 83, 86, 87, 89, 104, 105, 108, 110, 113, 119, 125, 128, 130, 132, 133–5, 137, 138, 143, 144, 145, 146, 158, 161, 162, 164, 165, 167, 168, 170, 171, 173, 182, 184, 185, 187, 191, 194, 195, 198, 206, 209, **229**

Neale, Sir John: 11

Nevill, Alexander: 77

Newdigate, B. H.: 149

Newton, Thomas: **230**

Nicholas, Pope: 9

Norden, John: vii–viii, 76

North, Sir Thomas: 103

Norton, Thomas: 90, 203, **230**

Northumberland, Earls of: 25, 31, 156

Nowell, Alexander: 107, 113

Occleve, Thomas: 155

Ocland, Christopher: 24–5, 118, 121, 143, 161

Ovid: 119

Oxford University Press: 42, 65, 83, 107–8

Page, publisher: 45

Paget, Lord: 236

Palgrave, Lord: 91

Paris, University of: 107

Parker, Archbishop Matthew: 66, 121, **230**

Parker, Henry, Lord Morley: 103, **230**

Parkins, Dr Charles: 40

Parnassus Plays: ix, 5, 6, 19–20, 35, 62, 72, 89, 96, 97, 101, 104, 113, 114, 119, 120, 124–5, 164, 169, 170, 187, 206, 209

Parry, Sir Thomas: 218

Parsons, Robert: 42, 45

Patriotism: **199 ff.**

Patronage: 5, **8 ff.,** 102 ff.

Peele, George: 25, 96, 128, 197, **230**
Peend, Thomas: **230**
Pepys, Samuel: 156
Percy, William: **230**
Persius: 119
Pestell, Thomas: **231**
Petrarch: 159
Pettie, George: 103, 158, **231**
Peyton, Sir E.: 157
Phaer, Thomas: **231**
Pilkington, John: 113
Plomer, H. R.: 46, 132
Plutarch: 67, 71, 139, 158
Politian: 158
Pollard, A. W.: 117
Ponsonby, William, publisher: **67, 68,** 86, 87, 122
Pope, Alexander: 144
Powell, A.: 31
Privileges: 11, **65 ff.**
Privy Council: **39 ff.,** 85, 161
Proctor, Thomas, publisher: **231**
Property, literary: **69 ff.**
Ptolemy: 8
Pullain, John: **231**
Puritanism: **90 ff.,** 161, 172 ff.
Puritan, The: 119, 166, 170, 185
Putnam, G. H.: 38, 77, 79
Puttenham, George: **231**
Pyne, W.: 115

Quarles, Francis: **231**

Rabelais: 135, 156, 194
Raleigh, Sir Walter: 27, 30, 33, 45, 49, 62, 128, 154, 168, 201, 215, 222, 226, **232,** 234
Randolph, Thomas: **232,** 236
Refutation of the Apology for Actors: 177–8
Reynolds, S. H.: 166, 202
Richmond, Duchess of: 218
Rickert, R. T.: 92
Ridley, Bishop Nicholas: 212, 223

Rimbault, E. F.: 50
Roberts, James, publisher: 65, 68, 74
Robertson, Jean: 74
Robinson, Richard: 103
Robinson, Richard, of Alton: 132
Rogers, J. Thorold: 3, 4
Rosenberg, Eleanor: vii
Rowe, Nicholas: 17
Rowlands, Samuel: 50, 61, 87, 105, 128, 143, 190
Rowley, Samuel: 97, 131
Rowley, William: 96, 97
Roydon, Matthew: **232**
Russia: 56–7

Sackville, Sir Edward: 12, 30
Sackville, Robert, Earl of Dorset: 235
Sackville, Thomas, Lord Buckhurst, Earl of Dorset: 90, **232**
St Leger, Sir Anthony: **232**
Sandys, Sir Edwin: **232**
Sandys, George: 129, 152, **233**
Satire: **47–8,** 169–71
Saunders, J. W.: 85, 131, 168, 174
Savile, Sir Henry: 103
Schelling, F. E.: 94
Schools: **115 ff.,** 159–60, 179–80
Scot, Reginald: 193
Scrope, Lord: 225
Seebohm, F.: 116
Selden, John: 44, 61, 142, 166
Seneca: 119
Seres, William, publisher: 65
Seymour, Edward, Duke of Somerset: 215, 216, 222, **233**
Shakespeare, John: 55
Shakespeare, William: 6, 11, 14, 16, 17, 18, 19, 29, 32–3, 46, 52, 55, 60, 61, 67, 69, 71, 81, 84, 89, 90, 91, 94, 96, 97, 98, 99, 100, 121, 128, 130, 131, 132, 133, 138, 139, 141, 149, 151, 157, 160, 163–4, 186, 191, 192, 193, 195, 197, 199, 200, 203, 204, 206, 207, **233**

Sharpham, Edward: 144
Sherburne, Sir Edward: 23
Shirley, James: 121, 126, 207, **233**
Shrewsbury, Earls of: 151–2, 154, 225
Sidney, Elizabeth, Countess of Rutland: 14–15, 114
Sidney, Mary, Countess of Pembroke: **13–14,** 67, 214, **224,** 225
Sidney, Sir Philip: **13,** 14, 34, 37, 67, 85, 100, 128, 131, 135, 137, 138, 148, 150, 151, 156, 165, 167, 168, 171, 182–3, 187, 188, 196, 209, 214, 221, **233**
Sidney, Sir Robert: 28
Simpson, Percy and Evelyn: x, **209**
Six Idyls from Theocritus: 108
Skelton, John: **233**
Smith, James: **233**
Smith, Sir John: 46–7, 61
Solemne, Antony de: 65
Somerset, Earls of: 117, 157
Southampton, Henry Wriothesley, Earl of: **16–17,** 29, 157, 217, 225, 232
Southwell, Robert: **233**
Spedding, J.: 33
Speght, Thomas: 107
Spenser, Edmund: viii, 13, 15–16, 17, 18, 19, 22, 23, 27, 30, 34, 61–2, 67, 86, 100, 103, 106, 122, 124, 128, 131, 132, 139, 151, 156, 158, 160, 165, 169, 174, 186, 192, 209, 211, **234**
S(tafford), W.: 4, 60, 109
Stanley, Thomas: **234**
Stanyhurst, Richard: **234**
Star Chamber: **39 ff.,** 70
Stationers' Company: **39 ff., 64 ff.,** 105, 107
Stationers' Register: **41 ff.,** 64 ff., 209
Sternhold, Thomas: viii, 165, **234**
Stevenson, William: **234**
Storer, Thomas: **234**
Stowe, John: 3, 60, 61

Strange and wonderful judgement of God upon a false swearer: 195
Strange, Lord: 91
Strode, William: **235**
Stubbes, John: 45
Stubbes, Katherine: 177, 197
Stubbes, Philip: 3, 49, 52, 61, 86, 116, 119, 122, 124, 161, 175–6, 177, 178, 184, 194–5, 197
Studley, John: **235**
Subscription patronage: **85–6**
Suckling, Sir John: **235**
Suffolk, Duchess of: 231
Sussex, Earls of: 232
Swift, Jonathan: 38
Sylvester, Joshua: 16, 18, 67, 151, **235**
Symmes, H. S.: 177, 181

Tarlton, Richard: 174–5, 205, 207, **235**
Tasso: 79
Taylor, John, the water poet: 14, 86, 128, 129, 140, **235**
Terence: 119, 161
Thomond, Earl of: 220
Thoms, W. J.: 197
Thomson, Hugh: 125
Thornton, John: 123
Thorpe, Thomas, publisher: 37, 68
Thucydides: 8
Tonson, Jacob, publisher: 86
Tottel, Richard, publisher: 65, 71
Tourneur, Cyril: **235**
Townshend, Aurelian: **235**
Translations: vii, 72, 77, **103,** 110, 119, 159
Trap, John: 116
Turberville, George: 103, 137, 142, **236**
Turner, Dr: 81
Tusser, Thomas: **236**

Udall, Nicholas: 90, 160, **236**

University education: **105 ff.**
Usher, Archbishop James: 31, 231

Vallans, William: 132
Vallinger, ? Stephen: 45
Vanbrugh, Sir John: 182
Vandernoodt, John: 139
Vaughan, Henry: **236**
Vaux, Thomas, Lord: **236**
Venice: 79
Vere, Edward de, Earl of Oxford: 128, 168, 222, 227, 229, **236**
Villiers, George, Earl (later Duke) of Buckingham, and Duchess: 154, 155, 163, 217, 224
Virgil: 119, 158
Vorstius, Conrad: 34

Waller, Edmund: **236**
Walsingham, Sir Francis: 228, 237
Walsingham, Sir Thomas: 44, 62, 157
Ward, Roger, printer: 70
Warner, Walter: 31
Warner, William: 151, **237**
Warwick, Earls of: 155–6, 237
Waterson, Simon, publisher: 86
Watkins, Richard, publisher: 65, 74
Watson, Thomas: 90, 130, 139, **237**
Webbe, William: 121, 171, 181, **237**
Webster, John: 36, 127, 128, 130, 141, 199, 204, **237**
Welldon, A.: 124
Wenman, Lord: 213
Whetstone, George: 181, **237**

White, Sir Thomas: 157
Whiteman, William: 156
Whitgift, Archbishop John: 42, 47, 48
Whiting, Nathaniel: **237**
Whitney, Geoffrey: **237**
Whittingham, William: **237**
Whyte, Roland: 28
Wilcox, Thomas: 177
Willoughby, Sir Henry: 221
Wilson, Arthur: 180
Wilson, F. P.: ix, **209**
Wilson, Robert: 96
Wilson, Thomas: 6, 165
Windsor, Lord Edward: 50
Wisdom, Robert: **237**
Wise, Andrew, publisher: 68
Wither, George: 16, 34–5, 48, 50–1, 59–60, 61, 64, 71, 72, 73, 76, 79, 81, 88, 103, 146, 165, **237**
Wolfe, John, publisher: 42, **66–7,** 69, 70, 87, 103
Wolsey, Cardinal: 215
Woodcock, Thomas, publisher: 87
Worcester, Earls of: 225
Wotton, Sir Henry: 16, 131, 168, **238**
Wright, T.: 40, 176
Wright, William, publisher: 86
Wriothesley, *vide* Southampton
Wyatt, Sir Thomas: **238**

Yeats, W. B.: 99, 158
Yoklavitch, J.: 197
Yorke, Sir John: 44
Young, Bartholomew: 82, **238**